E-GOVERNMENT OR OUT OF GOVERNMENT

Mark J. Barrenechea
Tom Jenkins

Barrenechea, Mark J.
Jenkins, Tom

e-Government or Out of Government

First Printing, April 2014
Printed in Canada
First Edition

ISBN
978-0-9936047-2-0

$29.00 U.S.

Published by
Open Text Corporation
275 Frank Tompa Drive
Waterloo, Ontario, Canada
N2L 0A1
(519) 888-7111
info@opentext.com
www.opentext.com

ACKNOWLEDGEMENTS

This book is dedicated to the staff, partners, and customers of OpenText Corporation and its subsidiaries. This book is possible due to their combined efforts, innovation, and collective vision.

We would like to thank the staff, users, and partners of OpenText Corporation for their contributions to this book.

Special thanks go to writer and editor Elizabeth Hanson, editors Ian E. Wilson and Rebecca Graves, and the following contributors:

Andrew Antal, Sanjay Aurora, Alex Benay, Eric Bencina, David Brott, Patricia Burke, Travis Cain, Suzanne Chiovitti, Kevin Cochrane, Jeff Cowan, Randy Crow, Eileen Cukier, Bill Cumby, Brian C. Davis, David Dunn, Sonia Florez Fernandez, Herb Hayde, Dave Hughes, Daniel Hopkin, Steven Keifer, Thomas Keuschnigg, Walter Koehler, Sabine Kusmierz, Christine Lesden, Sharon Malloch, Stephen Manniso, Jeff Martin, Alex Martinez, Ron Master, Deborah Miller, Gilles Mousseau, Stefanie Nastou, Kelly Nelson, Melissa Noto, Russ O' Neill, Donna Pearson, Brad Pederson, Hugh Ritchie, Anabel Sarrate, Andrea Sassenberg, Keith Sauve, Erin Schwab, Ray Schultz, Scott Schultz, Michael Shea, Michele Stevenson, Delphine Theolier, Kurtis Thomas, Ed Tracy, Nicole Wallenburg, Eying Wee, Gary Weiss, Michael Wilkerson, Nigel Williams, and Neil Wilson.

We would also like to thank Meagan Terrel, Srgjan Spasik, Jennifer Heisch, and Joe Dwyer for layout, design, and production.

Special resources are accredited in the Bibliography.

CONTENTS

INNOVATOR STORIES AND INTERVIEWS

FOREWORD

Let us be clear: society is changing. Mobile devices are globally ubiquitous, and their capabilities continue to advance rapidly. Apps and WiFi, big data coupled with semantic search, and proliferating social media profoundly impact not just our ways of storing information and communicating but also the fundamental nature of social interaction. This is not some passing fad but a meaningful transformation of the social fabric. Traditional business models—in the production and distribution of content, broadcasting, and news and in customer interaction, financial services, and other fields—are being disrupted and transformed. It is a time for creativity and innovation as new business models, structures, and even professions emerge to thrive or fail. It is an exhilarating time. It can also be painfully difficult. And it is unavoidable.

Large institutions, serving society for generations, are challenged to keep pace as we evolve as a digital society. Education, health care, defense, and public safety are at the forefront, but all governments are challenged to balance the traditions and values they were designed to uphold while adapting to lead in a digital environment. Layers of rules and regulations and long-established habits and assumptions combine with inertia to constrain the flexibility and nimble responses required. Bureaucracies have long worked within professional silos very comfortably and without the pressure of competition. But that too is shifting. The issues of a modern society cut across all disciplines and organizational structures, demanding collaboration and information sharing throughout the enterprise.

A government's online presence, services, and standards are now publicly clear and each can be assessed and measured against best practices. Citizens, now accustomed to interacting with their banks and retailers or easily finding information online, compare government services and information sources with these private sector transactions. The comparison becomes more prevalent as open government initiatives unleash data and private sector ingenuity finds new value by creating more cost-effective services. Industry associations and concerned citizens can now compete with the government hierarchies as experts, and crowdsourcing or engagement allows many voices to have a role in governance. We expect governments to offer truly citizen-centric services that do not forsake private sector convenience and ensure coordination across various programs and jurisdictions. Moreover, this coordination is further complicated by the imperatives of respecting privacy and information security.

The Honorable Kevin Lynch, former Head of the Public Service of Canada, has been clear that in a global trade environment, a professional public service is an essential and competitive asset. Support for innovation, negotiating multilateral trade agreements, border security, taxation systems, financial regulation, intellectual property protection, and fostering a creative economy relies on government. With demand for services and the expansion of government roles increasing at a time of financial constraint, productivity is fundamental to modern governments. And this depends on transforming bureaucracies into creative, empowered, and knowledge-based workforces. It requires a shift in the information culture, taking a whole-of-government approach to information assets. This is gradually being done and governments around the globe need to learn from each other.

This book, *e-Government or Out of Government*, is timely and practical. Information in all its myriad formats, from records to data, is the very life-blood of government. Most have recognized that all program managers are responsible for managing records as effectively as they have traditionally managed their other assets: money, people, and facilities. However, technology has been evolving rapidly in recent years as the cost of electronic storage has diminished and the power of semantic search becomes apparent. This book describes the current state of this technology and looks into the future, as technology continues to enhance program productivity. A wealth of practical examples drawn from various levels of government around the world vividly demonstrates how this technology is proving effective. But this is not a manual for CIOs: it is a user-friendly guidebook to the new technological frontier, meant to inspire all program managers to rethink and reinvigorate their approach. Key objectives resonate through all government structures: to collaborate, innovate, and move ahead with courage.

Ian E. Wilson
FORMER LIBRARIAN AND ARCHIVIST OF CANADA

INTRODUCTION

Digital changes everything. If you are not an e-Government, you are out of Government.

In a digital, information-based economy, governments must modernize to survive. If they don't they face becoming irrelevant. In democratic societies, when a government becomes irrelevant, it loses its effectiveness to govern.

The business advantages available through today's digital technologies are as powerful as they are plentiful. There is an abundance of evidence about the benefits of using technologies to address challenges in the private sector—from increased efficiency to reduced costs and a higher quality output of goods and services.

Similar benefits can be experienced in the public sector. Based on the application of Internet, web, and emerging technologies to government processes, e-government is the new digital imperative.

But are national, state, and local governments ready?

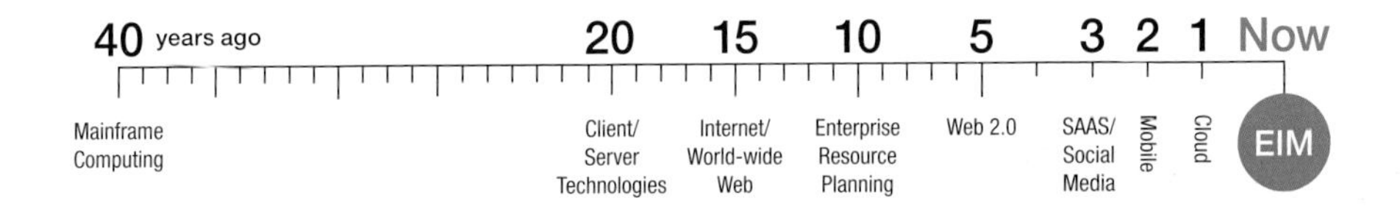

Information is Transforming Government

e-Government or Out of Government is a book about transformation.

Information drives business in the private sector. The public sector is no exception to this rule.

Like many businesses, governments maintain their information in different repositories. Information that flows across departments, agencies, and contractors is disconnected and processes are fragmented. Many agencies do not have a consolidated view of their information, which means they do not have a consolidated view of their customers, resources, or programs and services. Coordinating information and services across departments is as challenging as navigating through the complex levels of government.

e-Government replaces the paper-based system of the past with a single source of the truth. It digitizes and integrates information on a single platform with shared repositories and secure access, information and records management, and process management tools.

In the public sector, the value of content is only just being realized as an asset that must be managed. CIOs in both public and private sectors have been preoccupied with managing technology systems; today their focus is shifting to the strategic value of content. When managed effectively, information improves performance, informs better decision-making, increases citizen satisfaction, and reduces risks of litigation and non-compliance.

e-Government or Out of Government is a book about creating an agenda to transform your organization. We've included many provocative case studies highlighting those organizations that have begun their journey.

The public sector is a highly regulated industry in which privacy and transparency are not mutually exclusive, but are two sides of the same coin. e-Government helps agencies find the balance between open data initiatives and data security, between compliance to country-specific regulations like the Freedom of Information Act and the protection of both personal and business information in a cloud environment.

e-Government or Out of Government is a prescriptive book about best practices.

All around us there are examples of improved services through modernization and an information-centric approach to governing.

In both public and private sectors, the nature of information is changing. Bureaucratic boundaries are breaking down as information is shared in all formats across devices and in the cloud. With sites like Facebook® and WikiLeaks, government agencies are seeking full technology platforms that support everything from social media and multimedia to *ad hoc* process automation and secure information management.

Early adopters in government are already implementing solutions based on these technologies. This book contains over fifty examples of e-government applications from agencies around the world. It describes strategies for digital transformation.

While innovators in the public sector are crowdsourcing apps with citizens and making citizen services available on mobile devices, much of this is happening in isolation. A major obstacle in the adoption of e-government is the ability to create an environment that rewards innovation, allows risk, and tolerates failure as long as it is undertaken in the public interest. A consolidated effort is required if the government is to change the way it interacts with and provides services for its citizens.

e-Government is the platform for digital transformation. Read *e-Government or Out of Government* to reconcile e-government business strategies with traditional bricks-and-mortar approaches: to inspire employees and citizens to collaborate and co-create solutions, unlock the potential of your information to reveal insights and make better decisions, streamline and integrate processes, meet compliance and litigation requirements, reduce expenses and improve performance of mission activities—all while staying under budget.

Applicable across administrative, political, educational, and health care systems, the book includes models of innovation and measurements of performance in a global, flat, crowded, and digital economy.

Digital changes everything.

Mark J. Barrenechea
PRESIDENT & CEO,
OPENTEXT CORPORATION

Tom Jenkins
CHAIRMAN,
OPENTEXT CORPORATION

CHAPTER 1

THE BUSINESS NEED FOR E-GOVERNMENT

CHAPTER 1

The Business Need for e-Government

Governments around the world are mandated to serve their citizens—protecting lives and property, providing vital health and education services, stimulating economic growth and development and ensuring financial stability through regulatory reform and global policy review.

Mission drives agencies across all levels of government. Having access to accurate and secure information plays a critical role in mission activities—from giving employees access to the data they need, to citizens making public information requests, and contractors bidding on projects. In many aspects, the effective management of information is the central business of government.

FIGURE 1.1: Basic e-Government Framework

The world's governments, regardless of location, politics, and constitution share one common critical challenge: managing information overload in a highly regulated and citizen-focused environment.

A combination of digital technologies, budget realities, and public expectations is changing how information is being managed in the public sector. Many of these expectations are focused on digital technologies and how information is accessed, exchanged, and consumed: Which information is most important? What types of services do citizens expect? How and when do they want to exchange information? For governments to stay relevant they must keep pace with their constituents, otherwise they lose their effectiveness to govern.

But how can governments modernize their services with limited budgets? What are the key enablers? *e-Government or Out of Government* examines the critical need for electronic government, or e-government, in the public sector. This chapter traces the evolution of e-government, from outdated, analog practices to the digitization of services according to mission. It sets the stage for a later exploration of ways in which governments can deliver more satisfying digital experiences to all stakeholders.

Driving Mission at Every Level

FIGURE 1.2: Government Misson

Government agencies have requirements to deliver on their mission to:

- **Serve** by giving citizens the access they need to government programs, services, and information
- **Engage** by empowering citizens to participate in government services and policy development to impact decision making
- **Regulate** by providing information, processes, and programs to help businesses streamline regulatory processes and deliver safe products and services; by establishing and implementing laws that dictate how we live together as a society
- **Protect** by ensuring security, privacy, and the protection of every citizen

To balance accountability and transparency with the protection and security of information, governments must modernize their services. This necessitates re-engineering their enterprise architecture to engage citizens and democratize access to public information. Behind the scenes, an e-government infrastructure provides both online administrative services and a comprehensive database of corporate information. It informs and connects workers across multi-jurisdictional programs to improve productivity and services, while demonstrating the effective use of public funds.

The Call to Modernize Services

"A digital population cannot be well served by an analog government."[1]

Technology is transforming how we work and how we play. Advances in technologies like the cloud and mobile devices have given citizens greater access to online information and services. There are currently as many mobile subscriptions as there are people in the world, making expectations around accessing and sharing information immediate.[2] Citizens anticipate the same levels of responsiveness from their governments that they experience in the private sector.

[1] Paul Tellier and David Emerson, *"Seventh Report of the Prime Minister's Advisory Committee on the Public Service,"* Clerk of the Privy Council, March, 2013: *http://www.clerk.gc.ca/eng/feature.asp?pageId=314* (accessed December 2013).

[2] ITU, *"The World in 2013: ICT Facts and Figures"* International Telecommunication Union, *http://www.itu.int/en/ITU-D/Statistics/Pages/facts/default.aspx* (accessed December 2013).

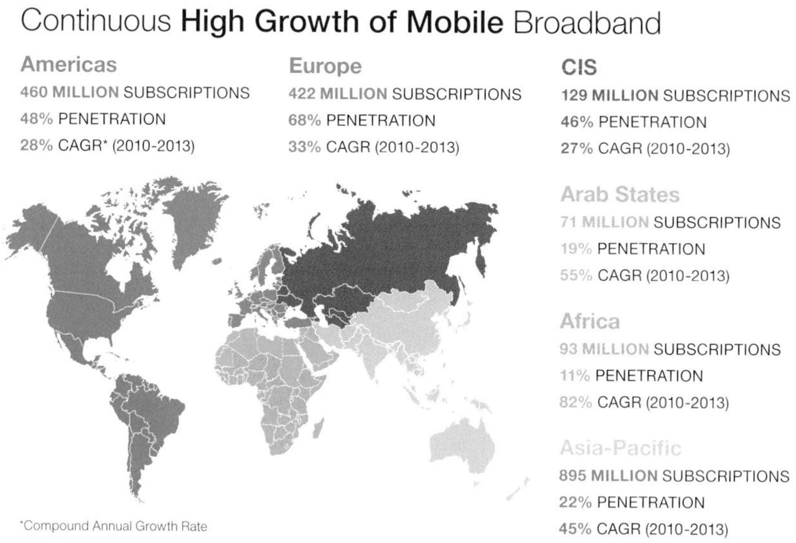

Continuous **High Growth of Mobile** Broadband
Americas
460 MILLION SUBSCRIPTIONS
48% PENETRATION
28% CAGR* (2010-2013)
Europe
422 MILLION SUBSCRIPTIONS
68% PENETRATION
33% CAGR (2010-2013)
CIS
129 MILLION SUBSCRIPTIONS
46% PENETRATION
27% CAGR (2010-2013)
Arab States
71 MILLION SUBSCRIPTIONS
19% PENETRATION
55% CAGR (2010-2013)
Africa
93 MILLION SUBSCRIPTIONS
11% PENETRATION
82% CAGR (2010-2013)
Asia-Pacific
895 MILLION SUBSCRIPTIONS
22% PENETRATION
45% CAGR (2010-2013)
*Compound Annual Growth Rate

FIGURE 1.3: Almost as Many Mobile Subscriptions as People in the World[3]

Factors like globalization, economic recession, and increasing regulation are forcing many governments to transform their programs and infrastructure. Aging populations around the world are placing additional strains on budgets, in terms of provisions for health care and a retiring workforce. Impacted by all of these converging forces, governments are faced with the challenge of transformation and the need to reinvent systems through Information and Communication Technologies (ICTs).

SOCIAL
BIG DATA
CONNECTIVITY & CONSOLIDATION
TRANSPARENCY
MOBILITY
EXPECTATIONS
!

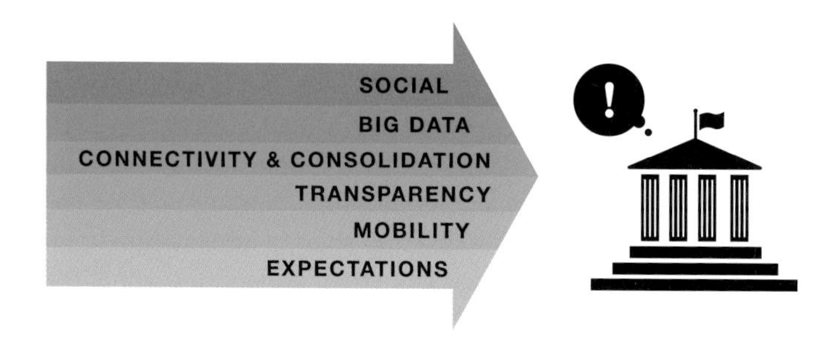

FIGURE 1.4: Converging Forces Impacting Government

e-Government refers to the use of ICTs, as well as Internet, web-based, or mobile technologies, to improve operational performance, engage with citizens, and deliver government services. It encompasses technologies for e-services, e-health, e-procurement, e-voting, e-management, e-democracy, and more.

[3] *Ibid.*

In scope, e-government moves beyond providing services online to encompass a holistic vision of electronic government that consolidates processes, resources, and information across agencies. It reaches beyond the firewall to incorporate external stakeholders and citizens for optimized efficiency, quality of service, and cost effectiveness.

Effective e-government requires coordination and collaboration across departments, sectors, jurisdictions, and policy domains; a host of changing relations and communication patterns; and a shift to citizen-centric service delivery. The desired outcome is a seamless government experience, supported by a technical infrastructure and connected users and citizens—as illustrated below in the Government of Aragón's effective implementation of e-government.

Modernizing the Mission: To Serve

e-Government helps agencies more effectively serve all stakeholders—from citizens to businesses and public servants. The U.S. Postal Service (USPS) is an example of an antiquated government service that is failing to transform itself to remain relevant to its consumers.

FIGURE 1.5: Early USPS Postman

The U.S. Postal Service

The USPS epitomizes a century-old, tried-and-true government service. "Neither snow nor rain nor heat nor gloom of night stays these couriers from the swift completion of their appointed rounds" reflects the USPS mission. Delivering a service that has endured for 238 years, the USPS has played a crucial role in uniting a nation and promoting commerce. Today, it has fallen behind in evolving to meet changing consumer needs.

Government of Aragón

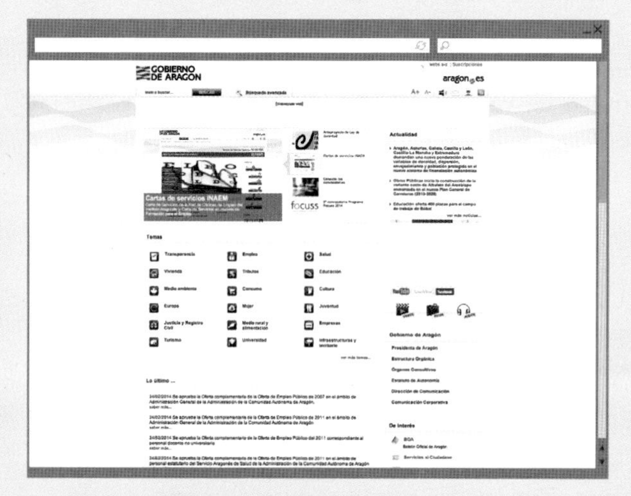

The portal embodies the values of e-government—offering improved transparency and service delivery that is available across every device.

FIGURE 1.6: Government of Aragón Portal

Aragón is an autonomous community in Spain that is made up of three provinces: Huesca, Zaragoza, and Teruel, and 33 comarcas or counties. Aragón is located in the northeast of Spain and has a rich history, including Roman and Arabic heritage, which constituted a large empire in the middle ages that ruled the Mediterranean Sea. Nowadays Aragón has a strong economy based on industry, services, and tourism. The Government of Aragón, through its IT agency Aragonesa de Servicios Telemáticos (AST), has modernized its citizen portal in a significant step toward implementing comprehensive e-government.

The portal provides a hub for the Government of Aragón and its citizens, partners, and businesses with a focus on creating a more fulfilling end-user experience. Access to information and services is more efficient, convenient, and contemporary. A new information architecture has simplified navigation, transforming the site into a portal that delivers a targeted experience for all visitors. Content is organized by topics of interest, such as jobs, taxes, health, justice, industry, culture, housing, and more—not according to government function. To migrate to the new platform, the Government's current content had to be classified and its processes modified. The platform gives the Government a flexible collaboration component that enables the agency to engage internally as well as externally with citizens and various service providers.

The Government is using the solution to manage its web content and has incorporated Web 2.0 tools, resulting in improved accessibility and usability. After launching, the portal received 350,000 visits in its first month, with three and a half million pages viewed. The portal embodies the values of e-government—offering improved transparency and service delivery that is available across every device. It is also one hundred percent accessible, meeting stringent UNE 139803:2004 and Accessibility Guidelines 1.0 Web Content defined by the W3C Web Accessibility Initiative (WAI).

According to sources, USPS mail volume has declined due to email and the Internet. Lower volumes mean lower revenue. In 2012, mail volume was at three-quarters of what it was in 2006. At the time of this study, the USPS was losing $25 million every single day.[4]

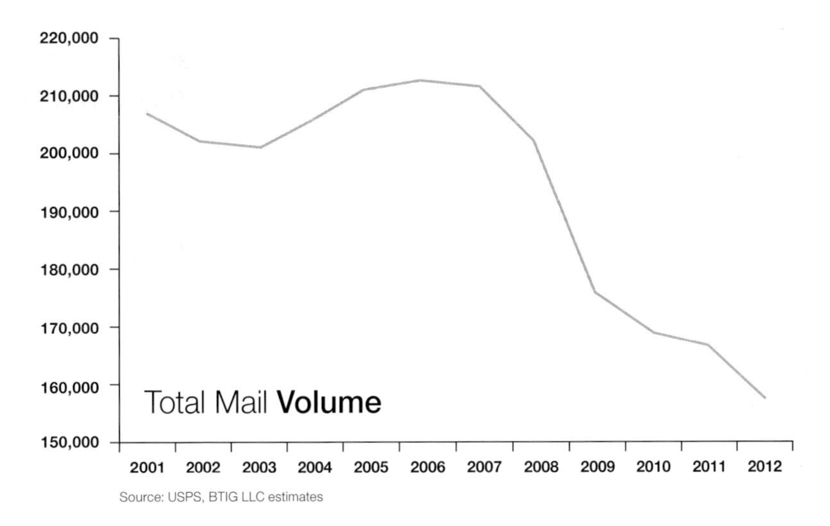

FIGURE 1.7: A Drop in U.S. Mail Volume

As we move toward becoming a paperless culture, the USPS in its current incarnation could become obsolete. Hand-written letters are a thing of the past. People are increasingly exchanging emails and texting one another instead of mailing letters. The publishing industry has had to shift drastically to accommodate a public that reads their newspapers, magazines, and books online.

As we have seen with the publishing (and other) industries, the digitization of information is a great leap forward (and often a first step) in adopting web-based models of service delivery. Digitization gives access to information in integrated and accessible ways to both support current use and encourage future use. e-Government facilitates the digitization of information in any format, so that it can be more readily accessed, managed, and stored.

To remain relevant, the USPS could capitalize on e-government technologies to pursue additional lines of business, as demonstrated in its recent partnership with Amazon.com to deliver online orders. Many postal services are leveraging technology to better meet consumer needs. In the following feature, the International Post Corporation (IPC) is using a combination of RFID tags and a global file transfer network to monitor and track the progress of mail to identify gaps in performance.

[4] *"U.S. Postal Service in trouble, losing $25 million daily"* CNN, Dec 10, 2012, *http://outfront.blogs.cnn.com/2012/12/10/u-s-postal-service-in-trouble-losing-25-million-daily/* (accessed Jan 2014).

International Post Corporation

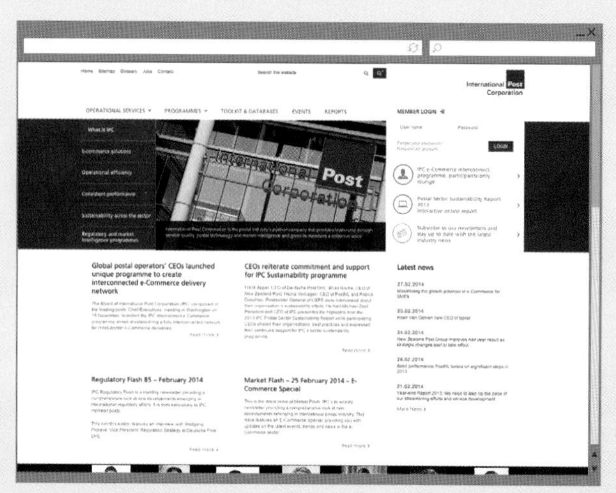

FIGURE 1.8: IPC Website

The proportion of international letters delivered within three days rose from an average of 69% to as high as 95%.

International Post Corporation (IPC) is a cooperative association of 24 postal organizations in Europe, North America, and Asia-Pacific, whose members handle 80 percent of the world's mail—some 330 billion letters each year. The organization is charged with improving the performance of mail and parcel delivery worldwide.

IPC employs Radio-frequency identification (RFID) technology to determine the amount of time it takes postal operators to deliver the international mail arriving in their territory. This measure is a key component of the formula used to calculate "terminal dues" (the fees postal operators pay to each other for the delivery of cross-border mail). Under agreements reached between international postal operators, the fees are tied to stringent quality-of-service standards. As a result, millions of dollars in fees are decided by the results of the RFID monitoring.

IPC deployed an RFID Network Manager Service on a global file transfer network that connects postal operators throughout the world and its centralized IT center. The network carries around 40,000 messages a day for IPC, peaking at 80,000 messages a day over the holiday season. Since IPC started tracking test letters, it has seen significant improvements in performance across Europe. The proportion of international letters delivered within three days rose from an average of 69 percent to as high as 95 percent. Using performance-related payments based on the RFID tracking data sent over the network has been a key factor in improving overall performance and helping the IPC improve service delivery.

Modernizing Mission: To Engage

Serve | **Engage** | Regulate | Protect

Connecting State and Citizen

The mission to engage has been the key focus of governments throughout the centuries. Some of the earliest forms of engagement between the state and citizen were in the form of town criers, who would proclaim bylaws, market days, tax increases, and news to a largely illiterate citizenry.

In the Peasant's Revolt in medieval England, a group of villagers travelled to London to petition King Richard II about abolishing the poll tax. A similar practice of engagement is described in the poem, "The Tale of the Eloquent Peasant" written in Egypt in 2160-2025 BC. A feudal lord confiscates a traveling peasant's goods. The peasant objects in an example of ancient civic engagement, making a series nine eloquent petitions to the king.

Citizens today play an active role in the collection and dissemination of state news and information. Civic engagement is evolving as conventional communications between state and citizen are being supplemented by e-government technologies.

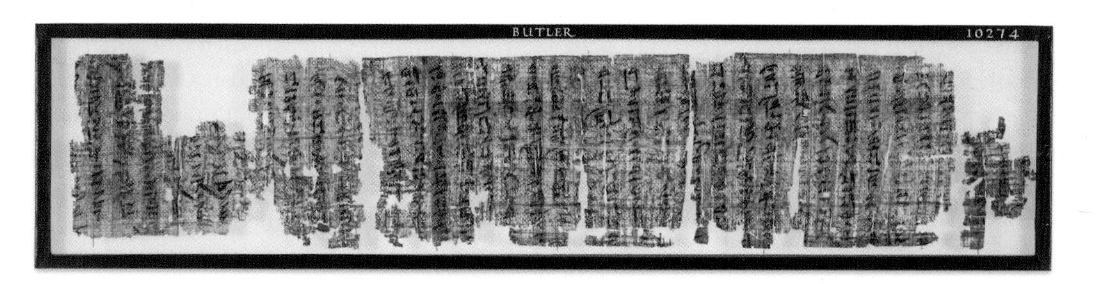

FIGURE 1.9: Excerpt of the Tale of the Eloquent Peasant[5]

The Shift to Citizen-Centric Engagement

The ability to connect citizens to the state has generated new programs that are transforming the public sector. Through its use of the Internet and mobile technologies, e-government can enhance democracy, revitalize civic engagement, and increase legitimacy. To achieve this, governments are using web portals to give citizens a single point of access to integrated government programs and services.

[5] Anonymous, *"Tale of the Eloquent Peasant"*, The British Museum, Egypt, 1800: *https://www.britishmuseum.org/explore/highlights/highlight_objects/aes/p/papyrus_with_part_of_the_tale.aspx* (accessed January 2014).

Delivering secure, improved, and online access addresses freedom of information requirements, bringing government agencies one step closer to developing renewable programs and practices. Citizens are empowered to comment on proposed regulations and participate in policy development. Surveys are available on government websites, allowing users to rate ease of use and services available. On some sites, mobile apps can be downloaded for direct mobile access to relevant information and services.

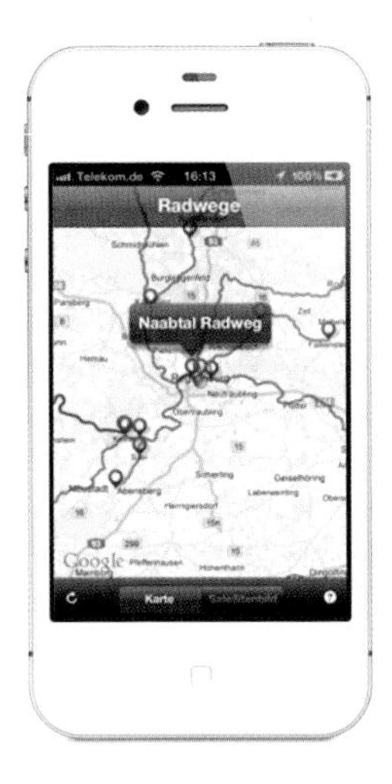

FIGURE 1.10: Apps for Deutschland on iTunes

The capacity of digital technology to expedite communication has already influenced the ways that people interact with their government. Participatory government ignites reform at the grassroots level to impact all levels of society. Social technologies organize human activity and promote the exchange of ideas. There are many examples of social media impacting social change, including both the Tunisian and Egyptian revolutions. The unstructured conversations that took place on social media platforms like Twitter,® YouTube® and Facebook® have had a direct impact on the action that took place on the ground. The opinions and voices expressed were amplified in a way that has never before been possible. This power can be channeled to advocate or improve products, services, and events. e-Government's potential extends beyond improving performance at lower costs to becoming a vehicle of transformation and change.

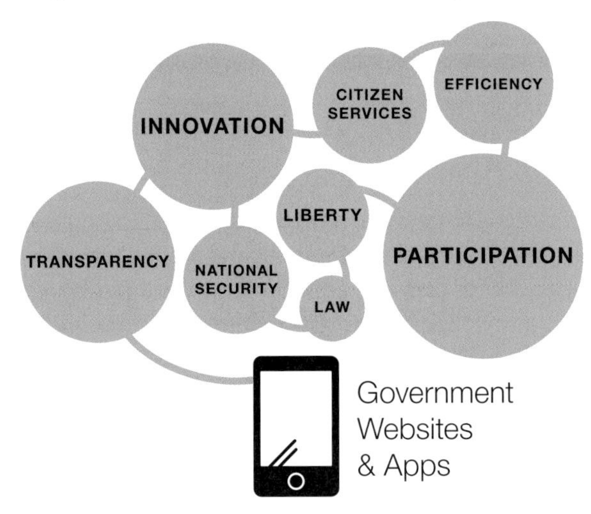

FIGURE 1.11: Government Websites and Apps Drive Citizen-Centric Services

Modernizing Mission: To Regulate

Regulations protect the health and safety of all citizens. They support the efficient operation of businesses in a competitive marketplace and help to preserve the environment. Regulations protect rights to ownership, enforce contractual agreements, and ensure that the fiscal system is functioning properly. Other common examples of regulation include labor standards, professional qualifications, transportation standards, health care regulations, and standards of production for certain goods.

With legislation like the Freedom of Information Act (FOIA) in the United States and its equivalent in Europe, the Data Protection Act, governments face external pressures to comply with regulations from regional, national, as well as international bodies like the International Organization for Standardization (ISO), World Trade Organization (WTO), international trade tribunals, and cross-jurisdictional courts. This legislation is critical to an informed electorate for keeping governmental activities transparent and accountable. Complying with regulations compels governments to adopt good recordkeeping practices, with the knowledge that information can be requested and by law must be produced.

More than 100,000 rules and regulations worldwide and growing

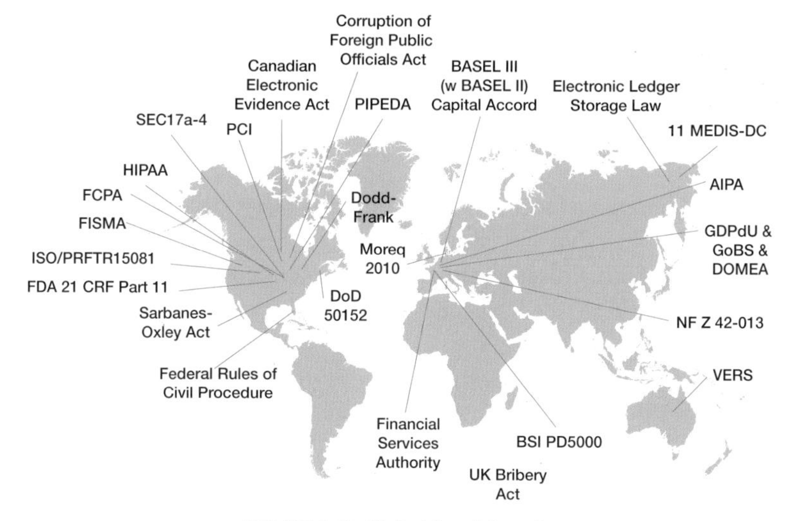

FIGURE 1.12: Global Regulatory Pressures

The Integrity of the Record

Early records of rights to ownership existed in a variety formats: a lease, will, agreement, writ, or grant of land. These records were typically preserved in a variety of contexts and housed in churches or cathedrals. One of the most complete and well-known examples of record-keeping is "The Domesday Book". It is England's very first public record, amassed in 1085 for William the Conqueror to identify who was responsible for land taxes.

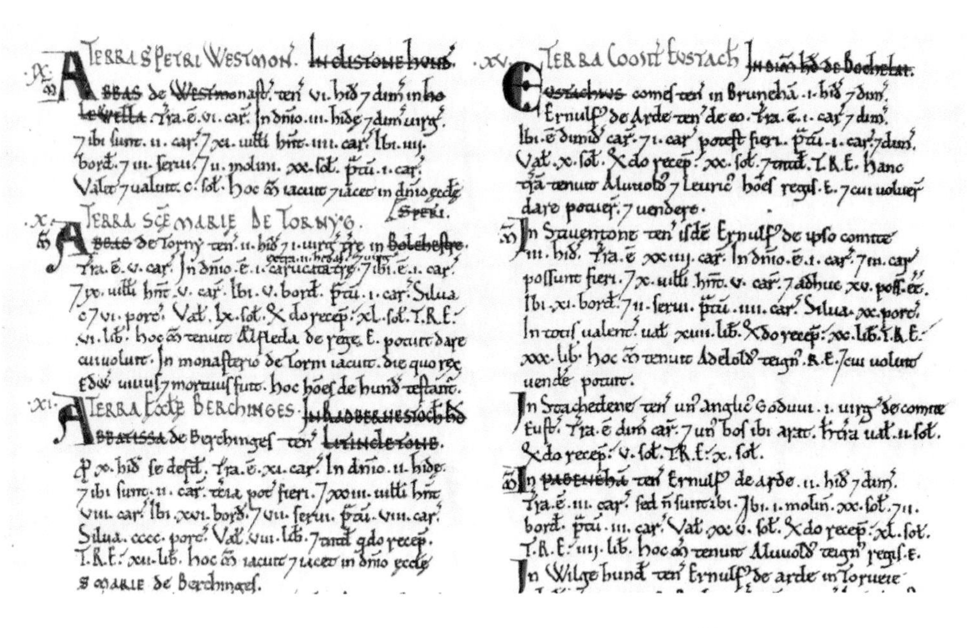

FIGURE 1.13: An Excerpt from the Domesday Book[6]

The Domesday Book embodies a facet of democratic government that holds true today: that accurate record of land ownership and citizenship are the fundamental basis for the rule of law. Without these, all is chaos. Preserving these records is critical to "keeping the peace." But we will never know how accurate the Domesday Book is as a record. In its entirety, it contains numerous obvious omissions and ambiguities. Certain areas of England were omitted from the survey as they were not yet conquered. Both the surveys and the book itself were compiled by people and were subject to human error. And finally, housing records in physical locations in paper format subjects them to the risk of being misplaced, destroyed, or even forgotten.

[6] *"The Domesday Book"*, National Archives, *http://www.nationalarchives.gov.uk/education/focuson/domesday/take-a-closer-look/* (accessed January 2014).

In spite of the risk of inaccuracy, our notion of history is based on the ability to access evidence from the past. Any overlooked or forgotten artifact alters a historical record forever. Consider how many records have been physically lost through the ages due to natural disasters, fires, wars, and so on. In government organizations across the globe records are being formally re-conceptualized as vital assets. With this recognition comes the realization that records need to be managed as rigorously as budgets, resources, and facilities. Public sector organizations are being held accountable and their ability to perform rests upon the integrity of the record.

In the digital age, accountability has taken on new force and meaning, reconfirming the necessity of effective recordkeeping. In litigious societies, responding to legal discovery requirements with proper records is as onerous as it is vital. Laws, such as the Patriot Act in the U.S., put additional strains on organizations to meet disclosure requirements. These requirements are driving the investments needed to develop records management solutions. This approach is rooted in the rapidly evolving international standards for maintaining authentic digital records and managing records in a modern administrative environment. As both hardware and software change rapidly, preserving email and complex documents requires both foresight and planning. There are no attics and basements, the refuge of many paper files, in e-government.

The security and protection of sensitive records is a mandatory requirement of governments that provide services to citizens. U.S. Federal agencies manage, on average, 209 million records—or 8.4 billion government-wide.[7] All around the world, governments are mandating the transition of permanent records to electronic recordkeeping in their agencies. President Obama's Managing Government Records Directive calls for all permanent records in Federal agencies in the U.S. to be managed electronically by 2019.

Public sector organizations face unique challenges in digitizing records and ensuring the fidelity of archived content. Data must be reliable, accurate, timely, and secure. e-Government helps agencies move from paper to electronic files, providing access to authorized users and ensuring the accuracy of content according to policy and regulation. Derby City Council, in the feature below, is using an e-government platform to run their digital mailroom and transform their services.

[7] MeriTalk,"*Federal Records Management: Navigating the Storm*", MeriTalk Press Release, March, 2013, *http://www.meritalk.com/pdfs/navigating-the-storm/MeriTalk_Navigating_the_Storm_Release.pdf* (accessed January, 2014).

Derby City Council

FIGURE 1.14: Derby City Council Website

The new, state-of-the-art mailroom has capacity to handle 8,000 items a day, converts over one million existing documents to digital format, and captures 90,000 to 100,000 pages per month.

Derby City Council is a city and unitary local authority in Derby, in the East Midlands region of England. The Council has around 8,000 employees, with around 2,000 working from their headquarters in Derby City to serve the local population of 250,000 residents.

In 2011, Derby looked to an e-government solution to reduce the amount of paper generated and stored and to facilitate their "One Derby One Council" strategic approach to the transformation of council services. Derby City Council selected an e-government platform for core document and records management functionality and a related solution to run their digital mailroom.

All inbound mail is now scanned and delivered electronically, reducing the reliance on email and expensive first-tier storage. The new, state-of-the-art mailroom has capacity to handle 8,000 items a day, converts over one million existing documents to digital format, and captures 90,000 to 100,000 pages per month. The team handles more inbound mail than ever before and even offers an outsource mail capture service to other organizations as an additional revenue stream. Back-office savings through consolidation and other efficiencies have contributed to savings of £20 million with no detrimental impact on front line services.

More than 2,000 in-house users are currently using the system, and this will extend to some 3,500 users. Digitized solutions are being applied in HR; to the Land Charges process; and to digitize recordkeeping for the Special Educational Needs (SEN) team, among others. e-Government is providing the Council with a solution that is efficient, intuitive, and scalable, helping them accomplish their core activities in a cost-effective, transparent, and timely manner.

Modernizing Mission: To Protect

To save lives, serve justice, and protect citizens, governments need effective tools to quickly pull together information and resources. Intelligence about suspected terrorists and known criminals often resides in disparate systems and databases, throughout various federal, state, and local government agencies. e-Government delivers full access to secure information, combining analysis with communications and messaging systems, collaboration, and statistical reporting—empowering government agencies to pool and share intelligence to protect citizens.

At the federal level, the military is tasked with delivering on their mission to protect. To coordinate and mobilize a phenomenal arsenal of resources, timely access to information and military logistics must be streamlined for effective execution. Speed and mobility are at the core of military and humanitarian operations. Even mere seconds could prove critical.

e-Government helps military organizations gather accurate intelligence and streamline operational procedures for greater mission achievement. It provides the ability to synchronize and analyze information gathered from diverse sources. Records and case management create the foundation for ensuring fast access to time-sensitive information, providing officers in the field with electronic access to arrest records, or geographical hotspots of crime and serial offending—information that helps detect, combat, and prevent crime.

We can see how fully integrated and effectively managed information helps to modernize on the mission to protect when we consider the tedious task and outdated method of collecting fingerprints. Using unique biological traits such as fingerprints, retina scans, and DNA to identify individuals often took weeks and even months to process. As technology becomes more portable, officers can use handheld scanners to identify individuals and compare these with records in databases to improve their effectiveness.

Timely access to critical information improves responsiveness and saves lives. Consolidating information from diverse systems (including mobile devices and video surveillance technologies), streamlines emergency management services for more rapid response. Officers and first responders can access, record, and disseminate important information no matter where they are. Using GPS technology, police and emergency personnel are able to pinpoint the exact location of a call and determine the fastest route to it, getting people the help they need quickly and efficiently.

Mobile access to data improves situational awareness and helps identify potentially dangerous situations. Public safety officials must focus on disaster mitigation, preparedness, response and recovery, while working within tight budgets constraints. e-Government technologies offer an improved level of access to information and disaster management resources. Through seamless communications, mobile access to real-time information, and analytics to provide insight into incidents, e-government is already being used on a global scale to spot threats to human life, from bush fires in California to disease outbreaks in Africa and even theft of nuclear material.

Technological advances will continue to transform mission activities to protect. Unmanned drones on patrol can deliver real-time information to dispatchers, crime analysts, and officers—alerting them to crimes as they happen. Social media is proving to be a useful crime-fighting tool in gathering intelligence. The applications are endless, and at this point inconceivable, but they all rely on fast, easy access to secure, accurate, and integrated information.

Embracing e-Government

Governments around the world are being impacted by a mix of disruptive technologies that include cloud computing, mobile devices, tablets, social media, and more. These technologies, while they pose security and other risks, also present great opportunity. As we have illustrated through examples of modernization, e-government gives agencies the opportunity to innovate more with fewer resources and better leverage data to improve the quality of services for citizens and other users.

e-Government increases efficiency and quality of mission, while minimizing operating costs and risks. But it can also do more. An integrated approach based on a strong information management strategy is the foundation on which modernization is built. It provides a platform to evolve citizen-engagement. It gives agency staff the tools they need to carry out their missions of engagement, service, regulation, and protection of all citizens. It democratizes data, unlocking the potential of information and encouraging a participatory government where citizens work with their governments to create a better place to live.

"A U.S. Department of Defense Organization

What follows is an excerpt from an interview between the Information Governance Lead for the Organization's CIO office and Tom Jenkins, Executive Chairman of OpenText. The interviewee works in a research, development, and acquisition Organization within the U.S. Department of Defense. Their workforce includes government civilians, military service members, and contractor personnel in multiple locations across the U.S. The Organization develops, tests, and fields system to protect deployed forces and allies.

TOM JENKINS: What prompted your Organization to search for an information management solution?

IG LEAD: *We required a DoD 5015.2 compliant Records Management Application (RMA) system that was cost effective, scalable, and could be integrated with our collaboration environment.*

How did you succeed with user adoption of your RMA system?

People are busy. We support people who provide mission services and they're always exchanging information. We do a lot of work with contractors, so information has to be secure. The solution had to be invisible, working behind the scenes, to auto-classify records.

What constitutes a record?

People have a tendency to want to keep data forever, but we know that context will change. The value of information created seven years ago is completely out of place in today's context. That has been a challenge, defining how long to keep information.

In the case of records management, our record champions within each department work with subject matter experts to develop a file plan—or determine what constitutes a record. For example let's say there is an event that has an associated working document. A subject matter expert can make the best decision on how important this information is based on the outcome of the event.

How do you balance security and the need for openness?

Each of the department heads helps us define the security requirements for access to content. Permissions are set differently depending on the need to access information to get the job done.

With most modern records and content management systems, people set permissions on access. It's not so much the technology but the management approach and policies.

Yes. And today's workforce is more mobile, more open about communications, so they expect to be able to access everything."

How do you see that transition unfolding? There is a huge generational shift going on in all industries.

It's fascinating, exciting, and overwhelming at the same time. As a citizen, transparency is important but there is also a need for privacy—we have to find a balance.

And that is the challenge: that the digital world is simply a reflection of our analog world, and we have to be careful to have a balance.

Governance is critical. Following our policies is very important in reducing risk and keeping storage costs low. But now we have new formats. Along with emails, there are RSS feeds, tweets, Facebook comments—and we have to determine how to manage these as records and ensure that they are secure. Several specific functions within our Organization have leveraged the content management lifecycle capability (with the 5015.2 securities) to build customized and dedicated libraries that could be restricted, controlled, and expanded to include workflow engines. While they have permitted secure access, these libraries have also saved the Organization thousands of hours in labor previously invested in a manual process.

"As a citizen, transparency is important but there is also a need for privacy—we have to find a balance."

CHAPTER 2

HOW GOVERNMENTS ARE ORGANIZED

CHAPTER 2

How Governments Are Organized

Governments at every level—national, regional, local—are grappling with changes brought on by the external influences of globalization, a worldwide economical crisis, shifting demographics, growing environmental concerns, and technological advances. Internally, government organizations are focused on increasing productivity, improving services that directly impact lives of citizens, and connecting information and services across the complex and overlapping levels of government that we have inherited.

Governments are adopting e-government solutions to promote teamwork and improve productivity across geographical, hierarchical, and organizational boundaries. They are having difficulty, however, changing from cumbersome, rule-laden and accountability-driven bureaucratic organizations into nimble, high-performing organizations. Culture, capacity, and authority are obstacles to transformation.

FIGURE 2.1: e-Government Framework—Mapping Mission to Organization: A Complex Mix of Objectives, Capacity, and Limitations

At its core, e-government is about redefining government relationships with all stakeholders: externally with citizens, businesses and other levels of government, non-government agencies, contractors and consultants; and internally with employees across departments and agencies; and even multilaterally across nations.

e-Government creates the space for new models of transparency, accountability, communication, and organization. Transformation occurs across many departments, with outcomes being driven by the citizen rather than function or program. Partnerships, networks, and e-markets improve performance and efficiencies and offset shrinking budgets.

This chapter describes how governments are organized, how they work together despite multiple, diverse, and parallel objectives, and how e-government has the potential to transform government organizations to facilitate efforts that cross borders, agencies, and even nations.

Systems of Government

Even at a simplified level, the pattern of executive functions within a government system is complex. In the model for the Westminster Parliamentary Government, the sovereign holds executive authority even though the Prime Minister and the Cabinet implement executive powers. The U.S. Government is technically defined as a federal republic, meaning that individual states have some power but central government has authority.

In most systems, executive authority is exercised by a Cabinet. In the U.S., the President presides over the executive branch as both head of state and the head of government. The executive branch includes the Vice President and the heads of 15 executive departments who make up the President's Cabinet, created to manage national and international affairs. The U.S. executive branch, an organization that today consists of roughly five million civil servants, is made up of myriad departments, including White House staff, the National Security Council, the Office of the U.S. Trade Representative, and more. Within the executive branch, there are also independent agencies, such as the U.S. Postal Service, the National Aeronautics and Space Administration (NASA), the Central Intelligence Agency (CIA), and the Environmental Protection Agency. In addition, at this level there are government-owned corporations such as the Federal Deposit Insurance Corporation.

COMMON LEVELS OF GOVERNMENT

In both the Westminster and U.S. Federal systems, there are three major levels of government. These are local or municipal governments (cities and counties), provincial or state governments (regions), and the federal or national government. The local governments typically put into practice policy directives that are specific to their communities. The provincial or state governments facilitate local governments and develop policies that involve more than one locality or region. The national government coordinates actions between the states, and between its country and other nations.

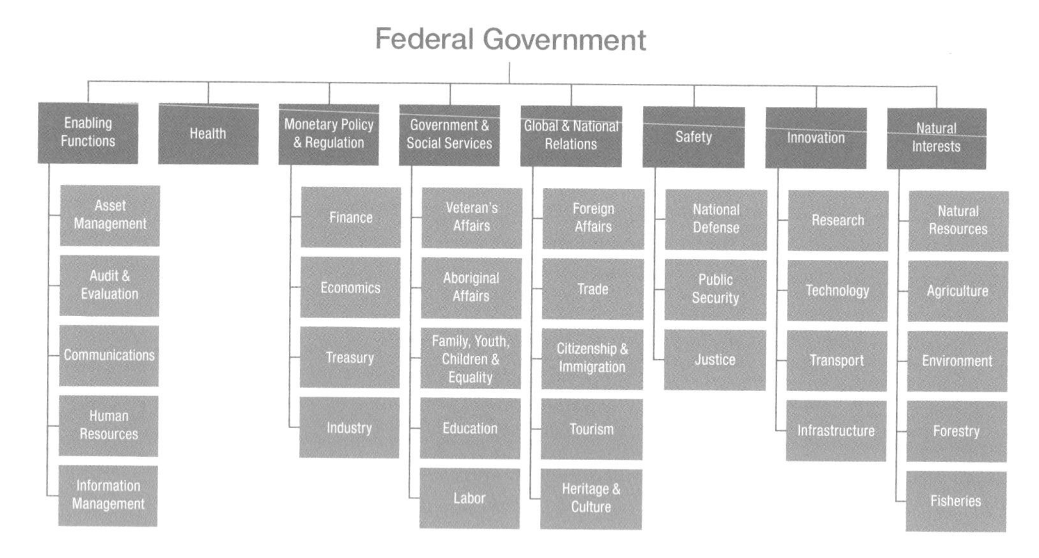

FIGURE 2.2: Federal Government Organization

How Governments Work Together

Both the Westminster and the U.S. Federal systems of government divide legislative powers between a central government and the governments of the provinces or states. Typically, the provinces may only pass laws in areas designated by the constitution, such as education, municipal government, and charitable institutions. Affairs that are not within the exclusive authority of the provincial legislatures fall under the federal parliament's power.

In many instances, there is overlap at the federal and provincial levels. In the U.S., different states have very different policies about how power is distributed to smaller jurisdictions. In some states, "Home Rule" delegates power to cities to regulate the laws within their borders. This has resulted in substantial diversity among the states with regard to every aspect of how their governments are organized. In Canada, there is similar overlap; both the federal and provincial parliaments can impose taxes, punish crimes, and regulate agriculture.

The division of powers between the Canadian federal and provincial governments is as follows[1]:

EXCLUSIVE FEDERAL JURISDICTION	JOINT FEDERAL AND PROVINCIAL POWERS	EXCLUSIVE PROVINCIAL JURISDICTION
- Peace, order, & good government - Any form of taxation - International/interprovincial trade & commerce, communications & transportation - Banking & currency - Foreign affairs (treaties) - Militia & defense - Criminal law & penitentiaries - Naturalization - Weights, measures, copyrights, patents - First Nations - Unemployment insurance & old age pensions	- Immigration - Agriculture - Pensions - Criminal law & penitentiaries - Taxation	- Anything local or private in nature - Direct taxation - Crown lands & natural resources - Hospitals (health sector) - Education - Welfare - Municipalities - Local works - Intra-provincial transportation & business - Administration of justice - Property & civil rights - Cooperatives & savings banks

Most states or provinces have at least two tiers of local government: counties and municipalities. The types and nature of municipalities vary from state to state. In addition to local governments, there may be local or regional special-purpose local governments, based on school districts, sewer service, public transportation, public libraries, and water resource management.

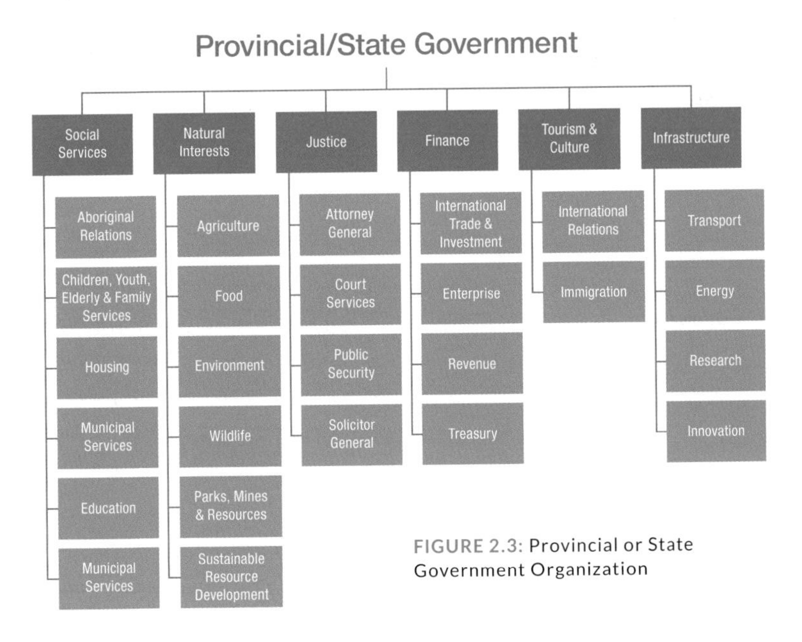

FIGURE 2.3: Provincial or State Government Organization

[1] Jay Makarenko, *"Federal Government in Canada: Organization, Institutions & Issues"*, March 4, 2009, Mapleleafweb, *http://mapleleafweb.com/features/federal-government-canada-organization-institutions-issues#federal* (accessed Jan 2014).

Local government refers to governmental jurisdictions below the level of the state. This category includes governments designated as cities, boroughs, towns, and villages. Municipalities range in size from the very small to the very large, and this is reflected in the range of types of municipal governments that exist in different areas. In most states, county and municipal governments exist as simultaneous entities. Municipal governments are administratively divided into several departments, that typically include urban planning and zoning, public works, public libraries, school boards, parks and recreation, police, emergency management, accounting/finance (tax collection and audits), administration, housing, and municipal court. Derbyshire County Council, in the following feature, is an example of a municipal government that has digitized its processes to better serve citizens.

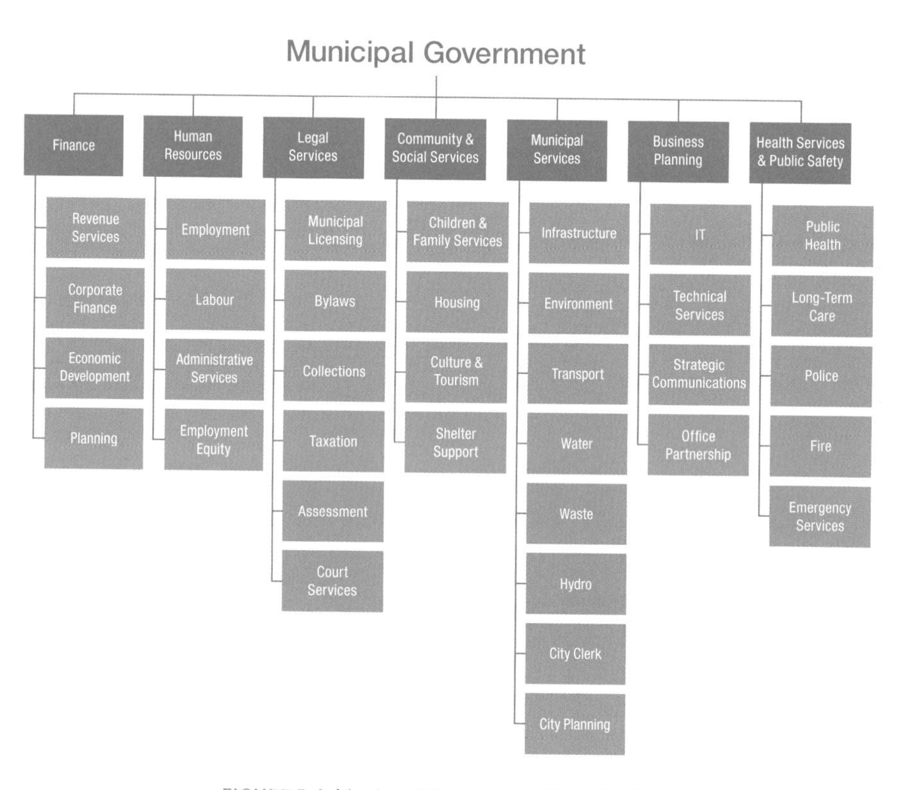

FIGURE 2.4: Municipal Government Organization

Derbyshire County Council

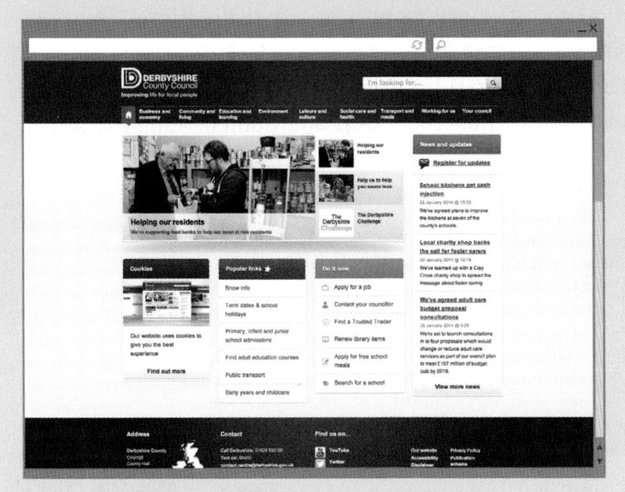

Digitization has helped reduce physical paper storage, eliminated duplication of effort, improved management reporting, and streamlined end-to-end "invoice-to-settle" process times.

FIGURE 2.5: Derbyshire County Council Website

Derbyshire County Council serves a population of 750,000 and employs around 37,000 staff. The Council is responsible for providing many services, including education, roads, and social care services. Some of the day-to-day finance activities of the Council produce a staggering volume of information with some 30,000 vendors, resulting in 250,000 invoices per year being handled by the Accounts Payable (AP) team.

Derbyshire made the decision to go digital and modernize their culture with an automated Invoice Management solution. Previous systems were manually based, causing a drain on internal resources. Manual keying of invoice data and resolution efforts involved time-consuming research, requests for additional information from multiple parties, manual routing, and the labor-intensive process of monitoring and providing update reports on the status of unpaid invoices.

The digital invoice management system optimizes the process of creating, managing, monitoring, and routing purchase orders and invoices for both accounts payable personnel and vendors. With the new solution, Derbyshire County Council manages invoices through a secure, browser-based interface where AP personnel and vendors can collaborate to resolve problems, obtain invoice status, check purchase order numbers, and submit invoices. As a result, invoices are processed more quickly and can be efficiently routed for problem resolution, approval, and payment. The system also provides more flexible, detailed reporting and analysis, which was previously hampered by the length of time report preparation took. Finally, full audit trail, retention, and disposition scheduling helps the council to ensure governance and regulatory compliance. Digitization has helped reduce physical paper storage, eliminated duplication of effort, improved management reporting, and streamlined end-to-end "invoice-to-settle" process times.

How Government Levels Relate to Each Other

Based on the governments systems explored earlier in this chapter, we can see that governments are structured into multiple levels, portfolio responsibilities, and jurisdictions—making any government a mix of goals, structures, and functions. Because government institutions are heavily structured, bounded by geographic districts, and dependent on thousands of representative institutions, their capacity to respond with agility to changing conditions is limited.

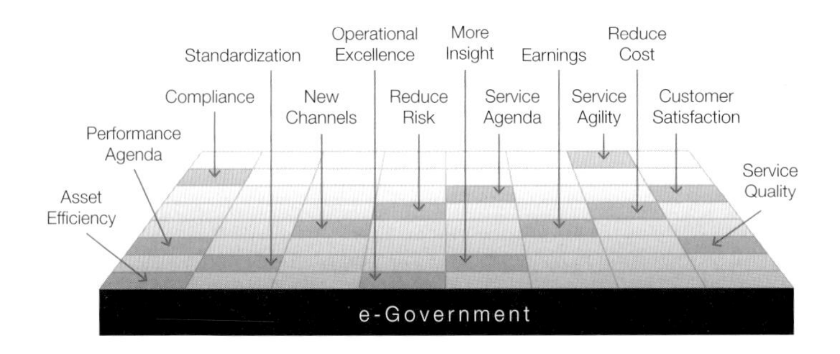

FIGURE 2.6: Diverse Agendas in e-Government

To be effective, especially in times of crisis, it is crucial that different levels of government work together. More often than not, relationships in government are mutually dependent and it is often not possible to separate responsibilities from outcomes between multiple levels. Government relationships are complicated by their inherent structure and diverse agendas—simultaneously vertical across different levels and horizontal at the same level of government, all connected through various networks.

As illustrated in the following table, collaboration must occur for policies to be successfully developed, supported, and implemented. Effective outcomes necessitate that the commitments assumed by central government are properly implemented at the local level. A lack of coordination results in policy gaps. Often, for example, provincial or state governments do not have the means (be it budget or capacity) to allocate resources to deliver public services. Other times, efforts can be duplicated with overlapping responsibilities, resulting in tremendous waste of effort, resources, and time.

Within governments across the globe, there is a constant struggle to integrate information and processes across jurisdictions (vertically), as well as across service lines-of-business (horizontally). Large populations need to be able to access government contacts as well as public information. Governments must regulate banks, government-owned businesses, private businesses, and their own internal policies and services. Managing relations and interdependencies between different levels of government is a requirement for successful outcomes.

LEVEL	RESOURCE MANAGEMENT	HEALTH CARE
International	Greenhouse gas emissions are discussed and international accords are negotiated and agreed upon (e.g., Kyoto, United Nations Environment Programme).	WHO and others monitor health outbreaks; national governments agree to global health development goals, etc.
National	National level government compiles input from all levels of government in their own country and represent internationally. Also responsible for managing certain aspects of resources such as international disputes, ocean resources, etc.	National governments set national health care policy, represent the country internationally, etc.
Regional	Responsible for managing natural resources and contributing to national and international plans and agreements. Directly manages natural resources such as oil-gas, forests, etc.	Delivery of health care against national and international policies and standards.
Local	Manages local waste and energy production according to provincial and national regulations and policies.	Local level health care delivery.

FIGURE 2.7: Collaboration Across Vertical and Horizontal Government Offices

e-Government supports opportunities to build collaboration and improve communications. Its technologies reinforce less centralized patterns of accountability, communication, decision-making, and social organization. New technologies like social networks, for example, have the potential to transform traditional public sector communications and organizational roles.

Policies, programs, and services can be more effectively implemented when resources are accessible, combined, and shared. Alignment between municipalities, provinces, and other sub-national organizations allows for greater coordination. Improving relations among vertical levels of government requires collaboration between ministries in charge of policies that impact at the sub-national or provincial levels. Horizontal cooperation at the local level can have a positive impact when governments share tools developed by other local authorities and join forces to improve economies of scale. Promoting collaboration among levels of government is critical for building capacity and sharing best practices.

e-Government helps public sector organizations find the balance between diverse agendas and shared processes to overcome fragmentation and duplication of effort. It provides a basis for dialogue, discussion, knowledge exchange, and learning that can help government levels identify common reference points to improve multi-level policy making and reduce disparities between departments. e-Government overcomes organizational silos to provide greater access to information, increase efficiencies and improve service delivery in a time of shrinking budgets and growing deficits.

The following feature on the Region of York in Canada illustrates how e-government supports a blended approach to business processes and department divisions to help overcome operational challenges and meet regulatory requirements.

Regional Municipality of York

FIGURE 2.8: Regional Municipality of York

> "As our implementation experience continued to mature, it became apparent that a blended approach of both business process and department/division strategy is required to be successful."
>
> **CORPORATE EDMS PROJECT MANAGER, YORK REGION**

The Regional Municipality of York is located just north of the City of Toronto, Canada. Comprised of nine municipalities, it has a population of approximately one million with 25,000 businesses located within its borders. The Region has an annual budget of $1.7 billion and employs 2,600 full-time staff.

York Region wanted an e-government solution that would help it improve business processes and address several operational challenges, as well as meet its obligations under new regulations established by the Municipal Freedom of Information and Protection of Privacy Act. Firstly, the Region wanted to bridge the information silos across regional departments and locations. Secondly, the Region recognized that a substantial shift from paper to electronic records was taking place. They needed a solution that could manage the wide range of document types being created. Fast searches were another consideration. And finally, the solution had to be cost competitive.

The Region's initial implementation strategy was based on identifying business processes that moved across the respective information silos within the organization, including the budgetary process, project management, reviews of legal agreements, construction projects, land use approvals, meeting agendas and notices, facility management, research and precedents, and even performance reviews. At last count, the system had 970 users. Over 500,000 electronic documents are managed in the system with some 300 added daily. There are close to 90,000 individual activities per month on the system. The total number of documents includes all Council and Committee records going back to 1971 when York Region was first established.

Models of Government Relationships

Transforming relationships is a fundamental part of e-government. According to the World Bank, e-government refers to "the use by government agencies of information technologies that have the ability to *transform relations* with citizens, businesses, and other arms of government. These technologies can serve a variety of different ends: better delivery of government services to citizens, improved interactions with business and industry, citizen empowerment through access to information, or more efficient government management."[2]

Broadly defined by the Gartner Group, e-government is "the continuous optimization of service delivery, constituency participation and governance by *transforming internal and external relationships* through technology, the Internet, and new media."[3] As an approach, e-government describes how technology facilitates deeper engagement between and among different levels of government, including Government-to-Citizen (G2C), Government-to-Employee (G2E), Government-to-Government (G2G), and Government-to- Business (G2B). Since these bi-directional relationships are inherent to the very definition of e-government, it is helpful to break them down into four primary models of engagement:

1. Government-to-Citizen (G2C)

This describes the interactions and transactions that take place between a citizen and their government, including the use of public services for individual or family use, such as the payment of taxes; payments of fines to local or state governments; personal records such as a passport, a new driver's license or a change of address; social security; public libraries; student loans; benefits; and any health-related services. Interactions are based on public information requests and administrative processes. G2C can take place at the federal, state, and local levels. Service delivery is either in person or online via a citizen-centric portal. Applications may include case management, correspondence management, process automation, secure information exchange, customer relationship management, customer experience management, portals, web content management, records management, social collaboration, and media management.

2. Government-to-Employee (G2E)

This model defines the relationships between governments, employees, and contractors. It describes the exchange of information at an interagency level between departments, management, and personnel regarding administrative tasks, performance, and mission activities. Applications include human capital management, performance management, program management, process and workflow management, information exchange, document and records management, collaboration, and knowledge management.

[2] Bruno Lanvin and Anat Lewin, *"The Next Frontier of E-Government: Local Governments May Hold the Keys to Global Competition"*, The World Bank, Oct, 2013. *http://siteresources.worldbank.org/EXTINFORMATIONANDCOMMUNICATIONANDTECHNOLOGIES/Resources/NextFrontierE_Government.pdf* (accessed February, 2014).

[3] Zhiyuan Fang, *"E-Government in Digital Era: Concept, Practice, and Development"*, International Journal of the Computer, the Internet and Management, August, 2002, Vol.10, Number 2.

3. Government-to-Government (G2G)

This model of engagement involves the exchange of information between government authorities regarding administration, laws, policy development, programs, and projects. G2G describes cross-agency interactions between government bodies; for example the municipal and the regional governments or the provincial government and First Nations in Canada as they collaborate to share information and services with a focus on more efficient service delivery, transparency, and performance. Applications include records management, workflow, process automation, secure information exchange, collaboration, and knowledge management.

4. Government-to-Business (G2B)

This relationship describes information and services that are used by entrepreneurs, businesses, and corporations for commercial use, including filing statements of incorporation, obtaining business licenses, customs declarations, business laws and regulations, wage reporting, patents and trademark filing, business or incentive programs, business policy, and workforce information. This relationship consists of commercial interactions between government and the private sector. Transactions range from acquiring and providing products and services, to placing and receiving orders, providing and obtaining information, and completing financial transactions. Applications include case management, invoice management (e-invoicing), e-procurement, information exchange, knowledge management, and records management.

e-Invoicing: Complying with Latin American Rules

Nearly every country in the world has legislation to regulate electronic invoicing or e-invoicing. The Brazilian and Mexican governments, for example, have very explicit rules on invoicing and mandate the use of government-sponsored systems to control the issue and receipt of e-invoices.

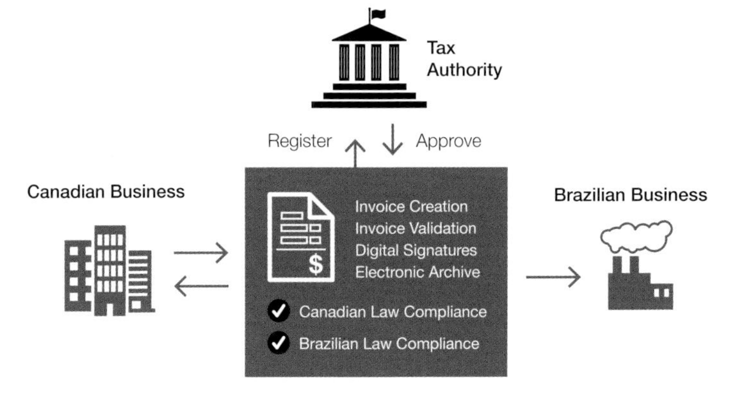

FIGURE 2.9: A Streamlined, Compliant e-Invoicing System

In Brazil or Mexico, any company sending or receiving invoices domestically must be aware of their legal obligations to use these electronic systems. In both countries, companies must integrate with government systems, use only approved certificate authorities (CA) for digital signatures, and adhere to specified data standards.

For global companies, the challenges of electronic invoicing compound as they manage multiple requirements for each value added tax (VAT) jurisdiction in which they do business. To issue invoices in Brazil, for example, an organization must integrate their accounting solution with the Brazilian Tax Authority (SEFAZ) electronic online system. Similarly, in Mexico, a company must integrate their accounting solution with the Mexican Tax Administration Service (SAT) electronic online system. Invoices sent to this system must be registered and approved by SAT.

A compliant solution enables organizations to send e-invoices to customers and receive them from suppliers, while achieving compliance with country-specific regulations. Supporting services include digital signatures, invoice creation, integration with government systems, and electronic archive. e-Government delivers a flexible, on-demand model for electronic invoicing that integrates an organization's accounts payable system with its suppliers to help meet compliance with e-invoicing regulations without investing in additional software and staffing resources.

Redefining Government Relations

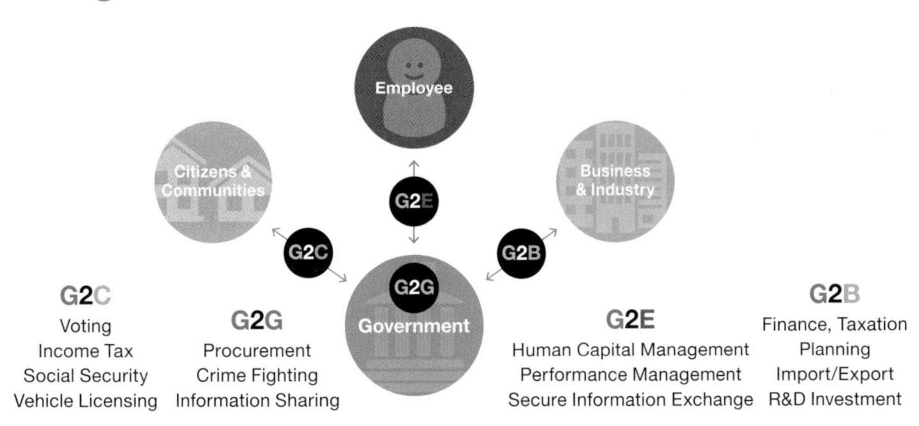

FIGURE 2.10: Digital Interactions in Government

The G2B model includes the relationship between government and not-for-profit organizations, which involves both inter- and intra-agency collaboration. It brings together countries, states, non-governmental organizations (NGOs) and multinational corporations to develop policies and solve multi-disciplinary issues such as globalization, ecological sustainability, nuclear proliferation, sanctions and trade regulations, global finance, terrorism, organized crime, and human rights. The practice of communication and negotiation between representatives of states requires e-government technologies to facilitate greater collaboration, interaction, and dialogue with global levels of security. We examine NGOs in more detail in Chapter 6.

The business of government is based on multiple interactions; internally between administrations, civil service, parliament, and judiciary functions; externally between central government and provincial, state, or local governments; and those that take place between citizens and their governments. e-Government supports new models of engagement at all levels of government. It streamlines the interactions and transactions between levels of government, making them more convenient, cost-effective, and transparent. This innovative approach to partnering is described in the following feature, in which the Institute of Public Administration of Canada introduces a new model of collaboration to raise the bar for policy development at a global level.

Redefining Employee Relationships

e-Government helps government organizations work more effectively together. By enabling new models of departmental interaction and multi-tiered collaboration, employees are empowered to work across boundaries to solve common issues.

As illustrated in the models of government relationships above, information is the fundamental commodity underlying effective e-government transformation. The exchange of information or data is central to government-based transactions and interactions. In its many formats and applications, however, information can hinder departmental collaboration in government and lead to fragmented policies, programs and processes.

Our Shifting Digital Landscape

Today's digital technologies offer us rich and immersive user experiences and opportunities to connect with others to communicate, collaborate, and create and share content. These digitally based relationships are changing how we interact—as friends, as colleagues, and as citizens. At the same time, our world is becoming smaller, more personalized, more connected, and accessible.

As technologies evolve and the ways that we communicate change, e-government presents an effective way for governments to move forward and redefine their relationships with stakeholders. Through the use of innovative ICT technologies, governments can:

- Deliver higher-quality services to citizens
- Improve collaboration with business, governments, and markets
- Comply with regulations
- Demonstrate accountability through transparency
- Empower citizens to participate in government
- Increase efficiencies and performance
- Do more with less

The Institute of Public Administration of Canada

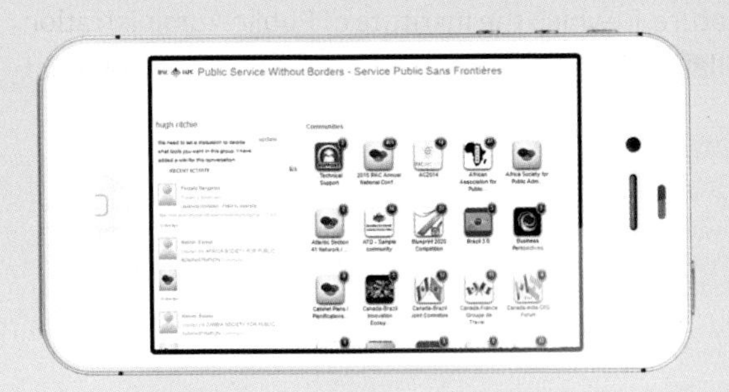

FIGURE 2.11: Cloud-Based Collaboration to Improve Program Excellence

"PSWB allows dialogue to happen in a safe and secure environment, encouraging the free flow of information and ideas.
We're finding that it is a support mechanism for networking across borders that users have probably never experienced before."

CHIEF EXECUTIVE OFFICER, INSTITUTE OF PUBLIC ADMINISTRATION OF CANADA

The Institute of Public Administration of Canada (IPAC) is dedicated to excellence in public service through the creation of knowledge networks and research. As a membership-based organization, IPAC consists of 18 chapters across Canada, partnering with all orders of government, aboriginals, and academia, as well as similar associations from around the world.

As communication methods between members have evolved, IPAC wanted to meet the call for more open government and greater transparency, while staying within the challenges of budgetary and security constraints. They were looking for a collaborative solution that was both secure and flexible enough to facilitate connectivity and interaction between individuals with specific needs and areas of expertise. IPAC found a cloud-based collaboration solution with PSWB.net, a social e-government platform. Public Service Without Borders (PSWB) provides a central location for all public servants to share information and collaborate in real time to advance the development of policies and citizen-centric services across the globe.

Within its first year, over 4,000 registered users engaged using PSWB in both public and private communities that focus on health care, social sciences, policy creation, and many other areas. Since its creation, 50 communities have been added. PSWB is accessible at anytime, anywhere in the world on mobile devices with information that is protected centrally, not at the device level. File sharing and synchronization are straightforward and permit access to critical content on the go, delivering a convenience that breaks down borders and time horizons. IPAC is confident that the cloud-based network will result in improved decision and policy making to promote open government.

The implementation of e-government, illustrated in stages in the figure below, begins with establishing an online presence that offers basic access to government-related information. A simple or static online presence is enhanced by offering services as well. This second stage evolves into giving citizens options to complete financial and non-financial transactions online. The final stage is the provision of a fully integrated, streamlined, citizen-focused experience based on optimized efficiencies and service delivery.

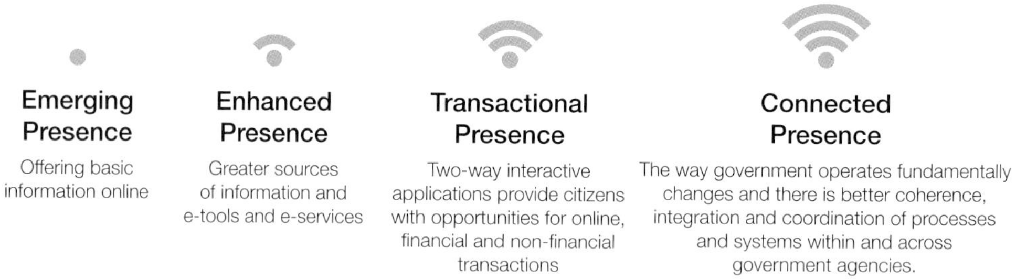

Emerging Presence

Offering basic information online

Enhanced Presence

Greater sources of information and e-tools and e-services

Transactional Presence

Two-way interactive applications provide citizens with opportunities for online, financial and non-financial transactions

Connected Presence

The way government operates fundamentally changes and there is better coherence, integration and coordination of processes and systems within and across government agencies.

FIGURE 2.12: The Stages of e-Government[4]

In the final stage of e-government deployment, websites are categorized by function not by internal organization or hierarchy or agency. Reflecting practices of the private sector, the focus is on the user and providing a seamless experience; citizens no longer need to know which agency or function of government is delivering a service. For this final stage to be achieved, interoperable connections between agencies, levels, and major stakeholder groups (G2C, G2B, G2E, and G2G) must be created.

This shift to a citizen-centric experience is impacting the nature of government administration and management. e-Government supports this shift by combining infrastructure and applications and presenting them in a portal that integrates the front office (citizen services) with the back office (employee collaboration, information, and processes). Many governments have embraced digital technologies, putting materials from publications and databases to government services online for use.

e-Government incorporates a number of digital applications across a broad range of government functions. Given the scale, scope, and multi-portfolio nature of governments and the transformational potential of e-government, the most effective approach is a holistic one. An e-government infrastructure combines: technologies for online service delivery, transactions and e-procurement, e-marketplace exchange of goods and services, the management of human capital and internal communications, secure external information exchange, records management and compliance, and a unified repository or repositories to support the paperless office. These are all examined in greater detail in the following chapter.

[4] Tanya Gupta. *"The UN E-Government Survey: Towards a More Citizen-Centric Approach"*, The World Bank, December 27, 2011, *http://blogs.worldbank.org/publicsphere/un-e-government-survey-towards-more-citizen-centric-approach* (accessed Jan 2014).

Governments are faced with the challenge of transformation and the need to reinvent their systems to deliver cost-effective services. The deployment of e-government solutions can only be successful if governments re-evaluate their mission activities and match these with new, automated, and streamlined processes, transactions, and interactions.

e-Government connects citizens and businesses with their governments. Through e-government, organizations in the public sector have the opportunity to transform relationships based on new forms of collaborating that empower citizens and help governments to transparently improve efficiencies and gain citizen trust.

CHAPTER 3

THE GOVERNMENT ICT LANDSCAPE

CHAPTER 3

The Government ICT Landscape

Governments rely on volumes of data to deliver programs and services. From crime prevention to defense, health care, and social services, government organizations struggle on a daily basis to manage growing amounts of information.

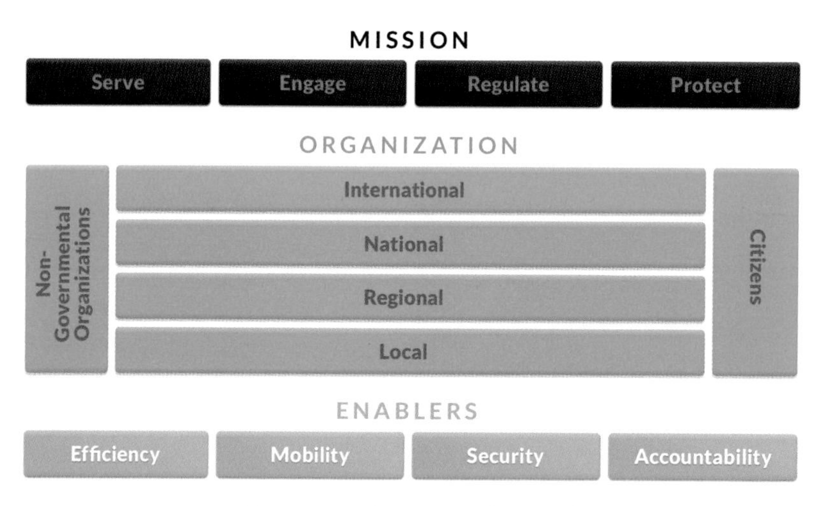

FIGURE 3.1: e-Government Framework

While the growth of information provides opportunities to improve efficiency and performance, it also represents significant risk. Information that is not managed can become a threat to an agency, often at enormous cost. Cases of records gone missing, failed audits, and lost information have resulted in recent scandals around data leaks or the deletion of mass emails. Governments today are required to ensure that information is secure and audited, intellectual property is not lost or compromised, processes are defensible, and data is discoverable.

e-Government helps all levels of government balance the need for transparency and innovation with requirements for privacy and information security. This chapter examines how e-government minimizes threats and improves efficiency, mobility, security, and accountability at all levels of government.

Information as a Commodity

Government agencies generate massive amounts of information. The average U.S. state and local agency stores 499 terabytes of data. This data ranges in format from structured to unstructured information contained in case-related documents, military and civilian personnel records, emails, website content, surveillance videos, and much more. In areas like health care, where 95 percent of data generated is in video format, thousands of times more bytes are generated than the text or numerical data generated in administration.[1]

In a recent study of U.S. state and local governments, CIOs and IT managers surveyed expect their data to grow by more than 50 percent over the next two years.[2] In the same study, only 47 percent of agencies are making strategic decisions based on their information. As the volume and complexity of this content increases, so does the need to understand, locate, and manage it. The potential for improvement is vast and required; the effective exchange of information is important to the continuity of business at any level of government.

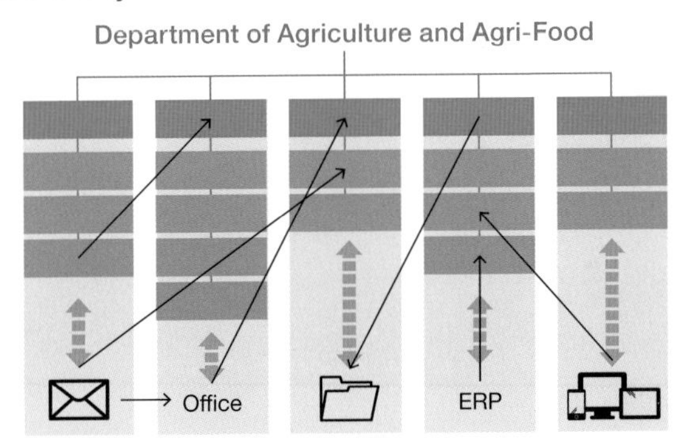

FIGURE 3.2: Integrating Information Across Silos Is a Common Challenge

The mismanagement of information hinders multi-level collaboration in government. Integrating information and processes across silos is a common challenge and is dependent on existing infrastructure and applications. An e-government solution centralizes information from many applications on a secure and interoperable platform, enabling departments to collaborate, make better decisions, manage correspondence, and streamline operations for higher efficiency and improved public service. In the story below, the Pinellas County Clerk of the Circuit Court office relies on e-government to improve case management processes and collaboration across different locations and stakeholders.

[1] James Manyika and Michael Chui, et al, *"Big data: The next frontier for innovation, competition, and productivity"*, McKinsey & Company, June 2011.

[2] MeriTalk, *"State and Local Agencies Expect Data to Double in Next Four Years; Show Little Adoption of Big Data"*, MeritTalk Press Release, April 29, 2013, *http://www.meritalk.com/pdfs/state-and-local-big-data/State_and_Local_Big_Data_Gap_Release.pdf* (accessed February 2014).

Clerk of the Circuit Court, Pinellas County

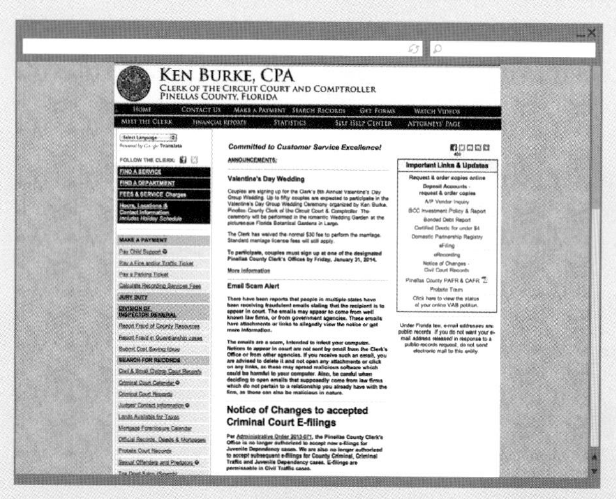

FIGURE 3.3: Clerk of the Circuit Court, Pinellas County Website

"We've been more efficient because we're doing the same amount of work, even a greater amount of work with fewer people. And we're effective because people are getting their files quicker and getting their orders in a timelier manner."

CLERK OF THE CIRCUIT COURT AND COMPTROLLER, PINELLAS COUNTY, FLORIDA

The Pinellas County government is made up of a unique mix of 25 governmental bodies that manage the county's 24 municipalities and unincorporated areas. The Pinellas County Clerk of the Circuit Court office is responsible for maintaining court records and pleadings, securing court evidence, collecting and disbursing court fines, and a variety of other functions within the County's judicial system. The Clerk's office is instrumental in ensuring that the County courts provide efficient services for citizens.

Like many counties experiencing rapid growth, Pinellas County experienced process inefficiencies that hampered its ability to achieve its "Excellence in Customer Satisfaction" mission. As well as experiencing bottlenecks in the paper-based traffic citation entry and verification processes, judges were still relying on manila folders with citation documentation to make their rulings. The County needed an automated solution to replace paper-based processes and improve efficiency in their traffic courtrooms.

A courtroom automation system based on a case management solution enables judges to manage a growing number of cases efficiently by easily accessing the history of an individual during court proceedings. The system provides judges with access to driving records, past citations, and Florida's centralized traffic systems. Integration of the solution with Pinellas County's information repository and in-car traffic ticketing system has enabled County officials to automate the entire information collecting process, saving hundreds of hours of data entry. As a result, officials are able to reallocate resources to other divisions. With this new solution, the County has been able to deliver on the State mandate for information sharing.

The Foundation for Holistic Government

From case management to contract management, budget formulation and execution, acquisition and procurement, and HR processes, government agencies rely on Enterprise Resource Planning (ERP) systems to provide support for day-to-day operations. These processes depend on large volumes of data. The value of this data lies not only in the individual transactions, but also in the supporting documentation that can reveal larger patterns of activity to confirm performance levels or evaluate compliance.

The decisive strength of e-government is its ability to cross department, content, and application silos. An e-government solution delivers out-of-the-box integration with existing ERP systems in an open landscape, uniting information across departments and making transactional information available for daily use. It embeds information management directly into processes like case management to give content a consistent context, and combines structured data with unstructured data (emails, social media, videos, images, and presentations) to align agency operations. As well as improving performance, an interoperable system reduces total cost of ownership, the reliance on paper-based processes, and the physical space required to store paper documents.

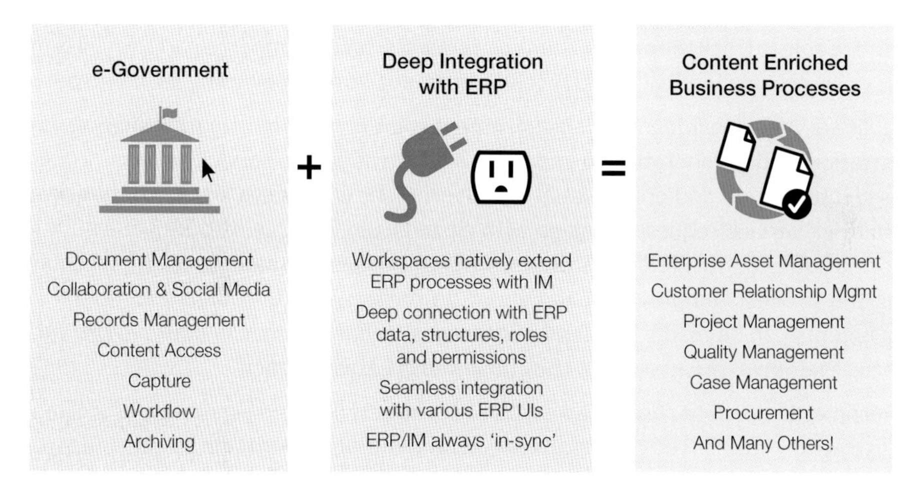

FIGURE 3.4: An Integrated and Interoperable Solution

Both the Canadian and U.S. governments, with their respective "Whole of Government" and "White House Digital Government Strategy" plans have emerged as leaders in the formal articulation of a holistic e-government approach—each recognizing that technology investments must be aligned with anticipated outcomes to support agency mission.

Efficient e-Government

In today's economic environment of uncertainty, citizens want a leaner, transparent, and more efficient government for maximum returns on taxpayer dollars. Both citizens and legislators are holding government leaders accountable for the results of public spending and programs. Are government efforts enhancing citizen service, economic activity, and quality of life? Citizens want to know and are increasingly empowered to find out.

e-Government facilitates a government-wide, integrated approach to service delivery. An e-government platform aggregates programs, processes, and information into a single public interface, connecting personnel and information across departments and agencies on the back end.

Empowerment Through a User-Centric Approach

Citizen services lie at the core of any government function. For citizens, e-government technology provides unprecedented transparency into the status of programs and services. An engaged government empowers citizens to access the services they need from any place, on any device, to create a seamless, self-service experience with every transaction.

Online citizen services, or e-services, deliver personalized views of individual or family services. Citizens are able to track the progress of their requests, access support, search for information and services, provide feedback, and receive automatic notification using an online portal.

For public servants, an integrated e-government solution links information sharing, process orchestration, and collaboration to improve administration and service delivery. Integrating back-end information and processes gives government employees access to the tools they need to track service requests, engage with citizens and improve responsiveness. The flow of information is controlled from the moment a request is made to its final resolution. During the process, employees can report on patterns and problems to reveal where improvements can be made. By identifying issues, departments can improve productivity and focus their investments where they have the greatest impact.

e-Government improves resource allocation, productivity, and accountability. Simplified administration reduces red tape, paperwork, and duplicated efforts to improve program alignment and service delivery. With information silos removed, decision-makers at any level can access information and share it with other agencies and users. By improving visibility, lining up resources against objectives, and measuring success against spending, governments can be more responsive to citizens' needs.

The General Council of the Judiciary, as described in the following feature, is using an e-government platform to deliver services in an integrated, user-centric portal.

General Council of the Judiciary

FIGURE 3.5: PoderJudicial.es

Web analytics help to measure the success of the site and overall performance, equipping the CGPJ with the tools it needs to present users with a relevent and responsive experience, supported by multimedia content.

The General Council of the Judiciary (Consejo General del Poder Judicial or CGPJ) was established by the Spanish Constitution in 1978 as the constitutional body that governs the Judiciary of Spain. The CGPJ wanted to combine its systems into an online portal to provide citizens with personalized access to the information and services they needed. The new portal would support a variety of communication channels in multiple languages. On the back end, the system would be required to integrate all corporate services of the Judiciary Council to streamline collaboration, provide integrated services such as online applications, allow for the secure management of information, and comply with current regulations around transparency, accessibility, multilingualism, Law 11/2007, and more.

An e-government solution was selected as the basis for the CGPJ website and judiciary extranet, providing the Council with a technologically sound and manageable platform for the future. The multilingual portal supports a substantial number of hits and is readily scalable. The web publishing process is more efficient; self-service capabilities have significantly reduced the time it takes to publish up-to-date information.

The system went live internally with 6,500 active users and 5,400 messages exchanged on its forums. Members of the Judiciary can participate and collaborate using the system's virtual environments, 45 communities of practices, and shared files. Secure access to integrated applications and services is provided through single sign-on and identity management. The system is customizable, allowing users to personalize and configure their working environment. Looking to the future, the CGPJ is planning to expand the platform to other departments in the Council and support mobile access.

www.opentext.com/e-Government/CGPJ

Mobile e-Government

The ubiquity of the Internet has been replaced by the ubiquity of the mobile device. In the private sector, the mobile Internet is already a driving source for productivity, efficiency, and output. In the public sector, however, many organizations have failed to keep pace in the adoption of disruptive technologies as productivity tools.

Mobile devices can make it easier for citizens to engage with their government for services and participate in program development. As part of automated service delivery, the mobile device is the final destination in a series of interactions with government that culminate in presenting citizens with an end-to-end, streamlined experience.

Mobile government extends services to citizens and other users via mobile devices. There are many different ways that mobile devices can be used for great benefit: to send out a mass alert via short service message (SMS) in the event of an emergency or natural disaster, to support communications between home and school, to provide registration for local events, to send out traffic alerts—the possibilities for government mobile applications are countless.

Likewise, the benefits of mobile government are many. Convenience and flexibility results in better service delivery and higher satisfaction levels for citizens. Easier access to information and processes improves productivity for public servants. In a crisis situation, the ability to reach a larger number of people has the potential to save more lives.

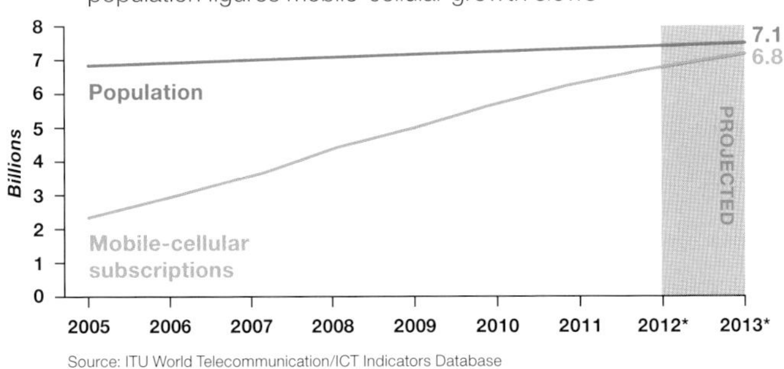

FIGURE 3.6: Mobile Subscriptions Approaching World Population[3]

[3] ITU, "*ITU releases latest global technology development figures*", February 27, 2013, *http://www.itu.int/net/pressoffice/press_releases/2013/05.aspx* (accessed January 2014).

Mobile Citizens and e-Services

Mobility bridges the digital divide between the haves and the have-nots by increasing access to government services. Mobile apps have opened up the exchange of information between people and their governments. The Border Wait Time app gives citizens estimated wait times for border crossings between Canada and the U.S., based on information made available by the Canada Border Services Agency.

FIGURE 3.7: Border Wait Time App

Some governments are already making it possible for citizens to complete transactions using their mobile devices. Only a secure e-government infrastructure—one that integrates with legacy applications and information—equips governments to align service delivery. Databases can be integrated, tasks centralized, and processes redesigned to reduce costs while improving service delivery. Mobile access is becoming the prime way that citizens engage with their governments. This is discussed in greater detail in Chapter 14 of this book.

Mobile Government Employees

In the private sector, the explosive growth of mobile devices and the popularity of mobile apps has many managers wondering how they can leverage the multi-functionality and portability of these devices to improve productivity. According to research, mobile apps can increase productivity, reduce cycles for decision-making, expedite processes, and improve customer service.

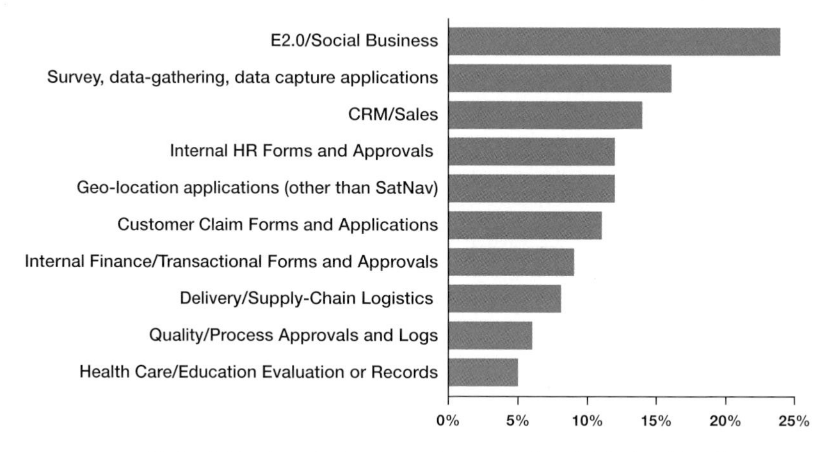

FIGURE 3.8: Organizations Are Embracing the Mobile App Trend[4]

[4] Doug Miles, *"Making the Most of Mobile - content on the move"*, AIIM/OpenText, 2011.

Just as organizations are providing secure, managed mobile access to enterprise systems, governments should extend their processes, information, and applications to public servants on mobile devices so that they can engage with the resources they need to do their jobs effectively.

Mobile technology helps government employees, especially front line workers, do more with less. Ideally suited for caseworkers, first responders, and law enforcement officers, mobile access increases responsiveness by providing critical information and resources on the go, 24/7. Time and money are saved through increased accuracy of information, expedited decision-making, minimized data entry, increased situational awareness, and the elimination of labor-intensive, manual paperwork.

Medical field workers in Africa, for example, are using their mobile phones to survey 200,000 inhabitants of the Kilifi District in Kenya, where the endemic rates of malaria are higher than anywhere in the world. Using the Mobile Demographic Surveillance System (MDSS) App, written by undergraduate students at the University of Nairobi, medical field workers can remotely interface with a hospital's database, conduct surveys, and remain in the field for longer periods of time, while bypassing the data-entry process altogether.[5]

Secure e-Government

The need for information security has never been more pressing with information fragmented across mobile devices, multiple applications, in both private and public clouds. In all sectors, the ever-present threat of security breaches is driving investments in secure information management.

With increased access to personal information, governments must consider security and privacy to ensure information systems are protected and individual rights are respected. Security refers to the protection of information systems and controlling access to the information itself. Privacy refers to respecting the right to have information attributed to an individual to be treated with the appropriate level of protection. Information privacy laws are in place to do just this.

Many government policies are focused around national security and privacy. In the U.S., these regulations include the USA PATRIOT Act, the Homeland Security Act, and the Health Insurance Portability & Accountability Act (HIPAA). Canada's counterpart is the Personal Information Protection and Electronic Documents Act (PIPEDA). European equivalents include the Data Protection Act (U.K.), the EU E-Privacy Directive, and Data Protection Directive.

[5] *"MDSS: Medical Data Collection on Mobiles"*, MDSS , May 2007, *http://www.media.mit.edu/ventures/EPROM/research.html* (accessed Feb 2014)

Security plays an integral role in e-government. For security to be effective, it must address risks, benefits, and processes at the organizational level and align these with policies and procedures, stakeholders, and resources. Protecting confidential information requires a risk management strategy that can also be leveraged to help optimize mission operations while minimizing threats.

Where Do Security Threats Come From?

In order to deliver on mandates like providing open access to data for citizens, it is imperative that agencies protect their information as a critical asset. But security threats have evolved alongside technology. From organized crime syndicates to hacktivists, vulnerabilities permeate all levels of government IT systems.

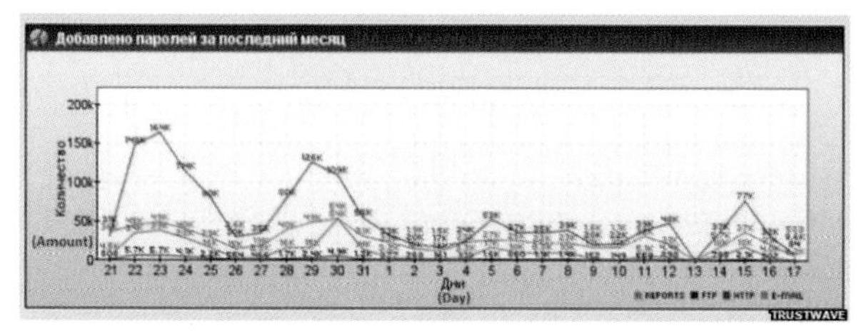

FIGURE 3.9: Malware Scraped Details from Users on a Daily Basis[6]

In December of 2013, more than two million stolen passwords used for sites such as Facebook, Google, Yahoo,® and other web services were posted online.[7] Login data was taken from computers that were infected with malicious software. The stolen information could be used to extract and then sell people's personal information. In February of the same year, Microsoft® announced that it had been hacked following a series of cyberattacks.[8]

Companies and their data are vulnerable. Despite external breaches, a recent study across industries reveals an interesting fact. While many organizations have good external defenses in place, the real threat of a security breach comes from unauthorized access by employees. As was the case with the WikiLeaks incident and the National Security Agency-PRISM scandal; the risk of security breach is often from the inside out.

[6] BBC News, *"Stolen Facebook and Yahoo passwords dumped online"*, December 4, 2013, *http://www.bbc.co.uk/news/technology-25213846* (accessed January 2014).

[7] *Ibid.*

[8] Damon Poeter, *"Microsoft Joins Ranks of the Tragically Hacked"*, PC Magazine, February 22, 2013.

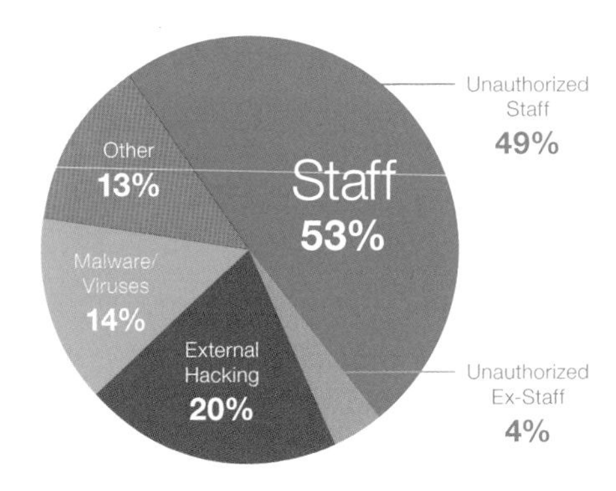

FIGURE 3.10: The Most Likely Source of a Security Breach[9]

The rise of the mobile workforce has also increased the threat of both intended and unintended security breaches—from a lack of clearly defined or implemented Bring Your Own Device (BYOD) policies to lost or stolen devices and data leaks of personal or confidential corporate information. The protection of government information should be holistic, covering all bases to avoid information risks that might violate legislation, cause non-compliance with regulations, or adversely impact the organization's ability to perform mission activities. Protecting sensitive data in a government IT environment is a continual challenge. Striking the right level of balance between the open flow of information and rigid control is a very important one. e-Government allows access on a "need to know" basis, while preserving an overall, federated archive of information.

Aspects of e-Government Security

Effective e-government is designed to protect information where it is used: at the point of interaction in the application itself. The following security mechanisms are built right into the system to secure content:

- Access and Permissions
- Secure Information Exchange
- Information Audit Capabilities
- Information Governance

Access and Permissions

A comprehensive e-government solution is designed for high-security environments, allowing organizations to configure security according to the level required for each information asset. Access controls ensure that users see only what they have permissions to see. In a granular system, access rights can be applied at the individual or group level to different stages in the lifecycle of content. By setting these controls, agencies can control data leaks and safely leverage emerging technologies such as social networking and mobile apps.

[9] Doug Miles, *"Making the Most of Mobile - content on the move"*, AIIM/OpenText, 2011.

Extended information security can be applied through an e-government system. When individuals request access to information, the system authenticates the individual, checking for additional identifiers like nationality, security clearance, and business role. Data sovereignty and privacy legislation in many countries requires that content be stored and accessed only in systems located in those countries. When content is marked with security clearance restricted to a given geography, the system will ensure that it is stored in that geography and that users can access it only when physically located in that country.

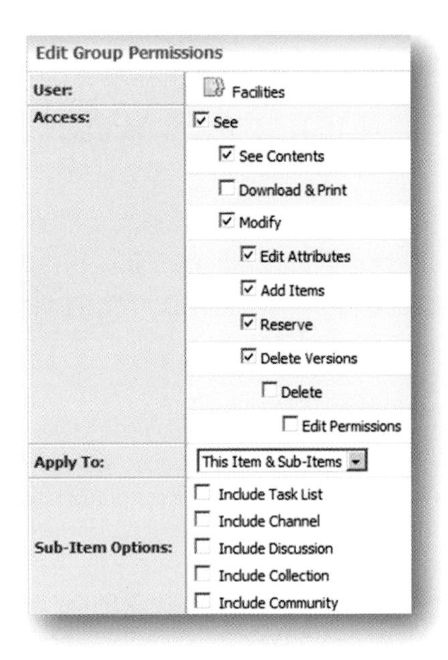

FIGURE 3.11: User Permissions

Information Audit Capabilities

Throughout its lifecycle, all content in an e-government system is tracked and all actions audited and logged. Audit capabilities are an additional layer designed to help manage security risks. These capabilities make all actions performed on a document or record transparent, from identifying who accessed the document to when it was downloaded, modified, or deleted, and when administrative settings were changed.

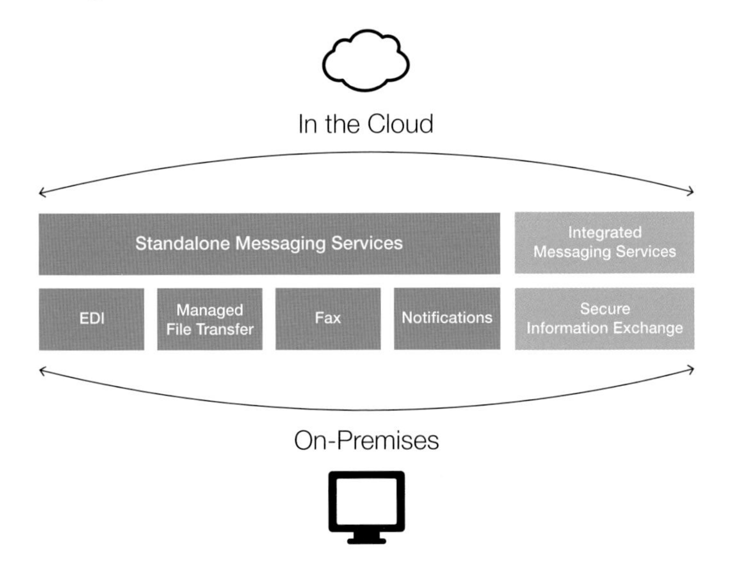

FIGURE 3.12: Secure Information Exchange

Melbourne Water

Using a secure and compliant information management system, users are able to interact and collaborate easily with each other, helping to ensure accuracy of information, regulatory compliance, and improved water services for the public.

Melbourne Water is owned by the Government of Victoria in Australia and is responsible for $8.4 billion in assets. Melbourne water required easy access to their information, particularly to help external bodies meet regulatory requirements or requests for information. Historically, information was siloed within the different departments or teams which resulted in the inability to share and provide accurate information. Business requirements placed an emphasis on managing their information electronically and securely.

Using a secure and compliant information management system, users are able to interact and collaborate easily with each other, helping to ensure accuracy of information, regulatory compliance, and improved water services for the public. All areas of the organization are benefiting from improved information management, from corporate governance departments like policy development and business services to the maintenance and operations team and civil works.

Records Management helps Melbourne Water to manage both their physical and electronic files, enabling them to request and process obligations but also respond to requests from their public records office and meet those obligations and compliance needs as well.

Secure Information Exchange

As part of an integrated e-government solution, information exchange helps agencies communicate and trade information securely. Sensitive data is protected during file transfer and daily information exchanges because it is encrypted at all times—both inside and outside of government enterprises.

Information Governance

e-Government provides a secure and integrated framework for effective information governance. It incorporates the tools needed to maintain policy in one central location and centrally manage the content and processes within their source systems. In the feature above, Melbourne Water is using e-government to keep its assets secure, transparent, and accurate so that it can deliver on its mission to provide water services to the public.

Accountable e-Government

While there are many good reasons for government organizations to implement information governance programs, regulatory compliance is a significant business driver. Other drivers include business continuity, savings on storage and infrastructure, unimpeded knowledge sharing, stronger security and privacy, and the ability to respond quickly and proactively to investigations of all types.

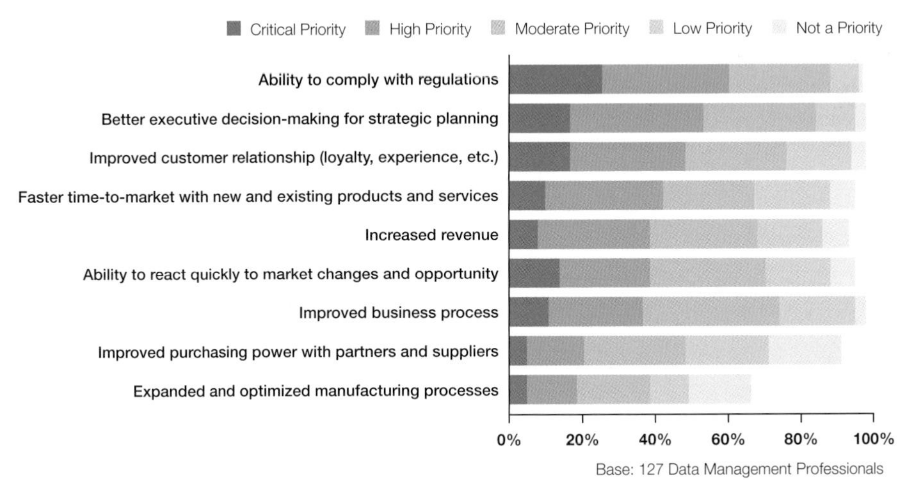

FIGURE 3.13: Compliance is a Key Driver[10]

[10] Michele Goetz, Henry Peyret and Alan Weintraub, *"Data Governance Equals Business Opportunity. No, Really"*, Forrester Research, May 20, 2013.

In all countries, countless government regulations, industry standards, and company procedures exist. Non-compliance can lead to poor performance, financial penalties, and even criminal charges. Transparent government requires well-documented processes with appropriate internal controls to ensure the legal and prudent use of taxpayer funds.

With increasing amounts of data, there is also the growing complexity of legal and regulatory requirements, including the mandate to convert hardcopy documents to digital format. Establishing a single source of the truth across multiple sources involves managing structured data, unstructured content, and emerging data types, such as social media, securely as records, both inside the firewall and in the cloud.

e-Government delivers a seamless compliance solution that connects procedural guidance with documentation, process execution tools, reporting and audits, and integration with ERP systems. It acts as a central nervous system to capture, track, and report on regulatory requirements. e-Government brings consistency and scale to the management and preservation of information by incorporating records management with solutions for archiving, email management, search, and e-discovery.

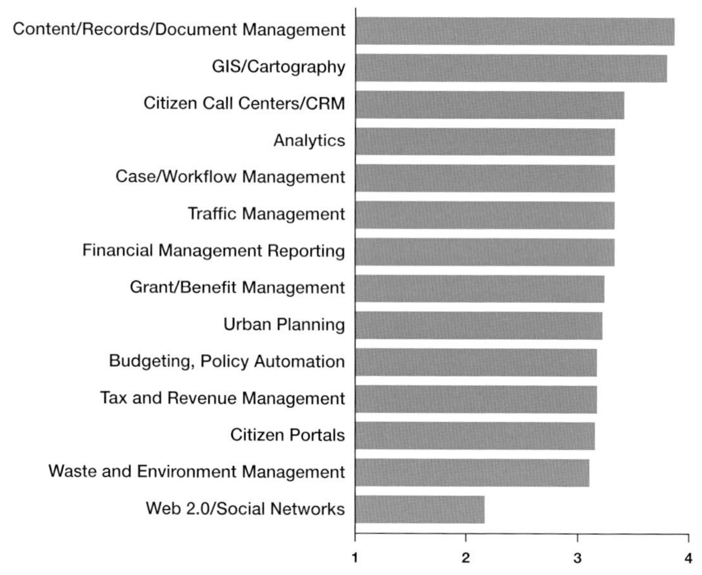

FIGURE 3.14: Records Management as a Top IT Investment Priority for Governments

Effective records management is not just about preservation; it is also about adding value to mainstream mission activities. Content such as emails, documents, and paper files can be classified as business records and managed from creation to deletion to comply with information governance and regulatory requirements, including DOD 5015.2 and MoReq 2010 v1.1.

As governments move applications and shared information to the cloud, they will be required to manage records in many locations. Records management provides visibility for IT governance and data management, and reduces risk by eliminating duplication and supporting automatic disposition of records according to agency policy. Records management gives accountability and accuracy of information new force and meaning for public sector organizations, which is why it ranks as a top IT investment priority.

FIGURE 3.15: Complete Lifecycle Management of Records

With growing open data initiatives, the process of disclosure (in accordance with the USA PATRIOT Act, for example), has become a tremendous challenge. The ability to assess relevant information where it resides using one central solution is critical to mitigating the risks and costs associated with disclosure. Litigation readiness involves identifying associated content, placing records under secure management and retention control, and defensibly deleting legacy content to save in storage costs. In the U.S., following revisions to the Federal Rules of Civil Procedure (FRCP), agencies have taken significant steps toward reducing the costs of e-discovery, at a potential cost of $15K per year, by implementing records management.

A holistic e-government approach includes archiving capabilities that interface with many content sources and locations where information is stored, such as file shares. Archiving information makes it much more accessible in the event of discovery or audit, reducing the time it takes to find information to hours as opposed to weeks. This is explored in the excerpt from an interview below with a Manager of Governance at a Canadian independent electricity operator.

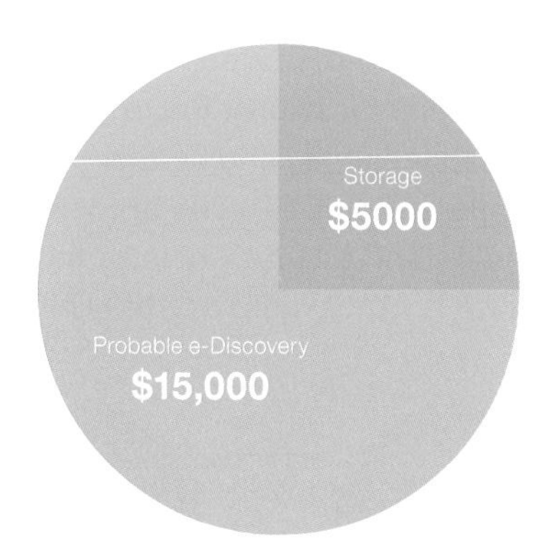

FIGURE 3.16: The Cost of eDiscovery[11]

As illustrated in the interview, e-government provides a high-capacity repository for storing and managing critical information while preserving context, structure, and links to associated content to add long-term, evidentiary value.

As well as accuracy, standards are critical to e-government deployment to ensure that all relevant elements of accountability are addressed. Some of the most commonly used standards include Control Objectives for Information and related Technology (COBIT), ISO 27001 (part of a growing family of ISO/IEC Information Security Management Systems), NERC 1300, the PCI DSS: Payment Card Industry Data Security Standard and others such as FIPS Publication 200 and NIST 800-53 in the U.S. As government organizations outsource services to the cloud, strategies around security have expanded to include data loss prevention (DLP) which is comprised of systems that identify, monitor, and protect data to minimize both intentional and unintentional data loss. Security in the cloud is explored in more detail in Chapter 14.

[11] Jake Frazier and Anthony Diana, *"Hoarders: The Corporate Data Edition"*, Law Technology News, December 19, 2012, *https://www.cgoc.com/resources/hoarders-the-corporate-data-edition* (accessed February, 2014).

Independent Electricity System Operator

Working at the heart of Ontario's power system, this not-for-profit entity connects all participants in the process of delivering power: generators that produce electricity, transmitters that send it across the province, retailers that buy and sell it, industries and businesses that use it in large quantities and local distribution companies that deliver it to people's homes. What follows is an excerpt from an interview with the Manager of Organizational Governance Support.

"We operate the real-time, bulk electric system for Ontario. We buy and sell electricity by the minute. While we do that, we have to maintain the reliability of the grid to ensure that everything is working well. We don't want any blackouts like the one in 2003, so we do a lot of procedural work to make sure that the information we use enables us to keep the grid working.

My focus is on governance—providing and enforcing the rules and regulations for all of the generators and transmitters in Ontario.

One of the biggest challenges we face from a governance perspective is keeping our information accurate, available, and accessible. Our previous records management solution was very difficult to use. As a result, the management of information, especially records, was haphazard and a big risk to the organization.

With our new system those risks have largely gone away because users can easily store, find, and manage information themselves. When we had to supply evidence to an auditor for example, we used to have to prepare months in advance to make sure that we had all the information we needed. Now it takes weeks or even days. In fact, when an auditor is in the room trying to assess whether or not we are compliant with regulations, we can pull information out of the records management system on the fly—a huge improvement for us. In fact, a lot of the information that we use to improve performance is based on evidence files that we keep for compliance purposes. The people that operate the grid can use information from the system in real time to keep the lights on. It's a huge advantage for us to have 24/7 availability of this information.

The system has given us process efficiency, information quality, and reliability. For example, for the year 2013, no overtime was required by our records management staff. But what the solution is also giving us, which wasn't anticipated, is increased transparency and trust with our market participants and stakeholders. The adoption rate and the excitement that people are showing for easier access to information is unbelievable. I get phone calls on a weekly basis from people who say, "This is really good, I want to do something more with it." And that to me is a really good sign of success."

CHAPTER 4

E-GOVERNMENT DRIVES PRODUCTIVITY

CHAPTER 4

e-Government Drives Productivity

FIGURE 4.1: e-Government Framework

According to research, productivity in the U.S. public sector has fallen by 50 percent.[1] Productivity in the Canadian public sector is on a similar annual decline—to the tune of costing the federal government $1.8 billion.[2] This total is based on a breakdown of time wasted by public servants looking for information, sifting through emails, toggling between applications and searching the web.

McKinsey & Company observed last year that if the G8 nations could increase public-sector productivity by 1.5 percent annually, they could generate benefits worth $1-trillion (U.S.) a year, which is equivalent to 1.5 percent to 2.5 percent of these nations' combined GDP.[3]

[1] William D. Eggers and Joshua Jaffe, *"Government on the go: Boosting public sector productivity by going mobile"*, Deloitte University Press, Feb 8, 2013.

[2] Chrystia Chudzak,*"The Digital Government,"* Video, September 1, 2013, *http://www.powtoon.com/p/dzzsQTV8lil/* (accessed Feb 2014).

[3] Neil Reynolds, *"Ottawa should do the math: Productivity trumps head counts"*, The Globe and Mail, April 23, 2013, *http://www.theglobeandmail.com/globe-debate/ottawa-should-do-the-math-productivity-trumps-head-counts/article4101797/* (accessed Feb 2014).

Productivity gains are critical on a global scale as governments cope with mandates to do more with less. An e-government solution powered by Enterprise Information Management (EIM) helps governments boost overall productivity through effective information retrieval and management, process automation, and user engagement.

EIM integrates information and expands its use to drive value as it moves through a government department or across agencies. EIM encompasses a full range of technologies to orchestrate information flows across government organizations. These technology suites include Enterprise Content Management (ECM), Business Process Management (BPM), Customer Experience Management (CEM), Information Exchange, and Discovery.

- **ECM** directs information flows effortlessly from capture through to archiving and disposition for more secure and consistent governance policies across any type of content in a government organization.
- **BPM** solutions empower employees, customers, and partners with Smart Process Applications and information to accelerate processes and build agile agencies.
- **CEM** solutions help governments deliver responsive, compelling, and relevant user experiences across multiple channels to improve productivity, services, and citizen satisfaction.
- **Information Exchange** solutions help people to accelerate and control how information is delivered—increasing the security and reliability of sensitive or complex communications.
- **Discovery** applications derive value from growing volumes of content trapped in silos across an organization to help organizations transition from query to insight to action.

EIM bundles all of these capabilities together into a government-wide information management approach. This chapter describes EIM as the underlying platform for e-government. It includes stories about organizations that have embraced EIM to address the challenges of information and capitalize on its potential. Each story illustrates the transformative power of e-government.

Govern Information with ECM

As the governance facet of EIM, Enterprise Content Management (ECM) delivers a breadth of offerings designed to manage the explosive growth of information and minimize the costs and risks associated with unmanaged content. ECM offers end-to-end management of information as it flows through mission-critical processes.

As enterprise information grows, the need have an effective ECM strategy in place becomes more critical. Access to increasing amounts of information requires a comprehensive ECM solution that can address demands for backups and auditing, tighter security, compliance, data classification (metadata), protection from threats of litigation, effective risk mitigation, and discovery technologies.

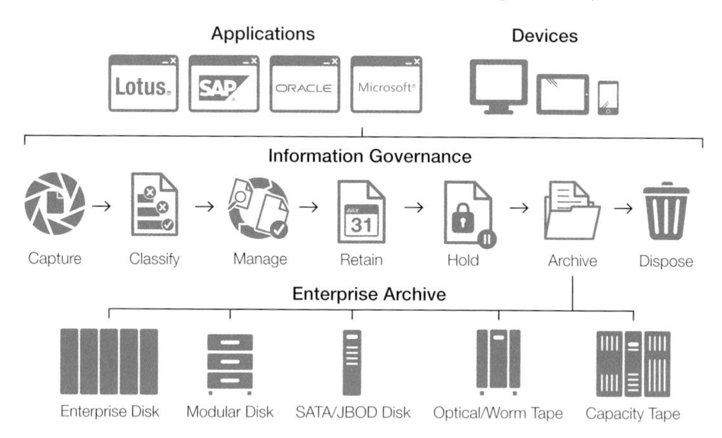

FIGURE 4.2: Managing the Full Lifecycle of Content

Content in Business Context

Public sector organizations look to their information systems to solve their business challenges, manage their business processes in the most efficient way possible, and ensure competitive advantage through operational excellence and innovation. Virtually all business functions have content associated with them.

Systems implemented to solve critical business problems can range from simple workflows to highly complex and long-running processes and complete business applications. These systems require collaboration and decision-making and automation wherever possible to ease the burden on staff and ensure consistency. Within business processes and applications, ECM plays an important role ensuring correct information is made available, actions on content are tracked and audited, and that security is maintained.

BPM combined with ECM drives timely decision-making and helps enforce compliance with corporate policy. Public sector organizations face increasing pressure to prove consistent compliance to policy while maintaining efficiency and ease of use for end users.

The following story about Hong Kong Polytechnic University demonstrates how ECM brings content to the fingertips of people and integrates critical content with business processes. ECM delivers a seamless experience across multiple environments, helping the University manage content and unlock the potential of its information for greater access and innovation.

Hong Kong Polytechnic University

FIGURE 4.3: Hong Kong PolyU

"Innovation is important to our University, and we aim to deliver state-of-the-art technology to support our teaching and administrative staff and enhance our students' learning experience. The solutions we are implementing will enable us to better manage and control the access of our documents, while enabling knowledge and information sharing across the university."

DIRECTOR OF INFORMATION TECHNOLOGY AT HONG KONG POLYU

Hong Kong Polytechnic University (PolyU) is the largest government-funded tertiary institution in Hong Kong with more than 30,000 students and nearly 3,500 teaching and non-teaching staff. It offers over 230 programs on campus. The growing student population, number of employees, and courses offered have increased at PolyU over the years and led to a huge growth in data generated. To better manage and leverage this information, individual units had implemented independent and isolated solutions.

These disparate document management systems were becoming harder to manage. Realizing that the ability to manage, control, and secure information is critical to their success, PolyU has implemented ECM. The seamless integration of content with collaboration tools and social media platforms will give the University better control over its content, ensure greater data integrity, and address its growing data needs.

Effectively managing information throughout its entire lifecycle creates business value and competitive advantage. From information capture to classification, management, storage, distribution, archiving, and disposition, ECM manages the flow of information across the University. Fast and seamless access from multiple environments (web, desktop, and mobile) within business processes and applications improves user productivity and organizational efficiency.

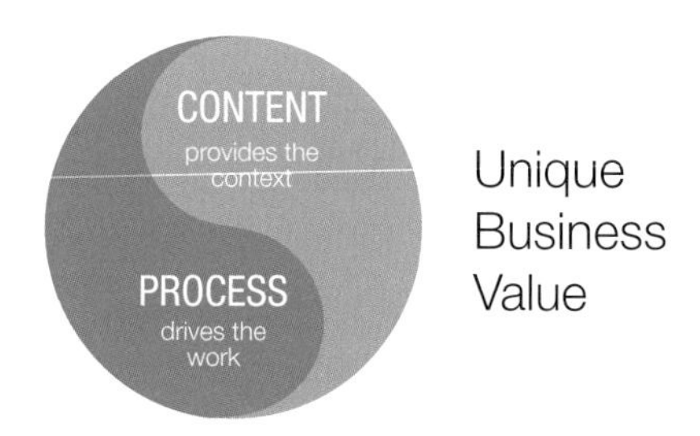

FIGURE 4.4: The Business Value of Integrated ECM and BPM

The ability to create and work with business processes is built into ECM. Agencies use processes to review and approve document sets, create and manage procedures, manage projects and cases, and more. These organizations look to BPM offerings together with ECM to support their process needs. Beyond process management, there are dedicated business applications built to address specific sets of business problems. Examples of these applications include contracts management, regulated documents, invoice management, employee file management, and learning management.

Accelerate Processes with BPM

Business Process Management (BPM) is one of the core technologies of EIM. Whether conducting thousands of high-volume processes per day for case management or running a lower volume of high-value procedures, BPM helps organizations better understand their operations, track the information that flows through those operations, recover costs, and optimize efficiencies.

1990	1995	2000	2005	2009	2010	2011	2012	2013
Business Process Integration • Workflow • Enterprise Application Integration	Business Rules Process Modeling Process Control	BPMS • Web Services	BPMS +SOA • Mobile Driven Development • BPMN	BPMS +MDD	BPMS +ACM Advanced Case Management (ACM)	BPMS +Social Social Networks	BPMS +Intelligence Business Intelligence + Process Mining	Smart Process & Predictive/ Diagnostic Analytics

Source: Forrester Research, Inc. Smart Process Applications Fill a Big Business Gap, August 2012

FIGURE 4.5: Workflow Evolves into Smart Process Applications

Enterprise Resource Planning (ERP) systems lie at the core of government processes—from financials and human capital management to case management, vendor invoicing, and other critical aspects. Administrative work, like case management, forms the basis of many government functions. This type of work is typically made up of government transactions and results in volumes of data housed in government databases.

Data generated by administrative activities is typically numerical and in many instances, this information is not easily accessible. While they do an admirable job of executing process and serving as the "system of record," ERP systems fall short in meeting the growing need to harness agility and adaptability to maintain competitive advantage.

Moving beyond legacy processes and workflows, effective BPM allows for the rapid modeling and automation of Smart Process Applications (SPAs) and the ability to constantly improve them. Next-generation SPAs provide agile solutions that are quickly developed and deployed to support both structured and unstructured business processes and adapt to rapidly changing business requirements.

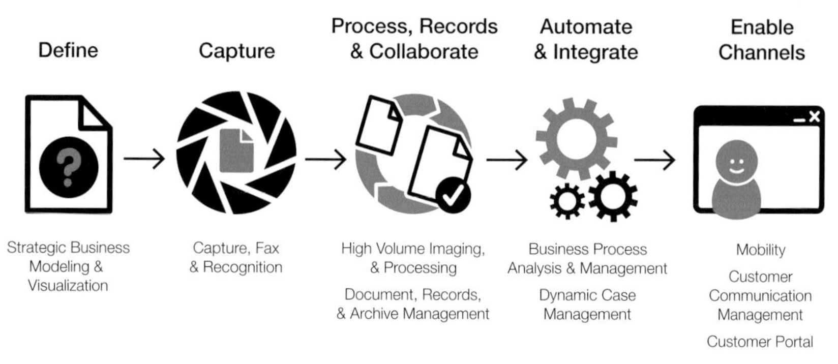

FIGURE 4.6: Integrated Processes and Information

The results of successfully extending BPM beyond its traditional role to allow for agile process improvement can be profound. Agencies like the U.S. Department of Justice, as described below, are embracing advanced BPM capabilities to improve processes and enhance operations for significant cost savings.

Deliver Exceptional Citizen Experience with CEM

As one of the five foundational pillars for EIM, Customer Experience Management (CEM) aims to create a richer, more interactive online experience—across multiple channels like websites, mobile devices, social networks, and more—without sacrificing the requirements for information governance. CEM powers the world's highest traffic brand sites, the most compelling mobile experiences, and the most recognized e-commerce portals on earth. The management of the citizen's experience, from visiting a government website and using a mobile app to conducting a transaction or viewing a city council meeting is vital to ensuring success. All of these interactions and the assets that surround them require more efficient management and use, which is what CEM is about.

U.S. Department of Justice

FIGURE 4.7: U.S. Department of Justice

...based on projected savings in the 82 districts, total approximated cost avoidance for all districts would be $38.8 million.

The U.S. Department of Justice, Office of the Federal Detention Trustee (OFDT) was established and activated in September 2001 by a directive of Congress in response to growing concerns regarding federal detention. It is the mission of the Federal Detention Trustee to provide for the safe, secure, and humane confinement of persons in federal custody awaiting trial or immigration proceedings. With an average daily population in excess of 55,000 detainees across 94 federal judicial districts and an annual federal detention budget exceeding one billion dollars, the goal of improving time and cost savings is paramount.

To reduce costs, OFDT set about automating the administrative prisoner designation process that involves the U.S. Federal Courts, the U.S. Marshals Service (USMS), and the Federal Bureau of Prisons (BOP) to help reduce detention costs. The process of designating a convicted felon requires information contained in numerous documents and controlled by several agencies. In the past, each step of the process involved moving paperwork between multiple agencies and geographic locations using fax, postal mail, and FedEx.® The manual nature of this process led to slow processing times and limited audit trail capability with no way of effectively tracking status information.

The Agency turned to e-government to support designation, while protecting sensitive prisoner information. The solution provides easy access to all employees regardless of location and enables the agency to track, report on, and measure ongoing performance metrics. With access to a web server, all agencies can check on the status of any prisoners' detention designation document in real time. It is cost-effective, saves time, reduces errors, and provides transparency around the process. The eDesignate system is operational in 82 districts and based on projected savings, total approximated cost avoidance for all districts would be $38.8 million.

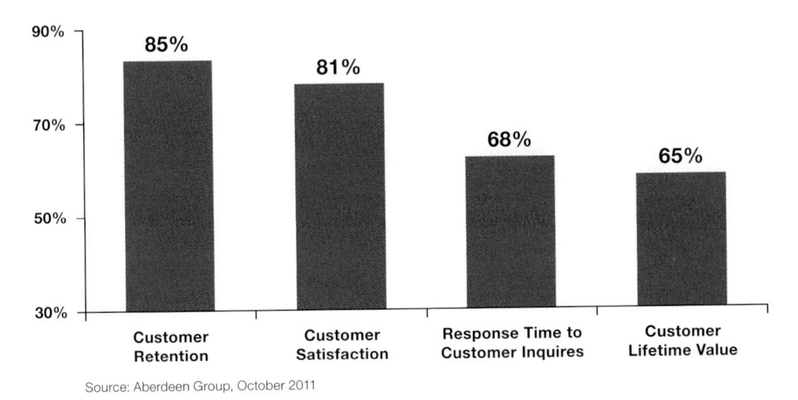

FIGURE 4.8: The Value of CEM

CEM gives government agencies the ability to transform information into a source of productivity. Media, website, and communications management combine to help public servants create, manage, share, and publish content with ease. With CEM, organizations like the City of Edmonton are creating online experiences to attract citizens, engage users, generate loyalty, and drive revenue.

Meet Budget Requirements with Secure Information Exchange

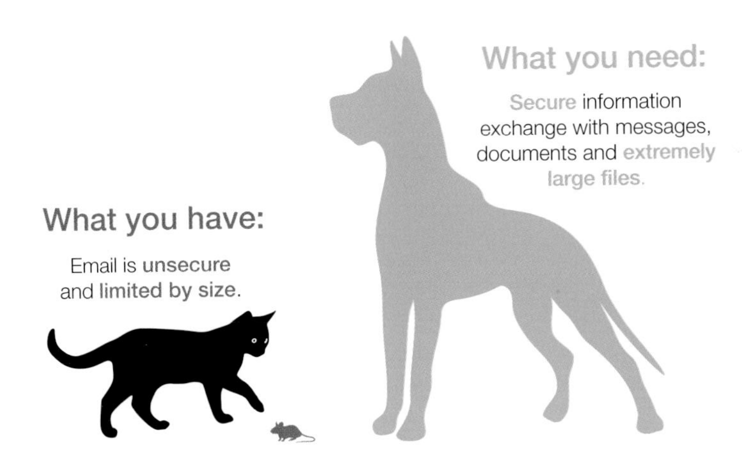

FIGURE 4.9: Secure Information Exchange

City of Edmonton

FIGURE 4.10: City of Edmonton's Website

"As Joe Citizen, I know that if I need a car towed away because it's parked illegally in my driveway, I phone the City. If I want to find out what time the bus is coming, I phone the City. If I need to find out what time they're picking up my garbage, I phone the City. I don't care how the City is organized inside; I just know I'm contacting the City. So, with our website, we wanted to follow the same line of thinking. Now it's a City website built entirely around how our customers expect to find information."

WEB OPERATIONS MANAGER, CITY OF EDMONTON

The City of Edmonton in Alberta, Canada is well known for its scenic river valley, oil and gas industry, and North America's largest shopping and entertainment complex, the West Edmonton Mall. Servicing more than one million residents in the area, the City of Edmonton's website was falling short of citizen's expectations. The City needed a website that reflected the vibrancy of the city while providing user-driven architecture, rich media support, social media compatibility, and easy-to-find, relevant information and services for citizens.

With a CEM website management solution, the site has transformed into a customer-oriented website, incorporating social media tools like blogs and wikis, with straightforward navigation and rich media like videos to showcase the community. The solution also offers the integration of legacy and future applications (written in a variety of programming languages), third-party search, and, most of all, ease of use for content authors to minimize training and accelerate adoption.

The marketing-driven website provides an efficient communications platform for citizens—giving them access to accurate, real-time information and services they need. As a result, the City of Edmonton is more responsive and the site has become the "number one" information source for citizens. Overall hits on the site increased by 19 percent in the first year and a visitor survey indicated a 92 percent satisfaction rate with the site by visitors.

Information Exchange is the practice of conversational data exchange. It defines a set of offerings that facilitate the efficient exchange of information inside and outside of a public sector organization, from electronic faxes and cloud services to Electronic Data Interchange (EDI) and large managed file transfers.

It securely manages transient, communicative exchanges of varying electronic format. This is the conversation of a government agency: internally among public servants and externally with its citizens and partner organizations. An information exchange can be described as a payload of data, moved between one or more parties for the purposes of communication, sharing, or transacting business. These services generate truly massive amounts of data and often are tied to other practices such as ECM with very specific collection parameters.

As an EIM category of offerings, information exchange solutions help safely move information from where it is to where it needs to be, regardless of which business systems it resides in, what devices it is required on, from user to user, company to customer, agency to citizen—from anywhere at any time. Data integrity and security are built in to protect against threats of internal information leaks and cyber attack.

The opportunities to drive business value through effective, secure information exchange are boundless, and demonstrated in the story about cost savings realized at Mumbai International Airport Limited.

Improve Insight Through Discovery

As a facet of EIM, Discovery solutions organize and visualize all relevant information to make it possible to find and learn about the right information at the right time and place. The integrated set of technologies that comprise discovery enhances an organization's capacity to "remember."

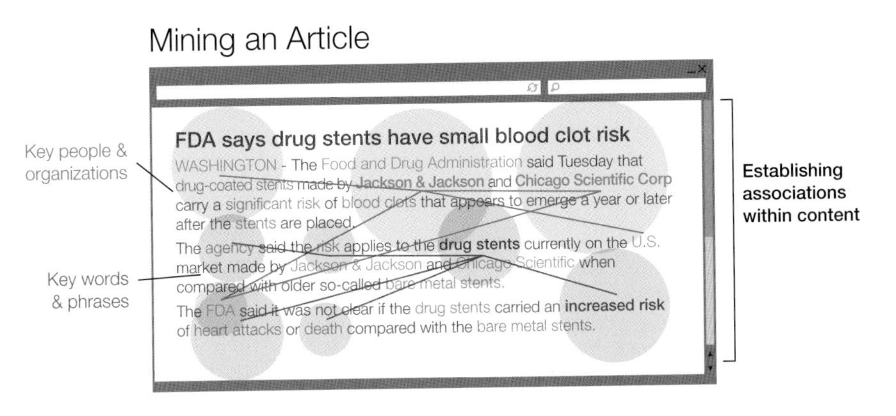

FIGURE 4.11: Semantic Pattern Recognition

Mumbai International Airport Limited

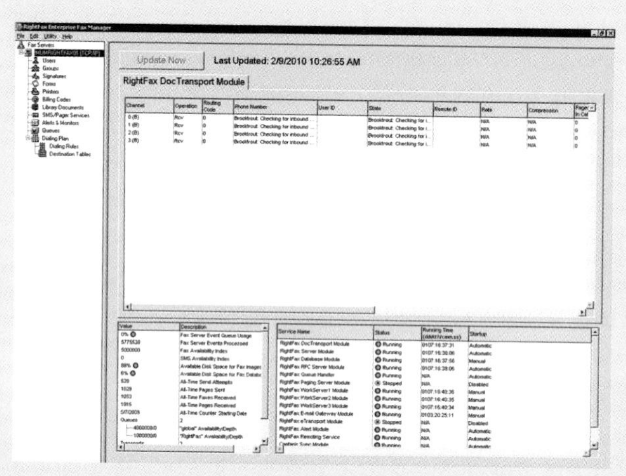

Faxes that used to take from 15 to 20 minutes to process are now delivered and tracked electronically within seconds.

FIGURE 4.12: Secure and Streamlined Information Exchange at MIAL

Mumbai International Airport Limited (MIAL) is a joint venture company owned by a GVK Industries-led consortium and Airports Authority of India working under the Ministry of Civil Aviation. The Company manages India's busiest airport, the Chhatrapati Shivaji International Airport (CSIA). Predictably, managing multiple projects across an airport that employs hundreds of people and spans an operational area of 1,450 acres demands both expeditious and secure communication. MIAL employees send and receive hundreds of faxes every month to and from vendors and government agencies. Previous paper-based faxing methods did not uphold timely turnaround or essential privacy. MIAL relied on close to 50 fax machines that required consistent and costly maintenance, as well as constant supply refills. Additionally, sensitive documents were neither private nor secure.

MIAL has eliminated fax machine queues and gained reliable security for all faxed documents with document delivery and fax software. MIAL employees now send and receive documents without leaving their workstations. Instead of printing pages to feed through fax machines, employees can fax documents right at their desktop computers. Integration with email allows any sent or received fax to appear alongside emails for secure and easy reference, forwarding, or storage.

The Company expects to eliminate close to 40 fax machines, with the remainder as backup devices in case of email failure. Expenses associated with maintaining dozens of fax machines are now designated as cost savings. Faxes that used to take from 15 to 20 minutes to process are now delivered and tracked electronically within seconds. Employees who link to the office via mobile devices when they are traveling can stay on top of urgent faxes and staff members have increased efficiency because the solution has optimized their time.

The expense and time associated with traditional legal or other information discovery is very high. Having a set of tools available to reduce and make more accurate the data sets retrieved in a discovery represents immediate savings for a public sector organization. Applying analytics to large data sets gives public sector organizations insights into productivity gaps and can provide techniques for improving efficiency.

Business insight is gained by capturing, combining, and transforming information to identify relationships, risk, and new opportunities for growth. Improved transparency into outcomes allows for the consistent measurement and monitoring of performance metrics, arming governments with the information they need to improve productivity and the quality of their programs. Unlocking this data is critical to identifying new opportunities for growth, minimizing risk, and promoting innovation—as illustrated in the open government initiatives currently underway in countries throughout the world.

With e-government solutions like semantic search and content analytics, organizations in the public sector like the Karlsruhe Institute of Technology (KIT) gain leading-edge capabilities, designed to mine, extract, and present the true value of information for improved research and analysis.

FIGURE 4.13: The Business Value of EIM

EIM: A Single Version of the Truth

The core sets of technologies adopted by the government organizations described in this chapter form a comprehensive platform for EIM. Despite the differing facets of technology, whether it is ECM, BPM, or CEM, each organization shares one common challenge: the impediment of information flows across the enterprise. Likewise, they shared a common solution to overcome their information challenges: EIM, which has helped them to more effectively manage and optimize the information flows that formulate the foundation of their operations.

Karlsruhe Institute of Technology

FIGURE 4.14: The Karlsruhe Institute of Technology (KIT)

With improved access to information and the ability to connect with researchers in similar areas of study, the website has evolved into an advanced research network that successfully meets the needs of all stakeholder groups.

The Karlsruhe Institute of Technology (KIT), one of the world's leading engineering research institutions, was founded in 2009 by a merger of Forschungszentrum Karlsruhe and Universität Karlsruhe. As a member of the Helmholtz Association, the largest science organization in Germany, KIT makes major contributions to top national and international research. According to its mission, the Organization operates along three strategic fields of action: research, teaching, and innovation. KIT currently has 9,000 employees and 24,000 students.

KIT needed a leading-edge solution that would give researchers, students, and the general public a faster way to find information across 600 websites and 200,000 associated web pages. On the back end, the institute wanted a robust website management solution that would support their 1,300 editors worldwide, on a day-to-day basis, by supplying metadata, key phrases, and the ability to automatically generate extracts of text. KIT also wanted a collaborative platform that would bring together researchers, scientists, and students.

KIT is using e-government technologies semantic navigation and content analytics in combination with website management to optimize web pages and provide relevant search results. Previously manual tasks that were labor intensive have been replaced by an automated solution that assigns metadata and supports entity extraction by generating teaser texts for new pages, saving users time and reducing error. Visitors are given personalized access to highly relevant information, facilitated by faceted search and related hits—resulting in a more satisfying end-user experience. With improved access to information and the ability to connect with researchers in similar areas of study, the website has evolved into an advanced research network that successfully meets the needs of all stakeholder groups.

EIM unlocks the potential for superior quality and less costly operations, reduced regulatory cost and risk, optimally efficient business processes, an engaging citizen and social experience, and more efficient online information exchange—on premise, in the cloud, and on mobile devices.

As an integrated suite of technologies, EIM delivers productivity-based benefits to organizations in the public sector—from higher quality programs and services, to increased efficiencies, improved resource and budget allocation, greater transparency and accountability, and higher levels of trust in government programs and services.

The following chapter describes these technologies in more detail.

CHAPTER 5

E-GOVERNMENT TECHNOLOGIES

CHAPTER 5

e-Government Technologies

As a collection of technology suites, Enterprise Information Management (EIM) integrates information and drives value as it moves through government departments and processes. The foundations of e-government are based on integration, interoperability, and a capacity to share and integrate information based on common standards.

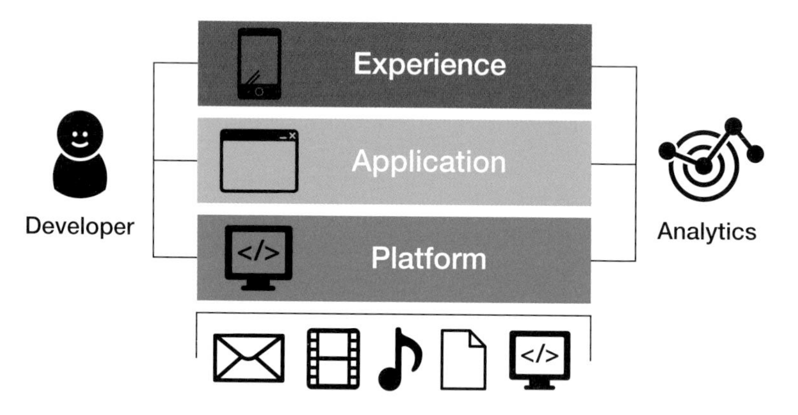

FIGURE 5.1: The e-Government Infrastructure

Within most governments, unstructured and structured content resides in many information sources. Platform technologies like records management, web experience management, and business process management help to create "smarter" and more useful documents, processes, and exchanges. Applications like case or correspondence management add value to information in context. A common technology infrastructure improves the flow of information across all processes, allowing it to flow from one context to another, from need to result, and opportunity to outcome.

Information is delivered as a responsive user experience for both employees and citizens through web browsers, desktops, and devices—all integrated with business applications SAP,® Oracle,® and Microsoft. The final piece of the technology puzzle is application development and the creation of a government app store facilitated by developer tools and a network. The result is a holistic e-government technology infrastructure. This is EIM.

FIGURE 5.2: Seamless Information Flows

e-Government enables connected government through technologies used to improve access, privacy, and security of information; establish networks across levels of government; provide online, mobile service delivery; and create opportunities for interactive democracy—at all levels of government.

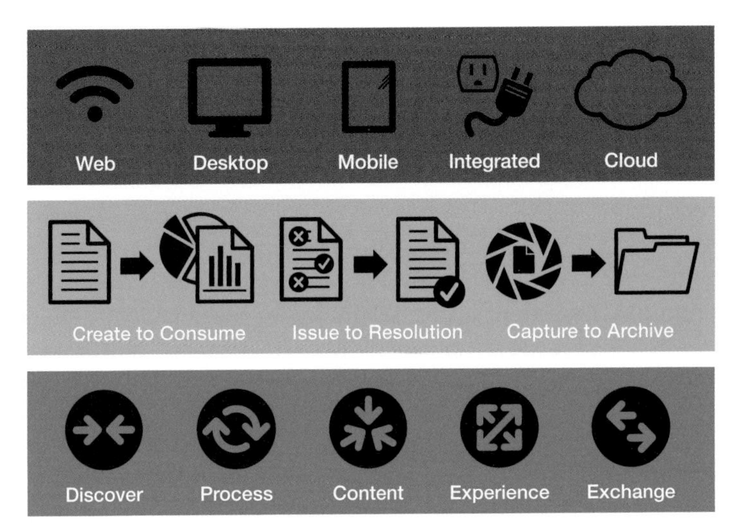

FIGURE 5.3: e-Government— A Seamless Experience

EIM delivers the platform for integrated e-government, bundling all of these capabilities together in a government-wide information management approach. What follows is a detailed description of these technology suites, including the following:

- Content Suite for Enterprise Content Management
- Process Suite for Business Process Management
- Experience Suite for Customer Experience Management
- Information Exchange Suite
- Discovery Suite

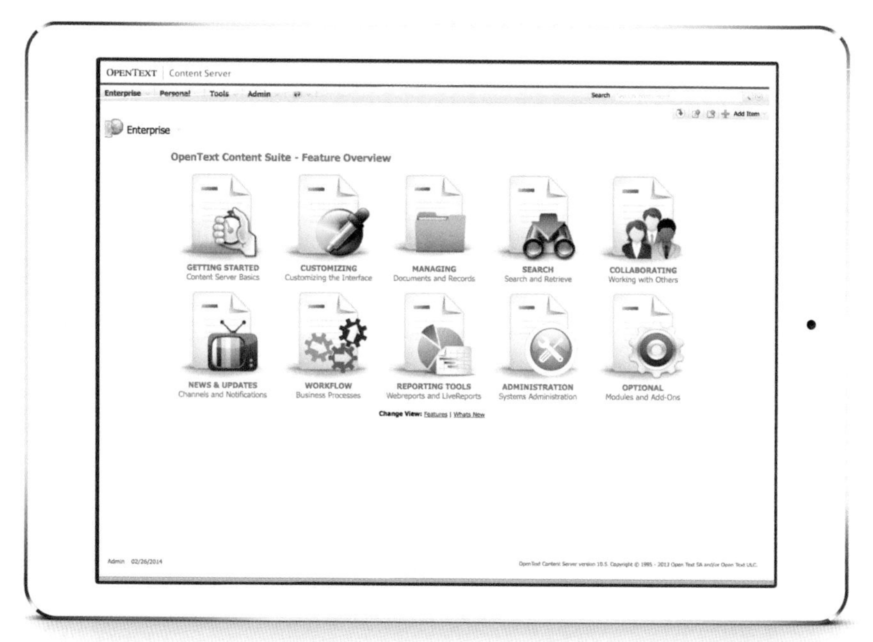

FIGURE 5.4: Document Management

Content Suite

Available on premises, across mobile devices, and in the cloud, Content Suite is a set of Enterprise Content Management (ECM) technologies that includes a platform to unite capture, document and records management, workflow, search, and archiving, as well as applications such as email, e-discovery, auto-classification, and contract management.

Document Management

Document management provides full lifecycle management for any type of electronic document in a single, authoritative repository for storing and organizing electronic documents. Using document management, organizations can manage any type of electronic document in any file format. Metadata is indexed and can be used to easily retrieve and generate reports on documents based on custom criteria. Each piece of metadata information is an attribute, and sets of attributes can be grouped into categories that can be associated with any document. Multiple taxonomic classifications can be associated with documents in their original locations.

Document management allows users to work directly between the repository and their desktop applications to open, edit, and save documents directly from the repository for optimal productivity. Document management also supports the WebDAV protocol, allowing users of WebDAV-compliant desktop applications to connect directly to the repository.

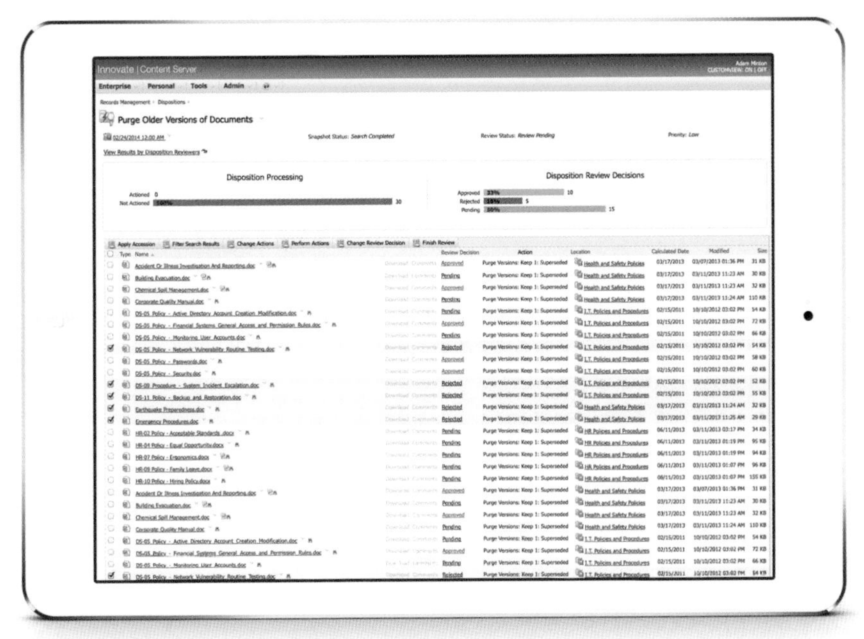

FIGURE 5.5: Records Management

Records Management

Organizations in the public sector can improve accountability, ensure compliance, and minimize the risk and cost of litigation with records management, an automated system that removes the complexities of electronic records management and makes the process completely transparent to end-users. The solution delivers a common records management file plan for all enterprise applications for retention and defensible disposition and the capabilities to classify all physical objects as records.

Archiving

Archiving empowers agencies to implement defensible, long-term archiving strategies to manage risk and intelligently govern today's data types and volumes while controlling costs. Using it, agencies can access a common, agnostic infrastructure for all retention and archival needs; ensure content integrity; avoid redundancy while meeting legal and compliance requirements; and cost-effectively store and retrieve content.

Coupled with industry-leading records management and auto-classification, archive supports rich capabilities to drive compliant retention and disposition policies. The following feature demonstrates how agencies are deploying a defensible, long-term strategy to comply with regulations, meet legal obligations, and reduce the overall costs associated with unmanaged content.

A Health and Human Services Entity

What follows are excerpts from an interview with the Chief Technology Officer of a Health and Human Services Entity, which is part of the National Institutes of Health (NIH) and the primary federal agency for conducting and supporting biomedical research.

"We focus our research on infectious diseases like HIV/AIDS, flu, tuberculosis, and malaria, as well as tropical diseases and a number of other infectious diseases. We work internationally in over 100 countries. We also have an administrative component, play a significant role in bio-defense, and conduct studies in re-emerging diseases.

The Organization is very diverse. We are a federal agency, but we function like a pharmaceutical company with our own lab where we manage the lifecycle of a drug from basic research through to modeling and clinical trials. Because we're a federal agency, we have to follow federal regulations. We have what we call a "validated environment" that has to comply with a complex collection of government and industry regulations such as the Federal Drug Administration Act, Freedom of Information Act, and Department of Defense (DoD) records management standards.

We work with a lot of manual paper processes and have to collaborate with sister agencies like the Ministry of Health and the Department of Health and Human Services, as well as with organizations at a global level. Many of our processes require signed approvals, and they were becoming too inefficient and prone to error. We implemented a document management solution to manage document-centric workflows and integrated this with e-sign technologies to expedite the approval process. Every process that we transform from paper to digital adds transparency and accountability and reveals where the bottlenecks are so we can address these to become more efficient. Using an application of this solution, we were able to reduce the bidding process on R&D contracts by 50 percent.

Transparency is good because it creates accountability in terms of open government. Many data sets that are available are not self-explanatory: they require experts to analyze and explain the data. A public cloud helps us promote the democratization of biomedical data. We have set up a comprehensive repository in the cloud with data about the human microbiome. Researchers who are interested can tap into the data in an open environment for research and analysis about the various microorganisms that live inside us."

" A public cloud helps us promote the democratization of biomedical data. "

Authentication, Audit, and Security

A comprehensive content management solution is designed for high-security environments, allowing agencies to:

- Configure security according to the level required for each information asset
- Protect content at rest inside the organization through encryption and authentication at the repository level, ensuring only authorized systems and users are able to gain access
- Ensure that users see only what they have permissions to see
- Apply access rights at the group or individual level to specific types of content and to different stages in the lifecycle of content

Bulk Imaging and Capture

Capture solutions help bridge the gap between the structured and unstructured world to harness what was previously untapped value. Agencies can use it to maximize efficiency and cost savings by capturing enterprise content and managing it consistently within information governance guidelines.

Imaging: A solution for capturing and displaying a complete range of business documents. Imaging helps organizations digitize paper documents to eliminate the costs of storing paper, increase productivity by making all documents easily accessible, and capture all documents in a secure, long-term archive.

Capture: A solution that automates the capture and interpretation of paper documents, scanned images, email, and faxes using sophisticated document and character recognition software. Agencies use it to fully digitize their processes, reduce manual keying and paper handling, and reduced the risk of non-compliance.

Annotation and Redaction

From scanning to printing, universal viewers and imaging tools handle the access, sharing, and distribution of technical and business information, enabling organizations to:

- Create, capture, view, redact, markup, and publish content to support business processes
- Integrate view-markup-print-edit functionality for hundreds of document types into networked database solutions or intranet/web solutions
- Handle document viewing requirements—from native file viewing and 3D CAD model viewing to direct scanning of paper documents, and document markup and revision
- Access, share, distribute, and cooperatively review documents across a department or agency and with partners and suppliers

Through its multi-faceted solutions, Content Suite lays the groundwork for a comprehensive e-government strategy by providing capabilities to digitize, manage, and secure documents and records. In the following feature, Metro Vancouver is using e-government to manage its records throughout their entire lifecycle, from creation and dissemination to final archive and disposition.

Metro Vancouver

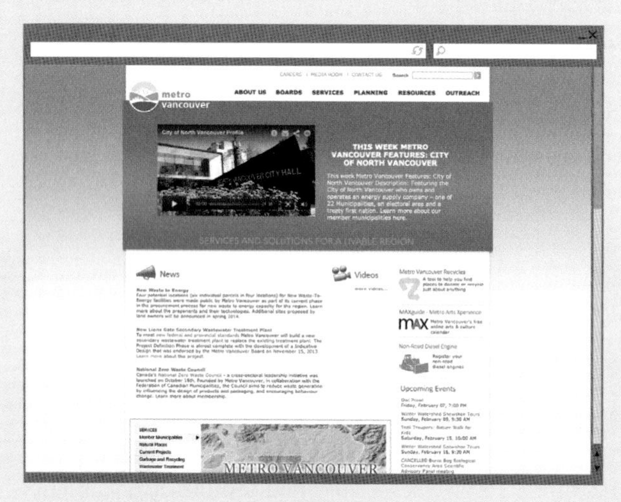

FIGURE 5.6: Metro Vancouver Website

The system is helping to make sure that the Region can prove through audits that the documents in the system are trustworthy records—and that they comply with statutes and regulations while promoting good business practice.

Metro Vancouver is one of 29 regional districts that were created by the provincial government to ensure that all British Columbia residents have equal access to commonly needed services. Regional parks, affordable housing, labor relations, and regional urban planning are significant services provided directly to the public. The Region has approximately 1,300 full-time employees and serves a population of 2.1 million.

The Region needed a central, secure repository for storing and distributing electronic records. An e-government solution would enable them to enforce retention periods and disposition rules based on preset periods to help control risks, reduce storage costs, and ensure regulatory compliance. They were also looking for an improved user experience for the profiling of documents that included automation and improved accuracy.

The system currently contains almost two million documents. An automated records management solution removes the complexities of electronic records management, making the process transparent to the end user. It maps record classifications to retention schedules, which fully automates the process of ensuring that records are kept as long as legally required and then destroyed when the time elapses. Enforcing governance across the region, each of its 14 departments is responsible to comply with policies, best practices, and procedures issued by the corporate records team. The system is helping to make sure that the Region can prove through audits that the documents in the system are trustworthy records—and that they comply with statutes and regulations while promoting good business practice.

Process Suite

Process Suite is a combination of Business Process Management (BPM) applications and solutions designed to help agencies work more efficiently, lower costs, and achieve business goals with real-time business insight. Governments can use them to reduce the time-to-value for deploying solutions; meet the changing needs of service requesters and providers; develop and deploy process applications to match business requirements, from packaged apps to model-driven development—on-premises, in the cloud, or using hybrid deployment.

Smart Process Applications

Smart Process Applications (SPAs) are created by configuring foundational processes and assembling pre-built components. Organizations use SPAs to create intuitive business services, case management, and efficient process transactions, and integrate data silos and back-office systems.

Out-of-the-box modules are available for:

- Service Center for web and mobile access
- Work Center environment for productivity
- Reporting Center for business insight
- Change Tools for process improvement
- Configuration Tools for services, assets, and people

Dynamic Case Management

Dynamic case management automates collaborative, people-driven and content-intensive processes, such as customer-facing or exception-handling processes. It gives agencies a 360-degree view of citizens to provide better service and improve response times. A persona-based user interface accesses the system to manage cases, while leveraging existing systems of record.

The Care Assessment Agency (CIZ) in the Netherlands is using BPM to effectively manage their caseloads and other processes for optimal efficiencies.

Experience Suite

Experience Suite is an integrated suite of Customer Experience Management (CEM) products delivered as a comprehensive platform to manage media, web, social, and interactive content to deliver a consistent user experience across multiple channels—while adhering to information governance policies and regulatory requirements.

Care Assessment Agency (CIZ)

CIZ is a Dutch Government organization responsible for handling the assessments of people who apply for care under the Exceptional Medical Expenses Act. They handle one million assessment cases a year and have approximately 1,200 internal and 17,000 external users of their systems. What follows are excerpts from an interview with the CIO of the CIZ, Robin van Iperen.

"Our key mission activities are to determine whether someone is entitled to care under the Exceptional Medical Expenses Act in Holland. We are the gatekeeper of 28.5 billion euros ($38.5 billion USD) spent annually under the Exceptional Medical Expenses Act.

Our old system was supported by 17 databases, which was neither effective nor efficient. When we selected a BPM platform to replace it, we were looking for a flexible platform that would automate our front- and back-end processes like case management and enable us to adapt our software systems to changing legislation. We wanted to create processes that would support interaction between business users and IT professionals.

The beauty of this platform is that you can use it to create a case model and showcase business users, who can recommend changes. These changes can be made immediately, rather than waiting for six months after the solution has been deployed to implement them. We put business users and IT developers together in one room and, as a result, we were able to develop a more effective case management solution. We ended up with a system that incorporated all of the business rules and presented users with an intuitive interface.

The system automates the primary processes of the CIZ and helps to facilitate policy development through improved decision making at the board level, based on accurate information. We have used it for case management, as a platform for our backup system, and as a messaging system to communicate with third-party organizations. Our future goal is to create applications that are fully adaptable to any device.

We are also looking at working with other agencies as well as private organizations. To this end, we have established a system that integrates our information with information from other organizations in the health care network—to help us oversee the processes behind the consumerization and financing of health care in Holland.

Many Dutch citizens conduct their business online. The Dutch Government has set a goal of 2017 to transform itself into a digital government, so we are now focusing our activities on making our processes and solution both digital and mobile for end users. In 2015 there will be changes made to the Dutch heath care system with many services transferred to the local government level. The adaptability of the software system is really important because we know that a lot of changes are coming our way."

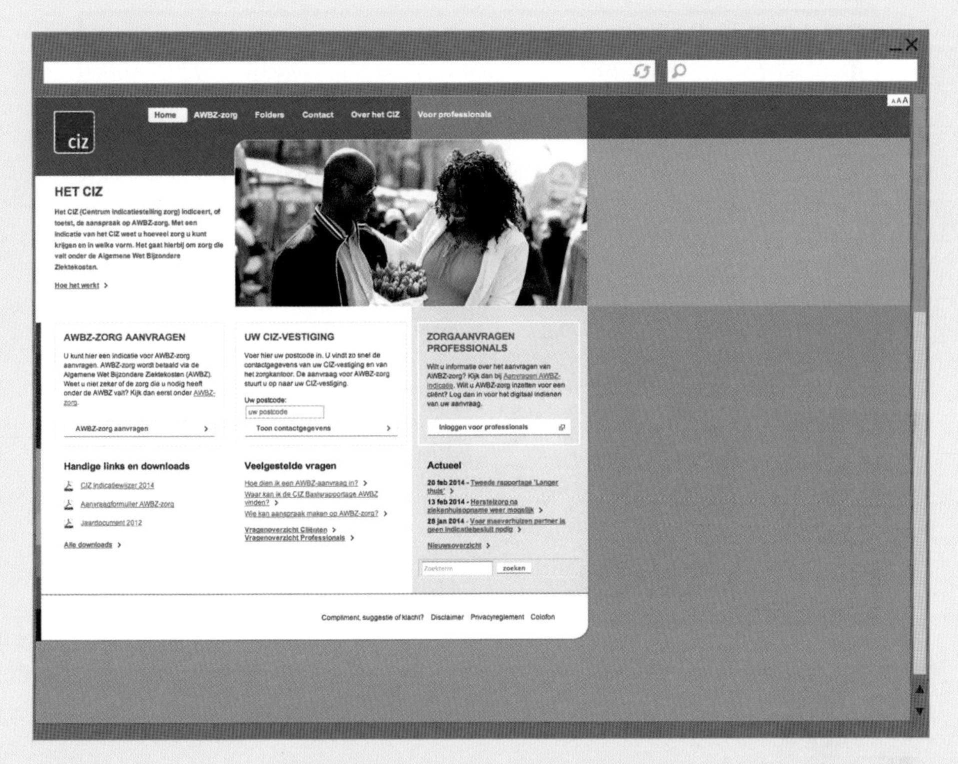

FIGURE 5.7: Care Assessment Agency (CIZ)

> The Dutch Government has set a goal of 2017 to transform itself into a digital government, so we are now focusing our activities on making our processes and solution both digital and mobile for end users.

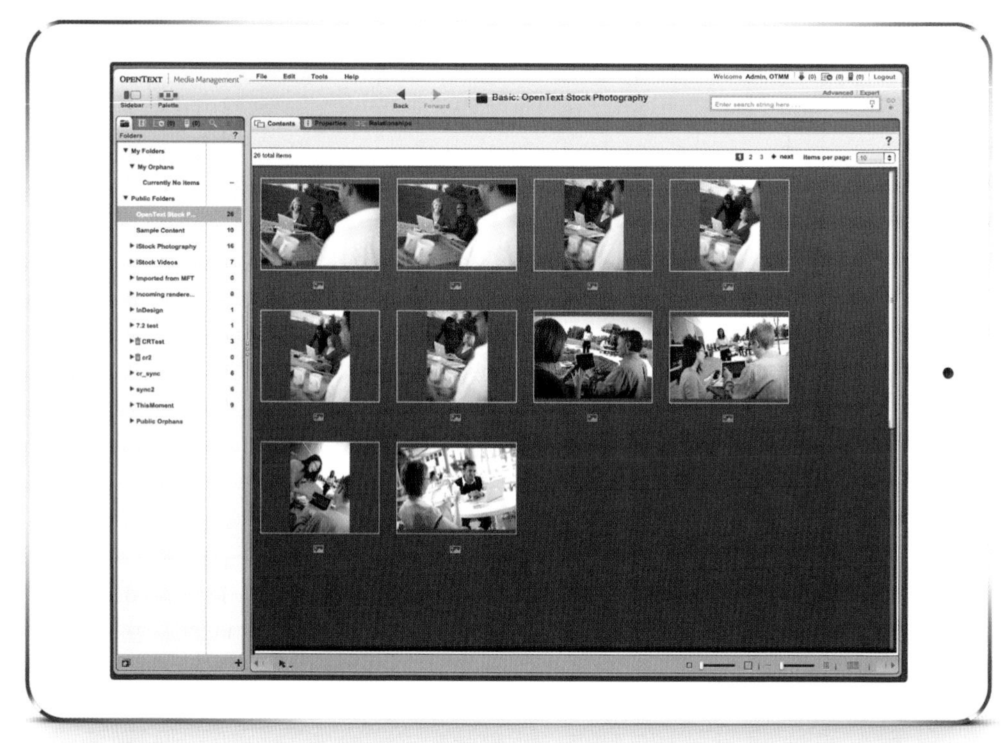

FIGURE 5.8: Media Management

Web Experience Management

Web Experience Management (WEM) is built for high-volume, transaction-oriented web applications across all customer-centric touch points—intranet or extranet, public or private. Public sector organizations can elevate the overall web experience and cater to the unique needs of all citizens with:

- Responsive design to display content consistently across mobile devices and platforms
- Compelling experiences and meaningful conversations
- Optimization of every citizen touch point with device neutral, content-centric experiences
- Alignment of IT and business digital strategies, processes, and technologies

Portal

Portals improve engagement with public servants, partners, and citizens through highly interactive and contextual online experiences. Portals can be used to create and deploy mashups and composite applications, implement microsites and global initiatives with ease, and improve citizen services with an online community.

Media Management

Media management is the proven and tested enterprise Digital Asset Management (DAM) solution, providing secure, cost-effective control of digital assets across multiple delivery channels and media platforms. With sophisticated search, navigation, and collaboration tools, media management provides a central repository and integrates with existing systems. Automated workflow capabilities ensure that production, reuse, and publication processes work together seamlessly.

Communications Management

Customer communications management improves citizen experience through the automation of communications. Personalized documents are created through rules-based dynamic assembly and presented to citizens, partners, and suppliers in multiple formats across multiple channels. From one-to-one contact to the high volume, mass production of documents, communications management simplifies and automates document-related business processes to improve business performance and efficiency.

Social

With e-government social capabilities, agencies can seamlessly integrate information governance with consumer-style file sharing and social collaboration apps to provide users with the best ways to engage without compromising security and compliance requirements. Productivity is enhanced by breaking down organizational barriers, facilitating the transfer of knowledge, and accelerating decision-making processes. A more socialized intranet or a social workplace allows teams to focus, work more efficiently, and connect with relevant resources and expertise by connecting employee-to-employee, citizen-to-citizen and employee-to-citizen.

Oakland County Michigan is using an e-government media management solution to integrate, manage, and digitize its media assets.

Oakland County Michigan

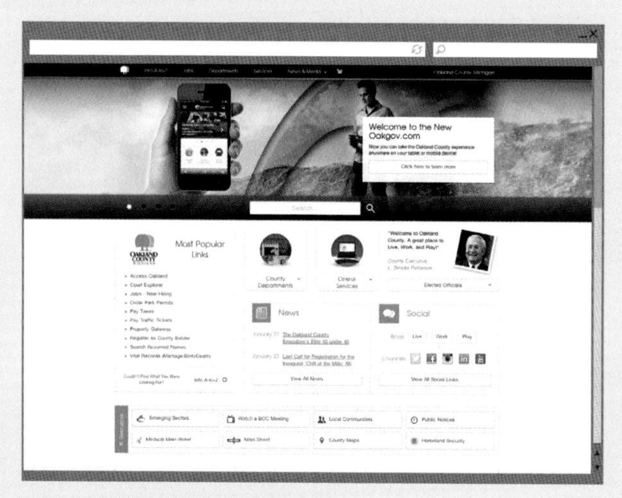

FIGURE 5.9: Oakland County Website

It has created a new level of usability by enabling County-wide access and ensuring efficiency in the production, reuse, and publication processes of all digital assets.

Oakland County, part of the Detroit, Michigan metropolitan area, is home to 62 cities, villages, and townships with a population of more than 1,200,000. The County's knowledge-based economic initiative, coined "Automation Alley," is one of the largest employment centers for engineering and related occupations in the United States.

Over the past several years, the County has built up an extensive digital library of assets that is used for newspaper advertisements, posters, brochures, event programs, the County website, and more. The County required a solution to manage over 40,000 digital assets and make them accessible to people in marketing, public relations, and other County departments.

Oakland County opted for a fully hosted e-government solution to provide a centralized repository for the storage, management, and distribution of approved digital content. With the hosted solution, the County is now able to manage their digital media assets without the need for internal IT support and resources. The County has effectively opened up access to their media to all County personnel, including those within the marketing and planning departments; also within parks and recreations and the health department. The system has saved users time—an estimated 30 percent—and the County money by improving overall productivity. It has created a new level of usability by enabling County-wide access and ensuring efficiency in the production, reuse, and publication processes of all digital assets.

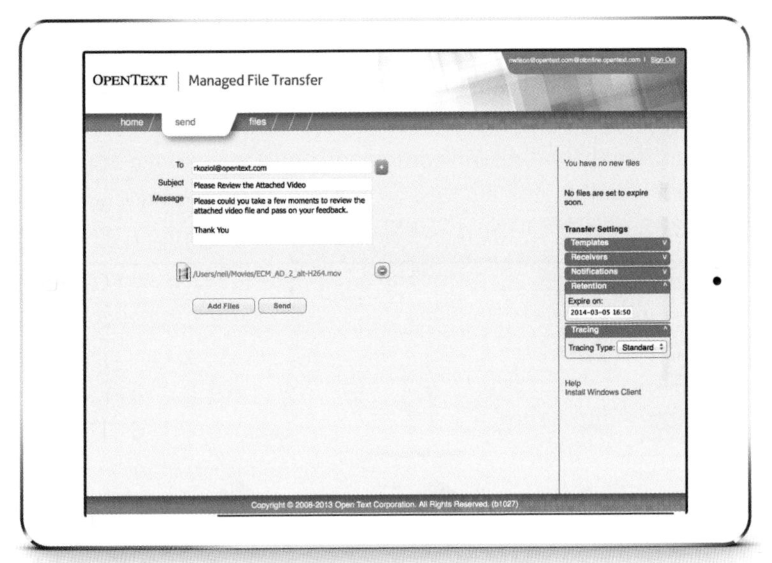

FIGURE 5.10: Managed File Transfer

Information Exchange Suite

Information Exchange Suite enables businesses to accelerate and control how information is delivered—increasing the security and reliability of sensitive or complex communications. Organizations can execute transactions quickly, easily, and with a higher level of confidence.

Managed File Transfer

Agencies can manage the secure exchange of large files inside and outside of the firewall with enterprise-level security and auditability, protocols to accelerate large file transfers, and a single file transfer solution for all ad-hoc and process-based requirements.

Fax and Distribution

Agencies can automate and integrate the exchange of business-critical documents on premise or in the cloud in order to increase productivity and lower operational costs. Using fax and distribution, organizations can transform paper-based operations into digital processes, reduce manual labor and automate information distribution, and send and receive faxes on premise and in the cloud.

B2B Integration Services

Agencies can optimize the reliability, reach, and cost-efficiency of supply chains with Electronic Data Interchange (EDI) and integration services with capacity beyond traditional Value Added Networks (VANs) with a world-class EDI transaction network.

Discovery Suite

Discovery Suite uses search and content analytics on enterprise information to accelerate time to value. It transforms big data from a costly byproduct of today's knowledge workers into a valuable resource that drives innovation and powers customer engagement.

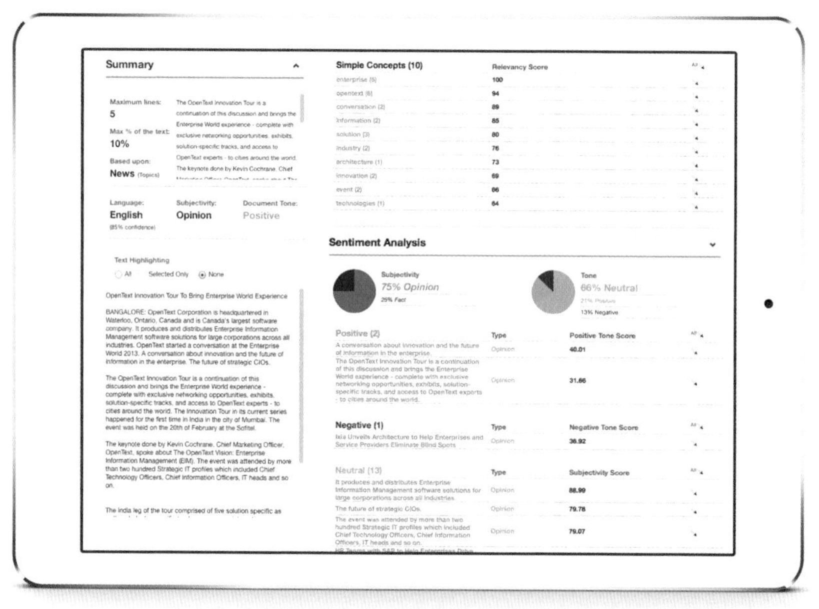

FIGURE 5.11: Content Analytics

Search

As a fundamental part of the Discovery Suite, robust search increases productivity, enhances knowledge capture and sharing initiatives, and produces accurate result sets so the right information is found when it is needed. Search provides unified access to internal and external information, helping agencies save money and reduce risk through secure, permissions-based search.

Content Analytics

Organizations use content analytics to extract meaning, nuance, and context from vast amounts of unstructured content to analyze it and harness its true business potential. The solution is being used to create machine-readable content from unstructured data, connect people with relevant content, discover accurate information to support decisions, and boost productivity. Features include concept extraction, entity extraction, categorization, sentiment analysis, summarization, language detection, similarity service, and a management console.

Semantic Navigation

Semantic navigation delivers highly relevant information to website visitors to drive engagement by automatically analyzing and tagging content to produce insightful facets, improve website conversion rates, and aggregate information from all systems for unified access.

Auto Classification

Using auto classification, agencies can establish a highly defensible, completely transparent records management program as part of a broader information governance strategy while automating policy application tasks for business users. Auto classification helps reduce litigation risk, e-discovery, and storage costs; improve compliance, security, and user productivity; and save time in addressing the need to classify huge volumes of legacy content, email, and social media.

InfoFusion: A Common Information Management Platform

InfoFusion delivers a new approach to managing, analyzing and understanding unstructured information with the ability to replace one-off information applications (and their associated indexes, connectors, hardware, and support) with a common information management platform.

InfoFusion helps to manage storage capacity, apply retention and lifecycle controls on terabytes of data, rationalize legacy applications and content, and provide unified access to content for end users. It significantly reduces the cost and complexity of individual systems and content sources through discrete applications for data integration, content migration, data archiving, and legacy decommissioning to help reduce the cost and complexity of individual systems and content.

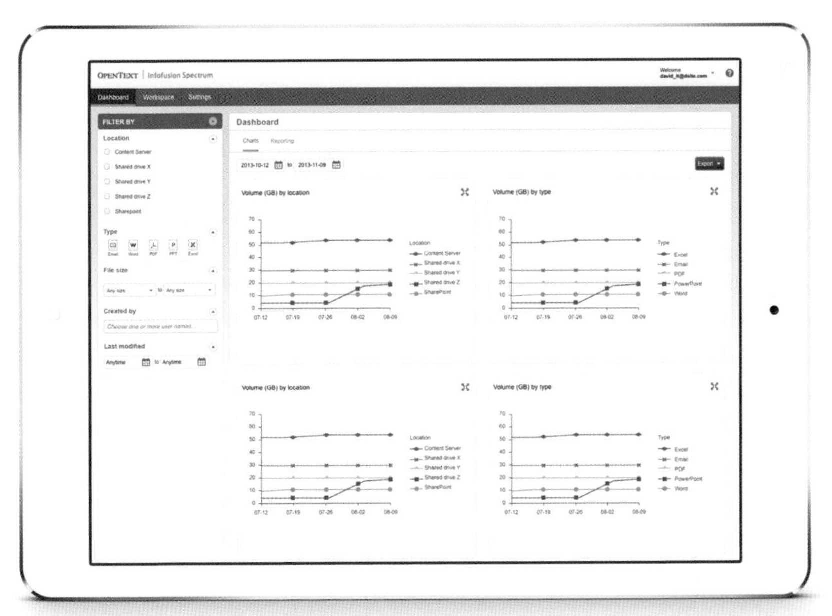

FIGURE 5.12: InfoFusion

e-Government Applications

The following e-government applications address business challenges with targeted public sector solutions.

Constituent Services

Agencies use this application to streamline service delivery with a single online portal that unifies front-end citizen requests with back-end services. The portal allows for personalized communications and delivers automated notifications on status and performance reports for managers. The application improves efficiency, citizen engagement, public servant productivity, and service delivery.

Public Information Request Tracking

This application automates information request processes and eliminates multiple touch-points, duplicated errors, and backlogs due to inaccuracies. Each request is captured, assigned an individualized tracking number, and processed using an automated workflow application. With this application, agencies can provide access to information accurately and efficiently to meet open government mandates.

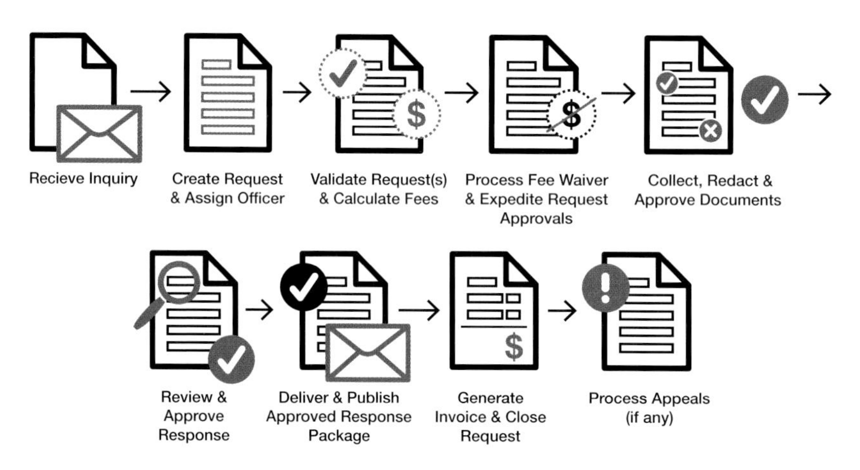

FIGURE 5.13: A Complete, Flexible Roles-Based Solution for Tracking Requests

Correspondence Tracking

Correspondence tracking ensures the effective capture, response, storage, and management of paper and electronic correspondence. A pre-packaged toolkit tracks and controls business correspondence from a variety of sources, including scanned letters, email messages, faxes, electronic documents, and hand-written notes. Correspondence is automatically routed to appropriate staff to meet response deadlines, while still following compliance standards.

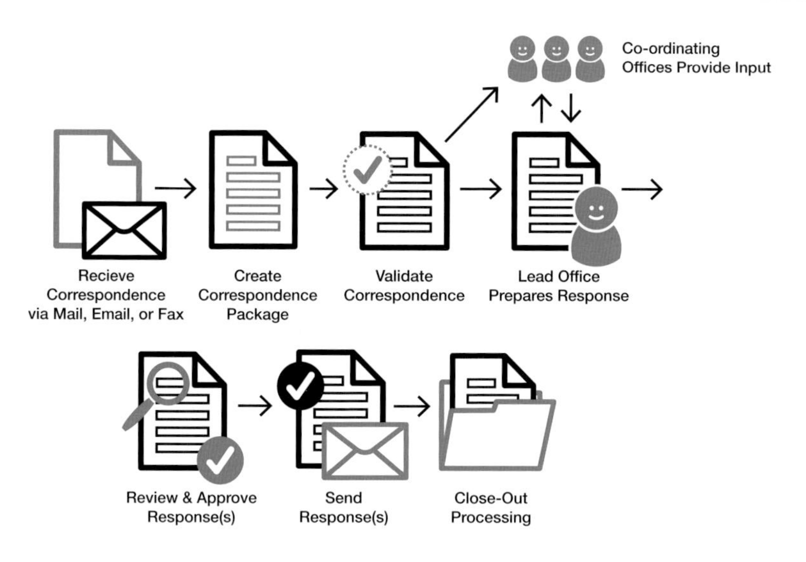

FIGURE 5.14: A Flexible, Role-based Correspondence Solution

Financial and Audit Compliance

This application was designed to meet the rigorous requirements of government accounting systems and audits. Agencies use this application to capture, search on, and access all purchasing and contract documentation. The impact of audits is reduced by the system which automatically assembles sample packages for audit, and streamlines the process to reduce cost.

Digital Records Compliance

Agencies use this application to capture and manage agency records in digital format, from email and documents to photos and social media. It helps to save time and money and improves performance by organizing information and associating it with daily tasks. Agencies can reduce the costs of e-discovery and meet records compliance mandates and standards (MoReq 2010, DOD 5015.2) with digital records compliance.

Digital Preservation of Culture

Digital preservation ensures that existing and new digital materials of value will be preserved and accessible for future generations. This application is comprised of a trusted repository, archiving, digital asset/media management, content lifecycle management, records management, metadata creation, and digital rights management. It can be used to manage information according to regulations and facilitates collaboration between the private and public sector through a sustained approach to archiving and managing national content.

Human Capital Management

Agencies use this application to streamline and improve human capital processes through services that support recruitment, on-boarding, training, benefits, appraisals, and more—out of the box. Agencies have experienced improved Human Resources (HR) staff productivity and performance visibility and eliminated paper-based processes using human capital management.

Many of these e-government technologies and applications will be described in further detail in the following chapters about e-government at the international, national, regional, and local levels.

CHAPTER 6

E-GOVERNMENT AT THE INTERNATIONAL LEVEL

CHAPTER 6

e-Government at the International Level

Globalization has made the world a smaller place. When national governments face challenges that exceed their capacity, they look across their national borders to embrace global partnerships. In this chapter, we examine the modernization of relationships between nations and multilateral organizations, non-governmental organizations (NGOs), and multinational corporations, with a focus on how e-government facilitates more effective, collaborative, and efficient international relations.

Multilateralism and bilateralism have roles to play in promoting a more just and environmentally sustainable global order. Bringing together international stakeholders to develop policies and solve multi-disciplinary issues such as globalization, sustainability, nuclear proliferation, sanctions and trade regulations, global finance, terrorism, and human rights requires robust, secure communications and technology infrastructure to support efficient coordination.

FIGURE 6.1: e-Government Framework

Examples of multinational organizations include the United Nations (UN), the World Trade Organization (WTO), the Group of Eight (G8), the Group of 20 (G20), the Organization of American States (OAS), the World Health Organization (WHO), and the Association of Southeast Asian Nations (ASEAN), as well as UN-related bodies like UNHCR. Additional examples include, the Commonwealth, the *Organisation internationale de la Francophonie* (OIF) (known more commonly as La Francophonie), the International Monetary Fund (IMF), and the Organisation for Economic Co-operation and Development (OECD). Multilateralism also describes joint military alliances, such as NATO.

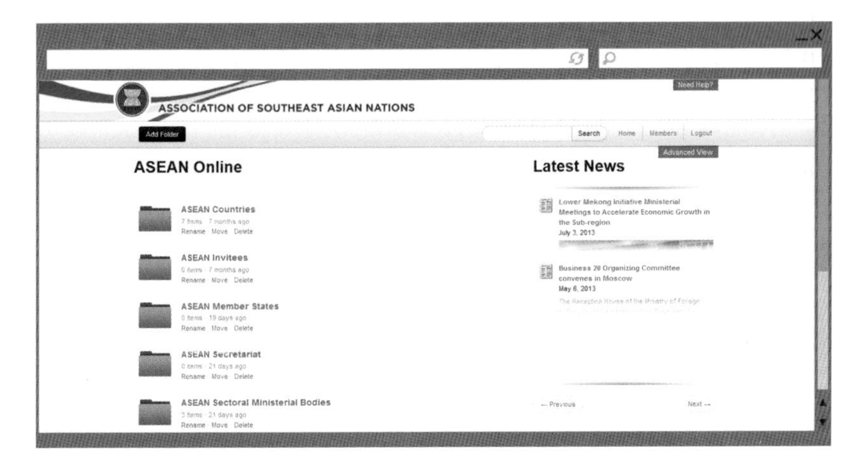

FIGURE 6.2: ASEAN Online

The government mandate for foreign affairs works to ensure that foreign policy advances national interests, enhances security, increases opportunity, and expands market access at bilateral, regional, and global levels. This depends on understanding, trust, and effective collaboration amongst a range of partners, both inside and outside of government. Communication and negotiation between representatives of states requires access to technologies that enable greater collaboration, interaction, and dialogue, with global levels of security.

From discussions on human rights to forums devoted to strong, sustainable, and balanced global growth, e-government delivers a global forum for open constructive dialogue and analysis. It enables rapid sharing of the latest research, statistics, and opinions for evidence-based decision making. It creates a secure and persistent presence for international events before, during, and after they have occurred to preserve intellectual capital, capture innovation and preserve best practices. And finally, it documents decisions and responsibilities.

Successful multilateral and bilateral ventures require new models of partnership between governments and nonprofit sectors, government and the for-profit sector, and other networked organizational forms. As a collaborative platform, e-government supports the growing role of private sector organizations in international affairs (which is discussed further in Chapter 10) and reinforces the rise of NGOs as central players in international development.

New Models of Engagement

Based on a need to collaborate across borders, NGOs have traditionally embraced innovative models of engagement. The anti-landmine movement that resulted in the signing of the Treaty to Ban Landmines and won the Nobel Peace Prize in 1997 was driven by the effective use of email. Other activists and lobby groups have been effective at the use of technology to organize efforts, usually much faster than governments.

e-Government flattens traditional geographical boundaries to tap into the power of networks, spanning the boundaries of government, citizens, and the private sector to engage globally for collaboration, transparency, and participation. In our networked world, the pace of change, the threat of risk, and the freedom of opportunity makes collaboration essential for success.

The emergence of a generation of digital natives (people who have grown up using digital technology) has made connectedness a fact of life. Citizens readily adopt new technologies to interact in new and more meaningful ways. Governments must follow suit. e-Government solutions pave the way to digitally-enabled collaboration and innovation. Adopting mobile, cloud, and social technologies will produce tangible benefits, helping governments, NGOs, and foundations to become more efficient, cost-effective, and agile.

In these times of economic crisis and globalization, it is imperative that nations work together. Managing relations between governments, NGOs, the private sector, and citizens is a necessity as countries become more decentralized. As illustrated in the following story, organizations like the LEND Network are using e-government solutions to transform government partnerships from a bricks-and-mortar model to virtual institutions to implement change in a matter of days, as opposed to years.

NGO Engagement

NGOs are complex in nature. They are based on a system that is a mix of collaborative and diverse groups that operate at many levels—from small, local operations to global multinational organizations. NGOs partner with governments, multilateral agencies, and the private sector, putting them in a unique position to help develop, influence, and implement international agendas based on interactions with various stakeholder groups.

The LEND Network

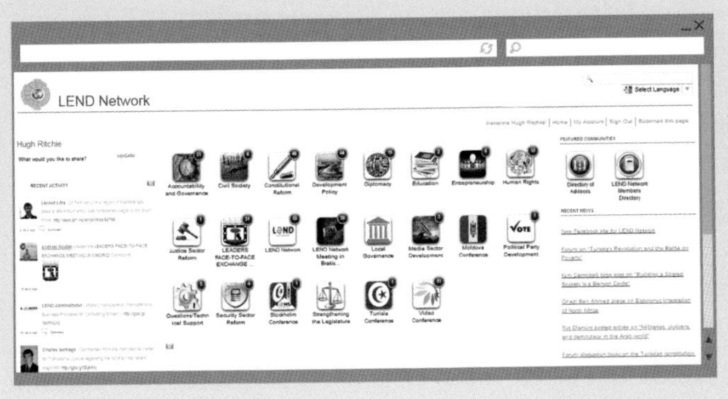

FIGURE 6.3: The LEND Network

The LEND Network employs the latest communications technology, including tablet computers and video conferencing, to create an online forum where leaders can securely exchange information.

The LEND (Leaders Engaged in New Democracies) Network is a groundbreaking new effort to support leaders in emerging democracies. It is a secure, self-perpetuating community that operates in a largely virtual setting. The LEND Network brings together key leaders from the world's newest democracies with former presidents, prime ministers, and others responsible for past transitions to democracy. It augments face-to-face meetings with ongoing peer-to-peer exchanges via a sophisticated, secure, virtual e-government platform.

The LEND Network fills a crucial need. It facilitates real-time information sharing amongst leaders in new democracies and those who have successfully navigated the challenges of democratization. The LEND Network employs the latest communications technology, including tablet computers and video conferencing, to create an online forum where leaders can securely exchange information. The project is designed to provide peer advice, peer support, and capacity building to political leaders and policy makers in key emerging democracies around the world.

By leveraging online voice, video, and text communication along with groundbreaking translation tools, the LEND Network addresses costly and logistical barriers that have limited such efforts in the past. It is accessible via mobile devices and hosted in the cloud. Approximately 20 countries are participating in the LEND Network with the goal of exchanging best practices and experience acquired during past transitions to democracy with senior officials working to consolidate democratic gains in today's newest democracies. The project received technology resources from companies including Google, OpenText, and DialCom-Spontania; funding from Sweden and the United States; and backing from many leading civil society organizations.

www.opentext.com/e-Government/LEND

For the most part, NGOs deliver bottom-up engagement projects that are typically co-financed by foundations, networks, or implemented by NGOs themselves. They aim to mobilize and gain support or deliver campaigns at the grass-roots level—often based on social media tools like networking and blogs that help to promote participatory government.

Traditionally, NGOs have focused on infrastructure projects (wells, bridges, habitat, etc.), but today they are looking more to education and technologies as long term enablers in a shift that puts NGOs ahead of governments in adoption. This is because they have critical links to all stakeholders, from local citizens and communities to governments and authorities who provide frameworks for policy development.

NGOs in the digital age have become more connected, integrated and skilled at running themselves as businesses, based on effective human capital management, strategic planning, performance management, social fundraising, and advocacy—all of which can be managed with e-government technologies.

e-Government solutions help NGOs to engage more effectively and securely, reducing the risks of corruption and mismanagement of funds and giving them the capacity to:

- Automate processes to maximize efficiency and minimize the risk of corruption
- Remove intermediaries that incur costs and follow their own agenda
- Improve collaboration and cooperation; reduce the red tape in public bureaucracies
- Increase transparency, accountability, and auditability through public transactions
- Preserve knowledge and enhance knowledge transfer through the exchange of best practices and secure repositories

A **Global** Footprint

FIGURE 6.4: e-Government Extends Multilateral Reach

e-Government helps to build a technically-oriented and governance-focused landscape for NGOs. It brings various stakeholders together to collaborate in real time, regardless of their location, time zone, or device. It builds knowledge capacity and advances aid development. Research programs are more readily established, grown, and globalized to deliver aid expediently and effectively.

Operating on an e-government unified platform, various stakeholder groups involved in international aid can be made more effective, accountable, and transparent. e-Government transforms the role of the NGO in promoting international aid, development, and democracy through increased stakeholder engagement and reducing the potential for corruption in international development programs.

Facilitating International Development

e-Government is a powerful tool to help developing economies realize the benefits of an emerging global information society. Sharing experiences and best practices for implementation, understanding why projects fail and why they succeed, and adapting solutions to the social and economic context of a nation will expedite the adoption of e-government in developing countries around the world.

As in the CARE Canada example below, e-government is revolutionizing the way governments interact with all their stakeholders. From the rural farmlands of India to villages in Africa, e-government is improving the quality of life for citizens in developing countries by increasing access to information that is useful in their daily lives, providing government services, establishing policies for development and aid, and offering new opportunities to participate in the political process.

e-Government gives governments the ability to forge new relationships among agencies, NGOs, and the private sector—which serves to make services and programs more accessible. Projects are easier to scale and collaboration amongst key stakeholders helps policymakers develop meaningful reforms based on knowledge of commerce, technology, and management. An e-government solution can help provide citizens in developing countries with access to:

- Programs and services through a government portal
- More participatory government through mobile-enabled social media
- Accurate and secure government-based information
- A digital platform for both citizens and public servants

All of these services can be provided in the cloud, saving governments millions in infrastructure costs. Although outsourcing to the cloud does raise data sovereignty issues, especially in light of the USA PATRIOT Act which potentially grants government access to data as soon as an organization interacts with a company in the U.S., the benefits outweigh the risk if the cloud vendor is based in a neutral country.

Care Canada

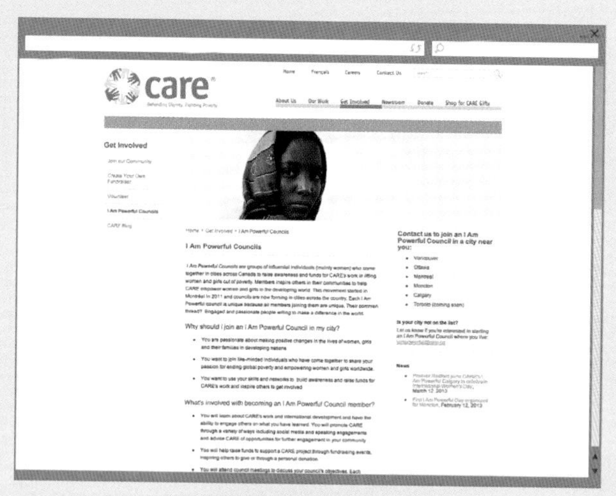

FIGURE 6.5: CARE's *I Am Powerful* Campaign

Many of CARE's contributors are not highly technical, so the solution has to be user friendly, interactive, and easily accessible.

CARE Canada is a non-profit and non-religious charitable organization. As a member of one of the world's largest independent relief and development federations, CARE International, CARE Canada's mission is to improve the provision of security and well being for the poor in developing regions and war-torn societies. For over half a century, CARE has been bringing emergency relief to those in need around the world.

CARE's community-based programs place a special focus on working with women because they are disproportionately affected by poverty and are crucial to fighting it. Based on this, CARE Canada has successfully initiated the *I Am Powerful* campaign to promote the empowerment of women internationally. Having trusted digital technology as the foundation for their intranet, CARE Canada revisited the solution, which they named Minerva, as their main tool for information storage, knowledge sharing, and distribution to help support the campaign.

Comprised of women responsible for spreading the *I Am Powerful* message within their own circles of the organization, users champion the repository. The reference group works in different departments, such as overseas programming or with emergencies or finance, in numerous sectors. Many of CARE's contributors are not highly technical, so the solution has to be user friendly, interactive, and easily accessible. The system contains documents for distribution, information for their personal use, and in-depth knowledge that is restricted to their view only. Minerva has proven to be a secure repository that encourages knowledge sharing and informational consistency within the reference group and throughout the CARE organization.

Many developing countries do not have the infrastructure necessary to deploy e-government solutions and services. These governments need to build out their Information and Communication Technology (ICT) infrastructure to solve issues around connectivity, privacy, accessibility, and security. Moving to a private cloud, as discussed in Chapter 14, helps make programs and services available in developing countries, without requiring investment in technology or resources. Service delivery is more affordable, time-to-value is realized quickly as solutions can be up and running quickly, and support for a system can be outsourced to further reduce costs.

International Standards and Regulations

NGOs and government agencies work together to develop global regulations, policies, and standards. International standards and regulations ensure that products and services are safe, reliable, and of good quality. For business, they serve as strategic tools to reduce costs by minimizing waste or error and increasing overall productivity. Standards and regulations help organizations access new markets, level the playing field for developing countries, and facilitate free and fair global trade.

As illustrated in the feature below about ISO, standards are developed through a consensus process. Experts from all over the world develop the standards that are required by their sector. They collaborate to share international experience and knowledge. e-Government solutions facilitate the secure exchange of knowledge, collaboration around this information, and the communication channels required to set standards and regulations across the globe.

Global Banking Regulations

Financial markets are globally integrated. The banking industry is connected and relies on national and global economies. For this reason, it is important for regulatory agencies to maintain control over the standardized practices of these institutions. The International Monetary Fund (IMF) is a multilateral organization that oversees the global financial system and monitors the economic and financial policies of its 188 member countries. Like the IMF, the World Bank is an international financial organization that provides loans to developing countries to promote foreign investment and international trade, and to help reduce poverty.

The consistent implementation of regulations results in a more effective global financial system. One of the challenges the global system faces is that while rules are established internationally, domestic regulators are responsible for enforcing them. As changes rapidly take place, the pace of domestic implementation is often not consistent at a global level.

International Organization for Standardization Central Secretariat

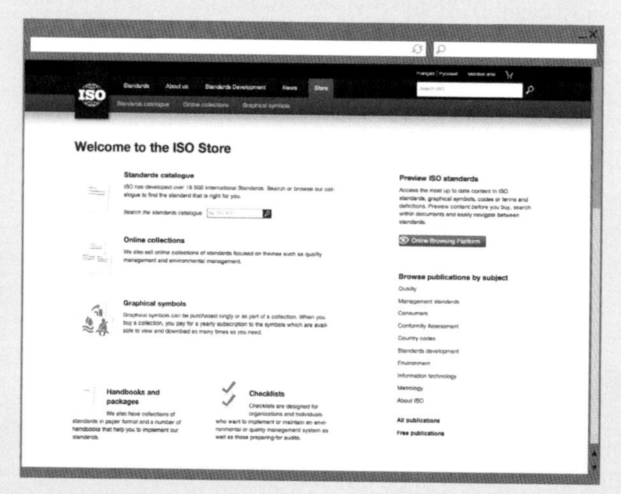

FIGURE 6.6: ISO Web Store

ISO has greatly reduced the time required to publish international standards, and can now manage all official documents and reports electronically.

The International Organization for Standardization Central Secretariat (ISO) is a worldwide federation of national standards bodies from 156 countries. Complying with ISO standards, such as ISO 9000 for quality management, is a must for any organization before it can compete in the modern global economy. Companies in every kind of business imaginable—from chemical to information technology—are required to comply with particular ISO standards as a prerequisite to doing business. Maintaining and publishing content on more than 15,000 ISO standards is no simple task. The very success of the ISO program depends on making sure that the most up-to-date, valid standards are made easily available to the countless number of worldwide users.

The ISO's Central Secretariat uses Enterprise Content Management (ECM) to effectively manage the entire standardization process—from development to distribution. ECM provides a long-term foundation for capturing knowledge and is web-based, so it can ease the process of distributing information over the ISO extranet. This means customers have instant access to information directly from their web browser, and they also have print-on-demand capability, which reduces operational costs. ISO uses ECM to manage content for its bilingual web site—www.iso.org—and also to manage content for its web store.

ISO has greatly reduced the time required to publish international standards, and can now manage all official documents and reports electronically. It is one of the largest virtual organizations in the world.

The recent global financial crisis wreaked havoc in the global financial system as banks became insolvent or received taxpayer-funded bailouts. The crisis resulted in significant regulatory changes made to the global banking sector to prevent a similar crisis from happening again. These changes demonstrate how interconnected the world is today, and the domino effect created when one system crashes and the others follow suit. This kind of interdependency requires extensive consultation, collaboration, and communications between governments, institutions, and organizations.

The following feature about the Office of the Superintendent of Financial Institutions illustrates how e-government solutions bring together key participants—from policymakers to regulatory officials—to expedite the decision-making process. Critical information is stored, shared, managed, and archived securely in an e-government system.

Private Sector and NGO Engagement

Global collaboration fosters a global perspective. A global perspective is needed to address many of the global crises we face today, such as the one billion children currently living in extreme poverty.[1] NGOs are particularly effective in this arena as they exert international influence and local presence. Government partnerships with NGOs and organizations in the private sector can help agencies around the world meet their mandates of increasing efficiency, expanding capacity, and improving the quality of life for all citizens.

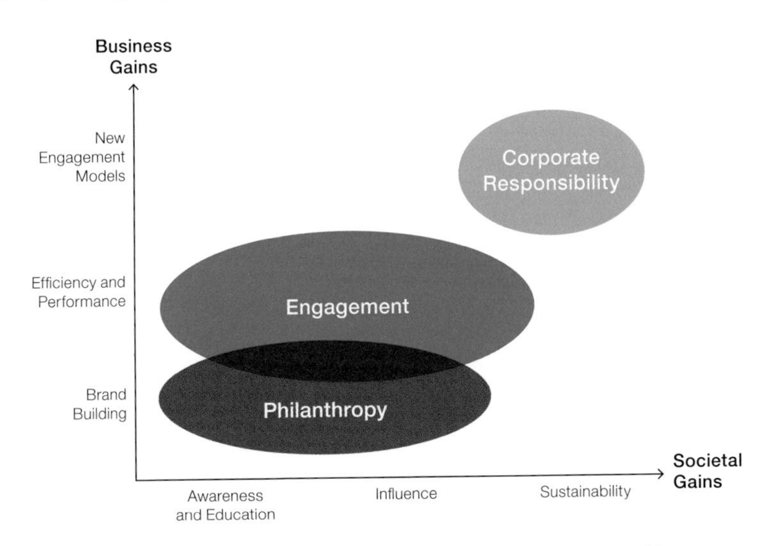

FIGURE 6:7: Outcomes of NGO and Private Sector Relationships

[1] Anup Shah, *"Poverty Facts and Stats"*, Global Issues, January 7, 2013, *http://www.globalissues.org/article/26/poverty-facts-and-stats* (accessed February 2014).

Office of the Superintendent of Financial Institutions

FIGURE 6.8: OFSI Website

OSFI's case management system makes it easy... to find and share case information, ensuring everyone is spending more time focusing on higher-value areas that require their expertise and judgment.

The Office of the Superintendent of Financial Institutions (OSFI), the regulator of federally registered financial institutions operating in Canada, needed to implement a system to streamline, standardize, and re-design internal processes and improve the management of information across the organization in response to government legislation, which specifies that certain types of cases are automatically "deemed approved" if OSFI does not render a decision within 30 days.

OSFI deployed ECM technology to create a central repository for managing unstructured content, as well as process workflows and collaborative workspaces. OSFI's case management system makes it easy for case officers and other expert reviewers to find and share case information, ensuring everyone is spending more time focusing on higher-value areas that require their expertise and judgment. In addition, OSFI's Business Systems Integration Initiative (BSII) provides a level of automation, so that OSFI employees can quickly and efficiently manage regulatory processes, improve risk management supervision, and speed responses to key stakeholders.

Partnerships between NGOs and the public and private sectors enable national policies to be expanded to the international level. From a governance perspective, an increasing number of NGOs are participating in multi-stakeholder initiatives and learning how to manage relations with all stakeholders—from government to private sector organizations. e-Government serves to expedite these relationships through facilitating systematic dialogue, shared programs, certification, consultation, and research cooperation.

Organizations in the private sector are attracted to these kinds of relationships based on opportunities to extend their reach globally and to fulfill the requirements of corporate responsibility. The benefits of this kind of relationship include brand or reputation enhancement, sustainability, and a rise in awareness of social, economic, and environmental issues.

An NGO and private sector partnership carries long-term outcomes above and beyond philanthropy. Potential outcomes of NGO and private sector engagement include the establishment of standards and guidelines, increased efficiencies through improved supply chain operations, greater employee satisfaction, the development of more effective business models and management tools, enhanced stakeholder engagement and support, and higher quality products and services based on shared innovation. These can result in greater economic, environmental and societal gains on the whole. e-Government provides the technology infrastructure needed to support new business models and foster collaboration and innovation to serve new markets and support communities locally through economic development and self sufficiency.

As illustrated in the stories below about the Vancouver Olympics and the RBS 6 Nations Championship, e-government facilitates organizers of international events, bringing together international sports federations (IFs), National Olympic Committees (NOCs), and organizing committees for each specific Olympic Games, corporations, citizens, and athletes.

e-Government delivers increased capacity and multilateral reach to national governments. From the Olympics to multilateral organizations and bilateral meetings, e-government helps nations cross geographic boundaries to sustain political engagement and establish working relationships based on trade, investment, and innovation. This is demonstrated in the current collaborative Canada-Mexico Partnership (CMP), which aims to promote collaboration not only between nations but between the public and private sectors as well, which is discussed further in Chapter 10.

Vancouver Olympics: 2010 Winter Games

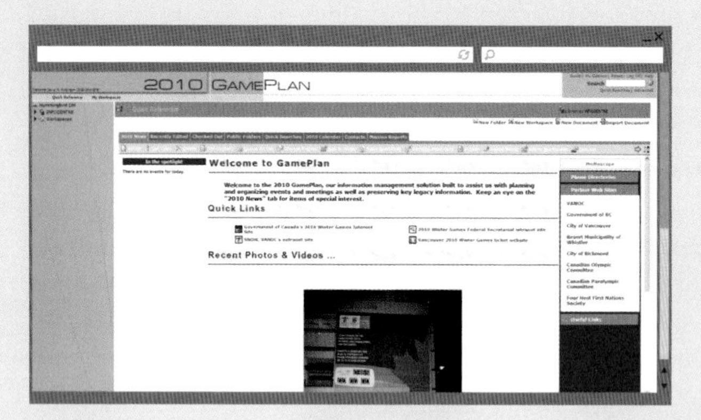

The system was fully bilingual, allowing people to work in either English or French.

FIGURE 6:9: Increasing Information Access at the Vancouver Olympic Games

To prepare for the Vancouver 2010 Olympic and Paralympic Winter Games, the Department of Canadian Heritage turned to an e-government solution to ensure safe, secure, and easily accessible records, documents, and collaboration. With numerous departments, and committees heavily involved (including the Vancouver Organizing Committee for the 2010 Olympic and Paralympic Winter Games [VANOC], the government of British Columbia, the City of Vancouver, and the resort municipality of Whistler), it was imperative that the latest documents were easily accessible, collaboration was safe and secure, and records of all the processes and documents were kept to ensure order and to share lessons learned and best practices with the team the next time the country hosts the Games.

The Government of Canada created a shared system initiative based on document management, records management, imaging, workflow, reporting, and e-mail integration products. Mobility was also important for the project to enable access to documents via the web.

The system was fully bilingual, allowing people to work in either English or French. A Francophone employee would be presented with a French environment and an Anglophone presented with an English environment. Employees could submit documentation or search in either language. Another advantage was that the system created a framework for how to manage information, whether it be email, paper, or electronic documents. One of the greatest benefits, however, was the assurance that content was secure.

Partnering to Preserve Culture and Heritage

NGOs, experts, centers of excellence, and research institutes play vital roles in safeguarding a nation's cultural heritage. At the national level, governments are working with NGOs to promote, identify, and preserve cultural heritage due to the social responsiveness, social focus, and cultural sensitivity NGOs have for the communities they serve.

It is true that governments are the stewards for digital preservation—integrating knowledge and creative materials into education, unleashing creativity in culture, providing an authoritative source for public policy development, and encouraging engagement around the world. However, the collaboration between NGOs and private and public sector organizations offers a unique approach to managing and promoting national content. And often one that is repeatable and marketable.

e-Government solutions that help to preserve national culture and heritage are made of technologies that interoperate and include a trusted repository, digital asset or media management, content lifecycle management, records management, web content management, metadata creation, and digital rights management.

By its definition, sustained digital preservation requires that preservation-related activities are technically, financially, organizationally, and culturally sound. The approach is rooted in collaboration between government, NGO, and private sector organizations and in the rapidly evolving international standards for managing authentic digital records and media in a modern administrative environment, as illustrated in the feature below.

e-Government facilitates a sustained approach to the preservation of culture to bridge generational and geographical divides. It enables citizens to be engaged and informed on national and international issues. It is also a means of sharing knowledge with the world and of providing access to resources in developing countries. Such knowledge resources must respect an honored tradition and continue as open, free public goods. This open government approach is explored in Chapter 12.

RBS 6 Nations Championship

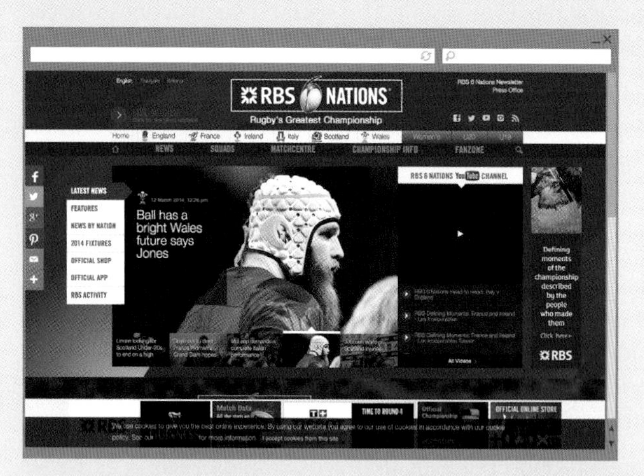

Mobile access solves a growing need in viewership experience, as last year over 51 percent of all site visits came from a mobile or tablet device.

FIGURE 6:10: RBS 6 Nations Rugby—Optimizing User Experience

The RBS 6 Nations Championship is the world's foremost annual international rugby event. Rugby teams from England, France, Ireland, Italy, Scotland, and Wales compete each year in a series of fiercely-contested matches. Each game is followed by tens of millions of rugby fans all over the world via television, radio, mobile devices, and the web.

The existing RBS 6 Nations Championship website was unable to meet the demands of its always-connected, international, mobile viewers. With so many international supporters visiting the site, there was also a need to extend its multilingual capabilities and provide information to the media in their local languages. The tournament organizers, Six Nations Rugby Ltd. decided to redesign the site.

The new site went live on a new digital platform in time for the RBS 6 Nations to kick off the 2014 Championship. The new platform, available in English, French and Italian, includes dynamic web and mobile sites, a Virtual Press Office, a Digital Media Guide, and a Judiciary Platform. The innovative platform uses the latest technology to ensure the ultimate user experience for those following the action. The site follows on-field action with live match coverage of all the games, in-game statistics, live images and commentary. It offers a wealth of historical statistics from the competition, as well as embedded YouTube video highlights from present and past fixtures. Complementing the website is the mobile friendly platform accessible from any smartphone or tablet. The content during matches focuses on the live action, defaulting the fans' view to the match center for instant updates on all the fixtures. Mobile access solves a growing need in viewership experience, as last year over 51 percent of all site visits came from a mobile or tablet device.

CHAPTER 7

E-GOVERNMENT AT THE NATIONAL LEVEL

CHAPTER 7

e-Government at the National Level

Although structure varies from country to country, federal governments perform essentially the same functions. They lead at the national level and are authorized to legislate across a country. National governments share common challenges based on their historically complex structures. This chapter examines how federal governments are using e-government to overcome these challenges—and improve operations through new patterns of decentralization and specialization, embedded in multi-faceted information systems and shared services between agencies.

FIGURE 7.1: e-Government Framework

As discussed in Chapter 2, the federal system of government divides legislative powers between a central government and the governments of the provinces or states. Creating a federal system of government requires working across many different layers, making for a very large and intricate system. Each province or state determines its own policies around citizen programs and benefits, which adds to an already fragmented system of government.

Canada, for example, is a highly decentralized federation. Power is diffused across the country with the provinces controlling primary areas of public policy. Under Canada's Constitution, the federal government's responsibilities cannot be altered by another level of government. This is also the case for provincial governments, which are recognized as autonomous entities under the Canadian Constitution. The federal and provincial governments represent political power within their respective jurisdictions. In Canada, municipal and regional governments are created and empowered by the provinces.

The roles of regional and federal governments represent an ongoing debate between centralists and decentralists. At one extreme, centralists advocate the federal government as a centralized, unified, and efficient governing force. Less power is relegated to the states in areas of policy creation and control. Decentralists, on the other hand, support authority and policy development at local levels of government with limited authority at the federal level. This approach is based on the belief that provincial and territorial governments are better positioned to promote local interests. e-Government has the potential to bridge levels of government, taking a citizen's perspective on access to services and making the differing jurisdictions transparent and seamless.

Accelerating Transformation

e-Government accelerates transformation by connecting vertical and horizontal levels of government with a focus on delivering services according to citizen need. The approach is citizen-centric rather than program-centric, and e-government is the enabler by providing new models of collaboration and a platform that works across functional boundaries to deliver e-services. As outlined in Chapter 1, the mission to protect citizens is a top priority for federal governments. In today's information-based society, security and protection are essential. For e-governance to be effective, national governments must focus on making their networks and services safe. e-Government delivers component technologies that support secure, transparent, and user-based identity management to help build trust in digitized services. This entails that governments educate citizens about the threats of cyber attacks and identity theft, and offer measures of prevention and protection.

Other safety measures managed at the federal level include the development of standards around digital governance and compliance with emerging regulations. Standardization and the application of open source software promote competence and use of information management technologies. The "Digital Agenda for Europe" identifies improving standards and interoperability as keys to future success in governance.

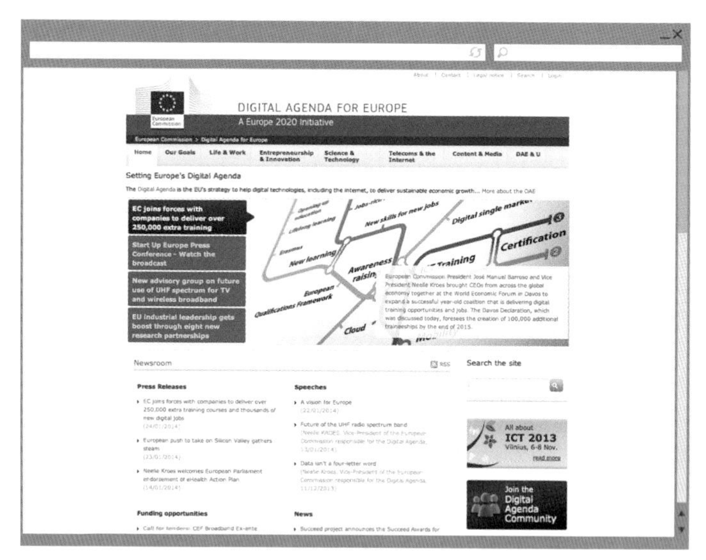

FIGURE 7.2: Digital Agenda for Europe

On the citizen side, secure e-government promotes deeper citizen engagement. Opening up government information to citizens and involving them in the decision-making process increases civic participation in policy and program development. Many governments around the world are using technology to unlock the power of data to improve transparency and efficiency through the co-creation of products and services. Open government and open data are discussed in greater detail in Chapter 12.

e-Government makes government leaders accessible through multiple channels of communication. In some elections in the U.S., town halls or debates have been hosted as live feeds. In a more specific example (see above illustration), the National Pipeline Mapping System makes information about pipeline safety available online to U.S. citizens. Any member of the public can view maps of pipelines accurate to about 150 meters across the country. Citizens can search by operator, pipeline, name, or even the status of the pipeline. Pipeline data about incidents is available and much of it can be downloaded. A homeowner can find information about any company, including how many barrels of oil were spilled in a year, associated property damage costs, and even details about company inspections.

Digital solutions generate growth in a digital economy. A crucial element for successful innovation-led development is quick and easy access to expertise and resources. e-Government facilitates the creation of communities of practice, bringing together entrepreneurs, subject matter experts (SMEs), researchers, and academics for efforts in research and development and the commercialization of products. Intellectual property rights for the development of technologies and services must be enforceable in the digital age. To prevent copyright infringements, federal governments need effective tools and processes for digitization and distribution.

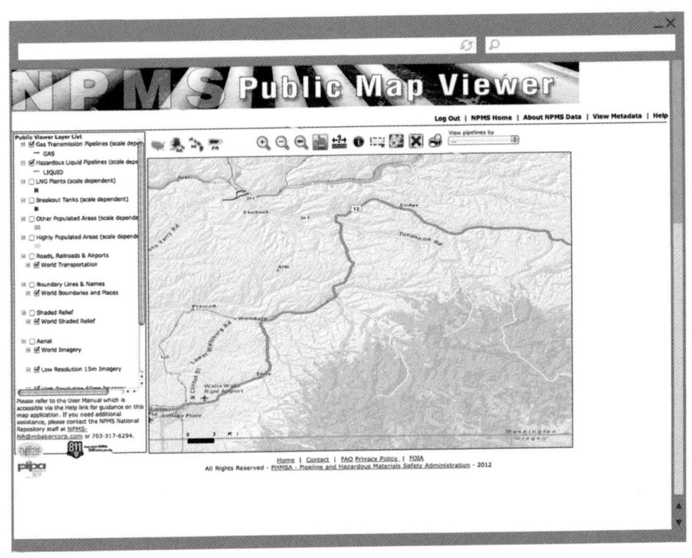

FIGURE 7.3: National Pipeline Mapping System[1]

Governments must adapt to the new digital world and manage information and technology appropriately. For e-government to be successful, certain conditions need to be in place. Digital infrastructure and networks must be expanded, and investments in research and development increased. To provide the necessary infrastructure, requirements for security, reliability, standardization, and interoperability should be established and implemented. The role of the Internet and other channels in regulatory and policy development should be determined.

The gap between governments and tech savvy citizens is widening, manifested in an unwillingness or inability to adopt new digital tools, processes, and approaches. Governments are realizing the key role that technology plays in modernizing services, and many countries have articulated e-government agendas such as the "Digital Agenda for Europe," the U.S. Government's "Building a 21st Century Platform to Better Serve the American People," and Canada's "Digital Economy Strategy." What follows is an overview of some international efforts toward implementing effective e-government, illustrated through example deployments in select countries around the world.

e-Government in Canada

In Canada, the federal cabinet determines priorities, sets tax levels and spending, and manages the administration of government departments. The prime minister appoints cabinet members, exerting influence on key priorities and policies to focus on. The federal level of government in Canada is made up of departments or ministries, along with over 130 agencies and crown corporations and the courts.

[1] "National Pipeline Mapping System", *https://www.npms.phmsa.dot.gov/PublicViewer/* (accessed February 2014).

Historically, e-government was established in Canada through the Government On-Line (GOL) initiative in 2006 to help connect the country to its citizens. The initiative accelerated the design and online delivery of 130 of the most commonly used government services. The objective was to focus on the Internet as a key channel for providing information and services to stakeholders, sharing experiences and best practices, and working toward building a secure electronic infrastructure that could be expanded to support sophisticated online transactions in the future.

The principles that guided the effort focused less on the organization and structure of government and more on citizen needs. Building partnerships among departments and agencies or with levels of governments to streamline service delivery was also an objective.

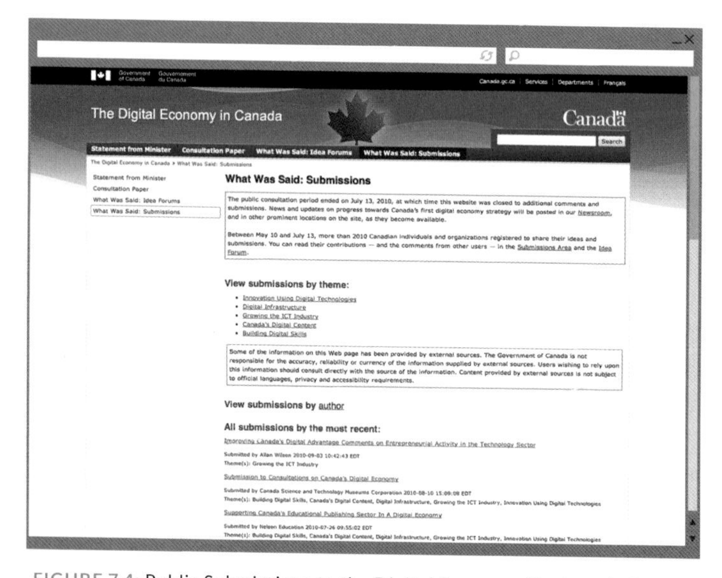

FIGURE 7.4: Public Submissions to the Digital Economy Strategy in Canada

To maintain the citizen-centric approach outlined in the GOL initiative and build confidence in online service delivery, the government reached out to the public to share their ideas and feedback for digitizing service delivery. The government is currently reviewing submissions, ideas, comments, and tweets—all of which have been collected and are accessible online. Once it has reviewed input, as well as the results of meetings with industry and federal, provincial, and territorial representatives, the Canadian government will develop an action plan for regaining Canada's leadership in the digital economy.

While Canada is recognized as a digital innovator, performance has slipped in some key dimensions. The Auditor General recently assessed that little has been added online since 2006. Growth rates have declined in the Canadian Information and Communications Technology (ICT) sector in the face of increasing international competition and Canada has fallen behind other countries in the adoption and use of digital technologies. In 2005, Canada ranked first among 190 countries in online service delivery, today it ranks eleventh. To prosper in the global digital economy, Canada is looking to build on its many strengths to seize new opportunities and regain its digital leadership.

Developing and implementing a digital strategy requires the active engagement of all stakeholders, including ICT vendors, consumers, researchers, educators, and users. It will also require cooperation across all levels of government. A stale approach, rooted in hierarchical bureaucracies, can impede the cooperation required to modernize government processes and services. As illustrated in the story below about Transport Canada, e-government transformation results in significant cost savings and efficiency gains.

e-Government in the United States

A main function of any federal government is to create and enforce laws to ensure order and stability within society.

FIGURE 7.5: The White House – Building a 21st Century Digital Government

Transport Canada

FIGURE 7.6: Transport Canada Website

Overall, Transport Canada has tripled productivity savings up to $4.6 million ... As a result, the system paid for itself in just 1.17 years.

Transport Canada's mission is to serve the public interest through the promotion of a safe, secure, efficient, and environmentally responsible transportation system in Canada. This requires effective information management to facilitate timely and informed decision-making among an extensive list of portfolio partners that include 15 Crown corporations, 17 port authorities, and 21 airport authorities, as well as other shared governance organizations.

Concerned about the dissemination of information through electronic means, privacy assurances, corporate memory loss due to employee turnover, and the need for real-time access to information to satisfy requests and litigation concerns, the Government of Canada (GC) championed an e-government solution based on records, documents, and information management. Transport Canada was the first Canadian government department to complete an e-government deployment, with more than four million records in a single library and 5,200 users to date at more than 117 sites—the largest single library deployment in the Canadian Public Sector.

Working as an integrated set of tools that facilitates the full use of electronic documentation—from capture and storage to organization, retrieval, sharing, reuse, protection, and disposal of information—the solution has become a mission-critical application for Transport Canada's managers and staff. It has helped the organization ensure the accuracy of its corporate records; unite a geographically dispersed and mobile workforce; meet legal obligations, including e-discovery requirements; improve productivity; and align information management with the GOL initiative. Using the system, Transport Canada has tripled productivity savings up to $4.6 million and expects further growth, staying on target to meet its annual cost avoidance savings estimate. As a result, the system paid for itself in just 1.17 years.

The Executive Office of the President (EOP) of the United States supports the government, and is staffed by the president's advisors. Current statistics support an EOP staff of close to 2,000 people. Similar in basic structure to the Canadian Government, the U.S. federal government is run by a cabinet that serves as an advisory board to the president, made up of 15 department heads.

On May 23, 2012, President Obama issued a directive called "Building a 21st Century Digital Government." The Administration launched a comprehensive digital government strategy aimed at delivering better services to the American people. The strategy builds on several initiatives, including Executive Order 13571, Streamlining Service Delivery and Improving Customer Service, and Executive Order 13576, Delivering an Efficient, Effective, and Accountable Government.

All U.S. Government departments and agencies are tasked to help build a 21st century digital government. Many departments and agencies, such as the organization in the Department of Defense (DoD) featured below, have produced their own digital agendas and are following these to improve their mission performance.

e-Government in Europe

European government administrations are being challenged to improve the efficiency, productivity, and quality of their services. They share the challenges experienced in governments around the world—struggling to deliver programs and services with reduced budgetary resources.

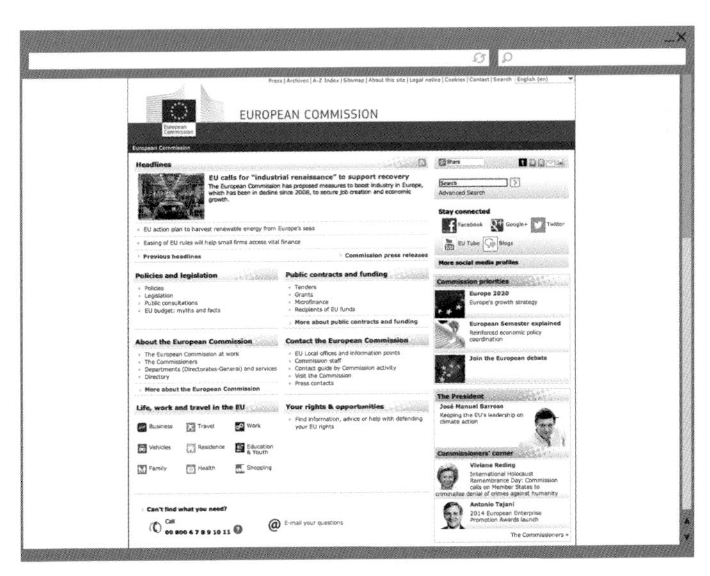

FIGURE 7.7: European Commission Website

An Enterprise in the Department of Defence (DoD)

For a decade now, the Organization has been relying on an e-government process automation solution to improve its performance and effectively fulfill its mission.

This U.S. Federal Agency is the Premier Security Assistance Enterprise in the Department of Defense (DoD). The mission of this Agency is to implement approved U.S. Army security assistance programs, including Foreign Military Sales (FMS) of defense articles and services to eligible foreign governments.

This Organization manages approximately 4,000 FMS cases valued at $49 billion, as well as co-production of Army materials. In addition, it is responsible for Army security assistance information management and financial policy, and provides logistics guidance to the Army security assistance community. Today, the Organization is increasingly responding to support the U.S. government in emergency assistance, humanitarian relief, and Operations Other Than War, including United Nations peacekeeping operations. The Organization's motto is "Strength in Cooperation."

An e-government process automation solution is being utilized to manage processes for foreign military sales. This involves the collaboration between the various support structures/commands within the Organization, as well as contractual control process with foreign militaries. For a decade now, it has been relying on an e-government process automation solution to improve its performance and effectively fulfill on its mission.

e-Government helps public administrators face numerous challenges. To be effective, it must be implemented in coordination with organizational changes and new skills to improve public services and enhance democratic processes. In practice, this means not only providing citizens with simplified official procedures and a citizen-friendly administration, but also facilitating engagement between private enterprise and public administration, as well as between administrations.

e-Government holds the key to modernizing public administration and encouraging stronger economic growth. European countries have realized this, and the European Commission is actively supporting e-government at both national and supranational levels. The Vice-President for Administrative Affairs is responsible for e-government implementations activities that follow the e-Commission strategy. e-Government initiatives include Access-eGov, EGovMoNet, and SemanticGov. The following feature about the European Court of Human Rights demonstrates how e-government helps consolidate information to ensure its accuracy and integration with key processes, reducing administrative burden and improving performance. As a result, agencies are better equipped to deliver on their mission to protect citizens.

e-Government in the United Kingdom

The United Kingdom (U.K.) "Government Digital Strategy" describes approaches to redesigning digital services to make them straightforward and convenient to use. It has been developed collaboratively across government as part of the Civil Service Reform Plan, followed by departmental digital strategies, which was published in December 2012.

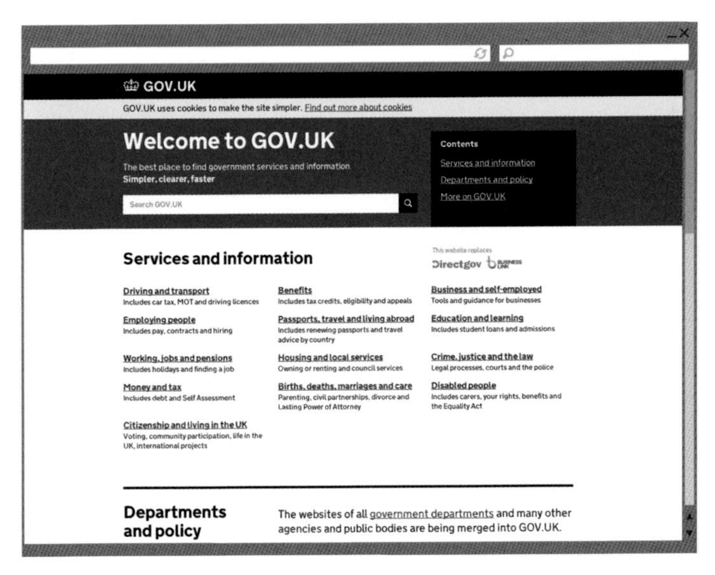

FIGURE 7.8: GOV.UK

European Court of Human Rights

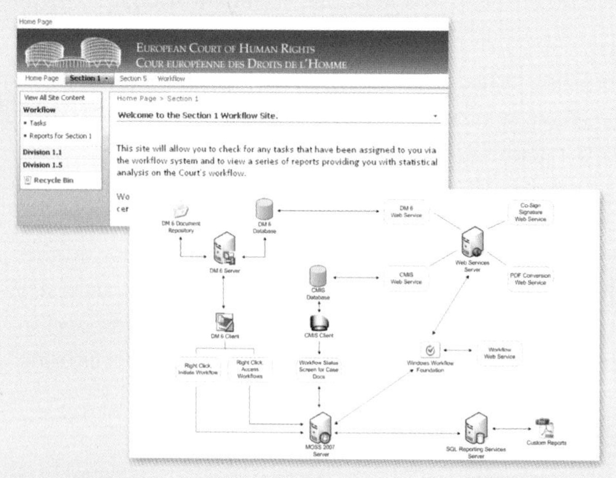

FIGURE 7.9: Streamlining Process at ECHR

The workflow solution helps manage the approval process for committee and chamber cases and provides the Court with a mechanism that radically streamlines its case management processes, further enhancing the productivity of the legal divisions.

The European Court of Human Rights (ECHR) is part of the Council of Europe, an international intergovernmental organization that was established in 1949 to promote political democracy and human rights, social progress, and European cultural identity continent-wide. Currently, the Council is made up of 47 member states that have all signed up to the system of human rights protection under the European Convention on Human Rights.

Over the last few years the Court's caseload has exploded, with the number of applications to the Court growing from 14,000 in 1997 to over 50,000 in 2009. Recognizing that it was time to streamline its internal approval processes in order to cope with the exploding caseload, the Court's IT department developed an in-house automated workflow solution. The workflow solution helps manage the approval process for committee and chamber cases and provides the Court with a mechanism that radically streamlines its case management processes, further enhancing the productivity of the legal divisions.

The system saves time, is easy to use, has led to less work for the legal assistants improving efficiencies, and is more streamlined than sending the committee notes by paper. Division assistants highlight the fact that the workflow solution automatically tracks the route of the workflow and that the dynamic reports make it easy for the divisions and sections to find out what stage a workflow is at. With the workflow solution for committee notes successfully underway, the Court now plans to begin piloting its workflow for chamber notes.

Despite the fact that 82 percent of the British population is online, people rarely access government services using the Internet. In response to this, the U.K. government is improving the way it provides information by consolidating programs and services on a single website, GOV.UK. Realizing that transactional services provide the biggest opportunity to save civilian time and government spending, the U.K. government provides more than 650 transactional services on this website.

The publishing activities of all 24 central government departments moved to GOV.UK in March 2013. The government has worked to raise awareness of their digital services so more people know about and use them. As an ongoing strategy, each department publishes its own departmental digital strategy with an action plan as a framework for continuing improvements in services. For continual review and refinement, the Cabinet Office operates an annual review process to track progress against action in this strategy.

e-Government in Germany

The German Federal parliament passed the e-Government Act in 2005 to promote more simplified, user-friendly, and efficient service delivery. Called BundOnline 2005, as the largest e-government program in Europe at the time, it was designed to ensure that each administration make 440 public services available online throughout the country. BundOnline applied central coordination with local responsibility for implementing public services. This meant that services were devised, implemented, and enhanced by ministries and their subordinate authorities, while responsibility for overall coordination belonged to the Federal Ministry of the Interior (FMI).

The digital government strategy was later defined in the e-Government 2.0 program as part of the more general strategic approach set out in the document *Focused on the Future: Innovations for Administration* concerning the overall modernization of the Public Administration. It included projects like electronic identity cards and digital signatures, a De-Mail system to facilitate the secure exchange of electronic documents among all stakeholders, and public services number (D115) as a direct line to public administration to obtain information about public services.

The German Federal Ministry of Economics and Technology has released an action plan for e-government called the *ICT Strategy of the German Federal Government: Digital Germany 2015*. It sets out the ICT policy framework for ministries to plan and implement the necessary measures for establishing digital strategies up to 2015. In parallel to modernization efforts focusing on the federal public administration, the plan outlines the priorities, tasks, and projects required to create a fully integrated e-government landscape in Germany throughout the federal government, federal-state governments, and municipal administrations. As illustrated in the following feature, Germany has standardized on an e-government platform to manage and consolidate its information.

DOMEA®

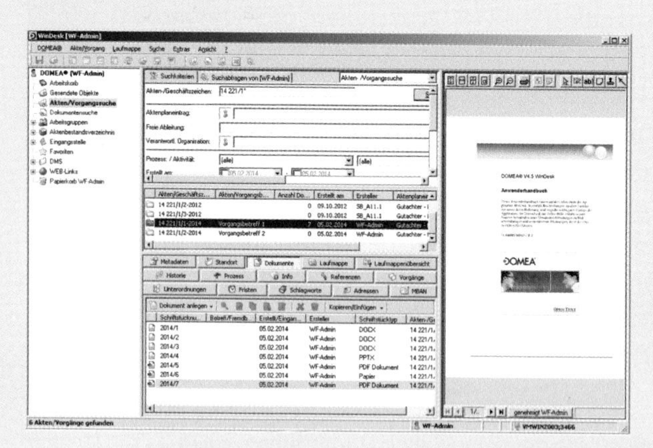

FIGURE 7.10: DOMEA

DOMEA helps government organizations reduce the costs, risks, and complexity of document, records, and content management.

The "Document Management and Electronic Archiving in Electronic Courses of Business" (DOMEA) concept introduced mandates for creating paperless offices in German government administrations. DOMEA® is the first product offering certified by the KBSt *(Koordinierungs- und Beratungsstelle der Bundesregierung für Informationstechnik in der Bundesverwaltung)*, or the Coordination and Advisory Agency of the Federal Government for Information Technology, to meet their requirements for document management and departmental coordination. In compliance with the Document Management and Archiving regulations issued by the KBSt in Germany, many e-government organizations rely on the innovative workflow-based document management capabilities provided by the DOMEA solution.

IT departments in the public sector were feeling pressured to make the most of their existing processes and file sharing systems. At the same time, they were required to eliminate paper-based systems, streamline business processes, and mitigate risk and cost containment. Serving more than 60,000 seats sold in the German e-government sector and nine out of 18 supreme German Federal Ministries, DOMEA supports the business of government and the transformational initiatives that the public sector is tasked with addressing.

DOMEA solutions are focused on information storage and exchange. Specifically, DOMEA helps government organizations improve internal processes and work with electronic documents rather than paper; promote information sharing and collaboration in and between government departments; ensure that administrative procedures are continuous, traceable, and revisable; reduce the costs, risks, and complexity of document, records, and content management; and improve agency and employee efficiency.

When used effectively, e-government can act as a catalyst toward economic development and sustainability. Many other countries around the world have identified the critical role that technology plays in delivering and transforming the operations of government. Australia, for example, released its Australian Public Service ICT Strategy in 2012. According to the 2012 *United Nations E-government Survey* rankings, the Republic of Korea is the world leader, followed by the Netherlands (see following feature), the United Kingdom, and Denmark, with the United States, Canada, France, Norway, Singapore, and Sweden close behind.[2]

The same survey confirms that member countries are moving from a single-purpose organizational model to an integrated, unified whole-of-government model for greater efficiencies. Despite progress made in general to implement e-government with a citizen-centric perspective, the gains are not spread evenly, especially across developing countries, which are still offering low levels of engagement.

In the following chapters, we examine how regional and local governments have recently invested considerable resources to transform public sector organizations and deliver services in a more efficient way.

[2] *"United Nations E-Government for the People: E-Government Survey 2012"* United Nations, 2012, *http://unpan1.un.org/intradoc/groups/public/documents/un/unpan048065.pdf* (accessed February 2014).

Netherlands Ministry of Defense

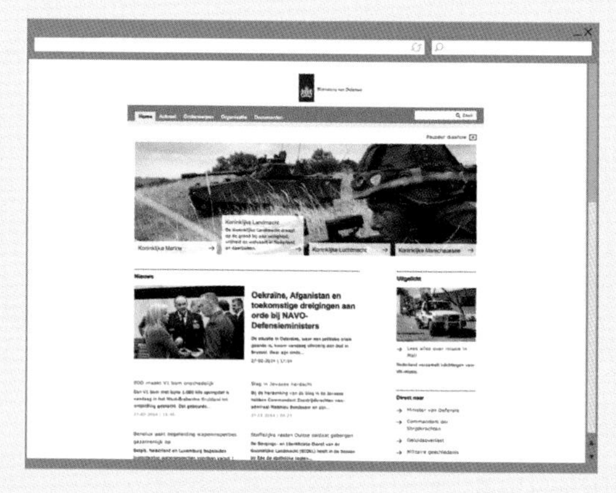

FIGURE 7.11: Dutch Ministry of Defense

The Netherlands Ministry of Defense comprises the Central Staff, the Royal Netherlands Navy, the Royal Netherlands Army, the Royal Netherlands Air Force, the Royal Netherlands Marechaussee, the Support Command, and the Defence Materiel Organisation.

What follows are excerpts from an interview with Lieutenant Colonel Erwin Huisman of the Dutch Ministry of Defense.

"As Information Manager for all of Human Resources (HR), I am responsible for 120,000 people in the organization, including civilians, reserve and military people, and veterans in areas such as medical, training, and education.

In early 2000, our budget was reduced and we had to completely reorganize the HR department. To support this, we deployed an Enterprise Resource Planning (ERP) system and integrated 14 different legacy systems. In 2010, we wanted to transition from an ERP system to business services, so we implemented a platform that enabled us to develop a solution based on a process engine which today serves as our new master data model.

Rules inside the defense organization change constantly, and we need a flexible process management system capable of supporting volumes like 3,000 applications for military operations support. With the new system, we were able to consolidate everything into a single interface in a single implementation. We have 2,000 different pieces of software communicating with each other, which required a lot of maintenance across different interfaces. With the new system, we were able to minimize costs through reduced maintenance and resource requirements. Cycles have improved with the adaptability of the system—what took months to implement now can happen in a week.

For example, when the military goes on a mission, a lot of things have to happen beforehand. Personnel typically need be inoculated, see the dentist, complete training, and more. Using process modeling, we were able to incorporate these steps into a single process, or transaction, that just needs to be initiated for all these things to happen automatically in the system.

The next generation of military personnel is using mobile devices. This use will only increase—which is why we are thinking about integrating the system with mobile devices. This will be the future."

CHAPTER 8

E-GOVERNMENT AT THE REGIONAL LEVEL

CHAPTER 8

e-Government at the Regional Level

Regional governments at state or provincial levels are responsible for policy development and service delivery in heath care, education, transportation, utilities, and natural resources. Many of the processes behind the administration of public service have been automated in varying degrees by e-government systems. This chapter explores how e-government streamlines and facilitates more effective services and operations in these industries through various deployments in the U.S., Canada, Europe, and the Middle East.

FIGURE 8.1: e-Government Framework

An e-government system is vital in ensuring that critical documents can be maintained, secured, and updated accurately as public records. Internally, an e-government system archives, stores, and secures all content according to policies. The critical function this serves is illustrated in the following excerpt based on an interview with a regional government organization that has a long-term strategic plan to enhance capacity and the quality of intercity travel by improving transportation services.

Overseeing Regional Transportation

This government entity was formed as a joint venture between the States of New York and New Jersey and authorized by the U.S. Congress that oversees much of the regional transportation infrastructure, including bridges, tunnels, airports, and seaports. Its network of aviation, rail, and surface transportation and seaport facilities annually moves millions of people and transports vital cargo throughout the New York/ New Jersey region.

What follows is an excerpt from an interview between the Enterprise Architect at this government organization and Tom Jenkins, Executive Chairman of OpenText:

TOM JENKINS:
What is your Organization's mission?

ENTERPRISE ARCHITECT: *The Organization was chartered by Congress in 1923. Its charter is bi-state transportation within a 25 mile radius of the Statue of Liberty. We own and operate JFK Airport, Newark Airport, LaGuardia Airport, the George Washington Bridge, the Lincoln Tunnel, the Holland tunnel, the World Trade Center site, as well as the PATH system. Recently we have actually taken on management of two other airports, the Atlantic City Airport and Stewart Airport and Air Force Base.*

There must be a lot of information associated with operating those assets. What kind of information management challenges does your Organization face?

We have massive amounts of information, usually based on very large projects that come on very quickly, such as the rebuilding of the World Trade Center.

After 9/11 you had such a tremendous challenge in front of you, rebuilding based on limited access to digital information. What did you learn from that?

Certainly we learned that electronic was easier to recover than physical. Our headquarters, all of our people, and our data center were at the World Trade Center site. We learned that offsite back up is very important. We had to reach out to our partners in order to help us recover.

You are continually building an enormous archive of information, and you are now getting to the point where you can harness that. How do you know which data to mine?

Some of it is reactive. Our customer is the general public. Let's take airport parking: if New York 3-1-1 [the non-emergency government phone number] wants to access our parking data and we're not using it, well, this demand forces us to use it.

How do you see your organization being impacted by big data and mobile devices?

Some of the predictive and auto-classification technologies, those are going to become very important to us. The toolsets for mining that data and relating structured and unstructured data are becoming much more powerful. But not one of those technologies is going to go far enough unless it's mobile-enabled. I think that's number one.

Digital Health Care Reform

Along with transportation services, provincial and state governments are responsible for delivering health care services. For countries throughout the world, an aging population, economic downturn, and increasingly expensive treatments are contributing to rising and unsustainable rates of health care. Health care executives face challenges in emerging and legacy technologies, data formats and access, and adopting new business models that can be integrated with existing ones. To offset cost pressures, the industry is adopting e-government solutions to enhance performance and improve the quality of health care services.

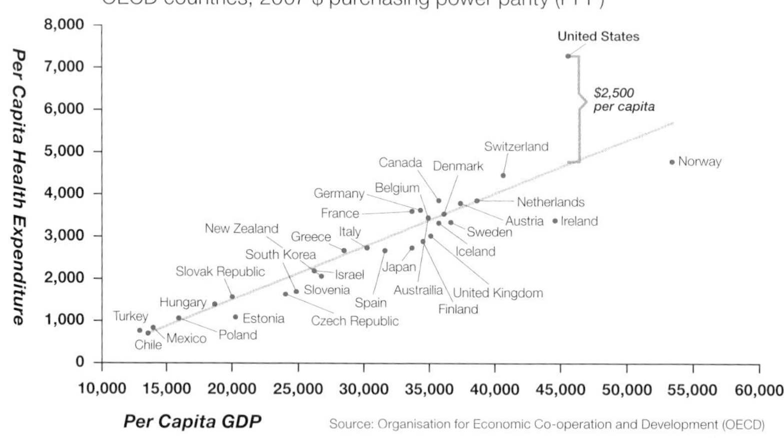

FIGURE 8.2: Potential for Efficiency Improvements in Health Care[1]

The health care industry includes multiple stakeholders such as doctors, institutions, and patients and encompasses pharmaceutical and life sciences industries. Each stakeholder group generates their own information, which is often disconnected across different systems. Much of this information is patient-focused, unstructured, and not easily incorporated into a database. Examples include paper records, digital x-rays, CT scans, and a variety of other clinical and diagnostic information. Data collected varies from region to region and country to country. Information is often trapped in silos maintained by Health Care Information Technology (HCIT) and Clinical Information Systems (CIS). Dispersed information hampers organizational processes and directly impacts patient care and hospital efficiency.

[1] Organisation for Economic Development and Co-operation (OECD), *http://www.oecd.org/statistics/* (accessed February 2014).

While the industry is in the early stages of digitizing health care data, the ability to integrate this information helps to achieve cost savings, increase efficiencies, and improve patient care. But in many cases, information cannot be shared across health care organizations due to incompatible systems and privacy laws or regulations.

A Complex Regulatory System

Health care is a highly regulated industry—almost every aspect is overseen by a regulatory body. In the U.S., HIPAA regulations require health care organizations to ensure the privacy of personal health information (PHI), run services efficiently, and offer high-quality health care. Similar legislation exists in other countries, including Canada's Personal Health Information Protection Act (PHIPA); Section 60 of the UK's Health and Social Care Act of 2001; France's Medical Privacy Act, Article L1110-4 of 2002; and Spain's Basic Law 41/200 of 2002. More general data privacy legislation in many countries also applies to patient information such as the European Union's Directive on Data Protection (95/46/EC).

Four distinct big data pools exist in the US health care domain today with **little overlap in ownership** and **low integration**

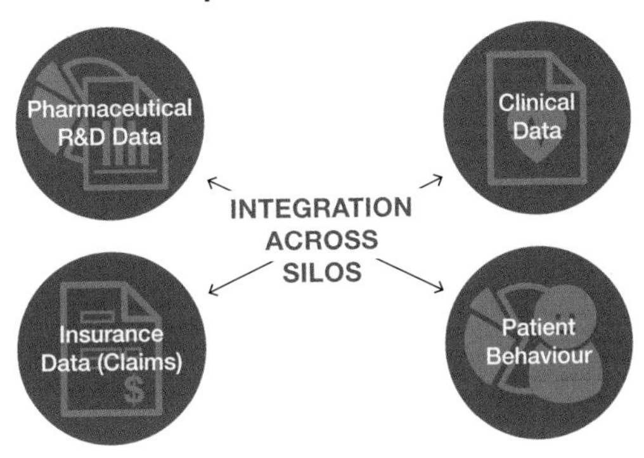

Source: McKinsey Global Institute analysis

FIGURE 8.3: Health Care Information Silos

Regulations are developed and enforced by all levels of government—federal, state, and local, as well as by a variety of private organizations. Both organizations (e.g., pharmaceutical) and individuals (e.g., physicians) are subject to regulations by multiple authorities. To be effective, e-government solutions must comply with regulations, while still allowing for easy data access and collaboration. A centralized, media-agnostic e-government system balances access to health care information with security and privacy requirements.

Secure, Compliant, and Accurate Patient Records

Health care has been impacted by the development of Electronic Health Records (EHR) systems and standards. The purpose of an EHR is to improve the quality of care through the coordination of multiple sources of a patient's clinical information. Effectively maintained EHR mean that patient information is accurate and up to date and results in better outcomes.

Every patient leaves a paper trail. An e-government system brings together both structured and unstructured patient records, aggregating and synthesizing patient, diagnostic, and treatment records from lab results to images and doctors' notes. These can be integrated with non-clinical records, such as insurance, billing, and other administrative records to streamline care and provide a complete, holistic view of the patient.

By making available the data collected on a patient, hospitals can share records with other professionals and institutions, strengthening their network and improving their service. Allowing specialists to collaborate on difficult cases is critical to the advancement of the medical industry. Keeping this information secure and available is crucial.

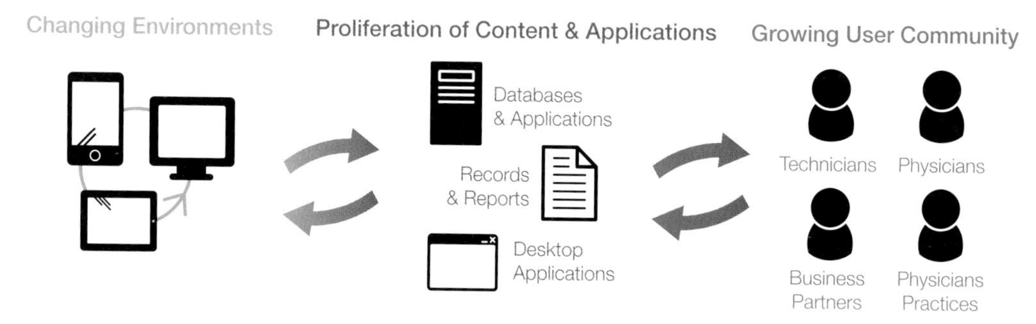

FIGURE 8.4: The Health Care Industry

In the following example, Geisinger Heath System has created an environment in which doctors and patients can easily access records. The system captures, organizes, and makes all content available through a single interface. This "one patient, one record" approach provides on-demand access to information. In a mobile society, this allows for a patient-centric approach to care, wherever the patient requires treatment.

Optimizing Treatment Pathways

In today's health care organizations, hundreds of clinical and non-clinical processes occur each day, from filling out a patient information form to assigning patient records for review, administering drugs, and releasing patient information. Very specific process requirements encompass the treatment of patients. These are referred to as "treatment pathways" and are comprised of automated workflow and information management components. Treatment pathways recommend and track the best possible treatment and care for a patient.

Geisinger Health System

FIGURE 8.5: Geisinger Health System

It has proven to be extremely reliable and cost effective, making it possible for Geisinger to save more than $1.2 million a year via a custom-developed capture solution with additional savings realized in clinical document storage and retrieval costs.

Founded in 1915, Geisinger is an integrated, physician-led health services organization serving 2.6 million people throughout 44 counties in central and northeastern Pennsylvania. With 44 primary care sites, 34 specialty care sites, six medical centers, more than 1,000 physicians, and 20,000 employees, Geisinger performs more than 46,000 surgeries and facilitates more than 2.2 million patient visits each year.

Geisinger identified a need for an enterprise-wide paperless office using a single integrated system to manage all files, including Human Resources (HR), billing and insurance records, CT scans, MRIs, nuclear medicine, general X-rays, and ultrasounds. To find a solution, Geisinger looked into expanding its infrastructure. The goal: to provide end users with the most complete record of information to empower them to perform their jobs at an exceptional level.

Today, an integrated e-health system is the cornerstone of Geisinger's operations. Patient histories, test results, and payment information are now instantly available at any Geisinger facility, providing patients with better and faster medical care. Users enjoy a simple, seamless experience as the integrated solution manages information from multiple areas and formats. Automated logs and audit trails ensure regulatory compliance by managing the lifecycle of the patient record. The solution exceeds two billion documents/objects and more than 100 terabytes of online storage. It has proven to be extremely reliable and cost effective, making it possible for Geisinger to save more than $1.2 million a year via a custom-developed capture solution with additional savings realized in clinical document storage and retrieval costs. Geisinger is a leading example of how a system can improve its health services performance, patient and community reputation, and operational performance through the integration of advanced technologies.

www.opentext.com/e-Government/Geisinger

It is critical for health care providers to be able to modify treatment pathways easily and on-the-fly. Though their treatment pathways may be similar, every patient is different. With smart process application tools, health care organizations can incorporate relevant resources—users and content—into ad hoc processes to customize pathways.

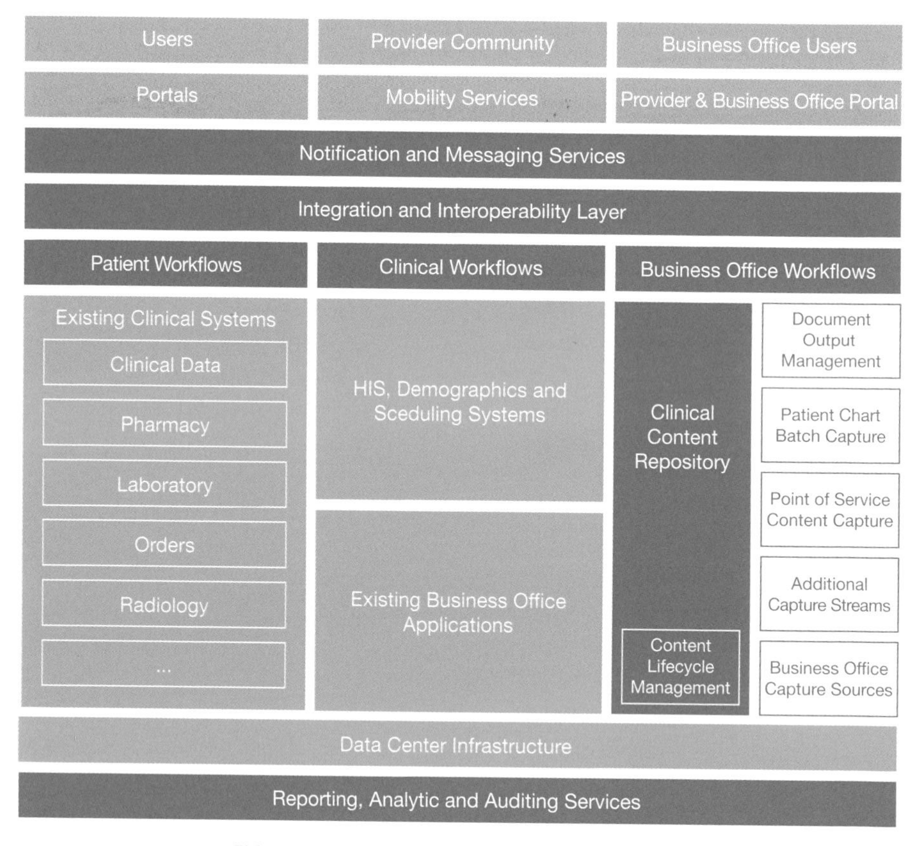

FIGURE 8.6: e-Government Health Care Architecture

To operate effectively, business processes supporting access and quality of patient information must transition from a paper-based to a digital environment. e-Government prevents the overtreatment and the under-treatment of patients by improving the availability of information. Online portals and communities like PatientsLikeMe.com help to promote participatory health care by enabling individuals to share experience and doctors to share medical insights. In a shift to more personalized treatment, patients experience lower costs for better care and have broader access to health care information. This is particularly compelling in low-service areas and with long-term-care patients.

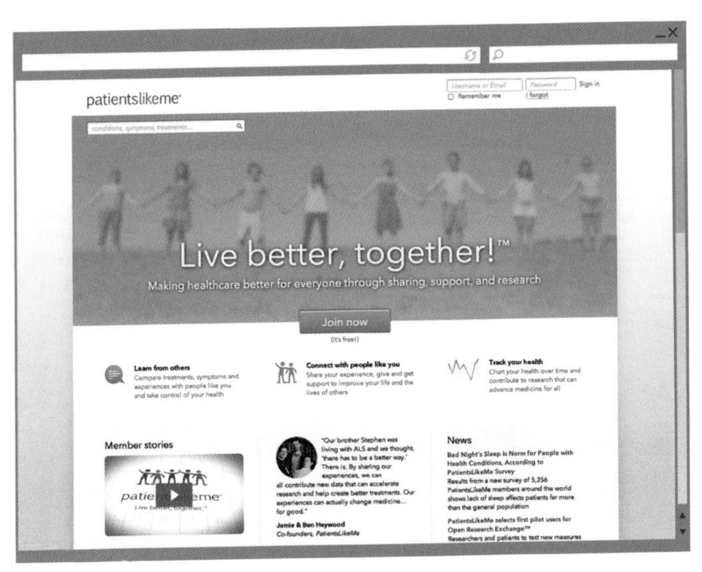

FIGURE 8.7: PatientsLikeMe.com

e-Government provides an infrastructure for the management of big data, which holds great promise in advancing health care processes and services. Physicians can apply analytics like predictive modeling to patient information to help with disease management programs across nations and to identify candidates for treatment, those at risk, and potential clinical trial participants. They can only do so using technologies that are integrated, interoperable, and based on established standards. The application of big data is covered in greater detail in Chapter 13 of this book.

e-Government integrates information and processes, bridging the gap between systems, functions, and stakeholders in one seamless platform. As illustrated in the following feature on Western Cape Government Health, digitizing health records results in significant costs savings.

e-Government for Education

Like health care institutions, educational institutions are applying digital technologies to create more effective, impactful, and efficient environments. For educational institutions, the drive for improvement comes both from within organizations and from government bodies that oversee and fund them. Currently, there is pressure on educational institutions to integrate digital technologies into their organizational structure and curriculum to better serve the "always-connected" student.

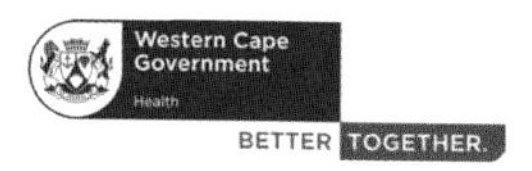

Western Cape Government Health

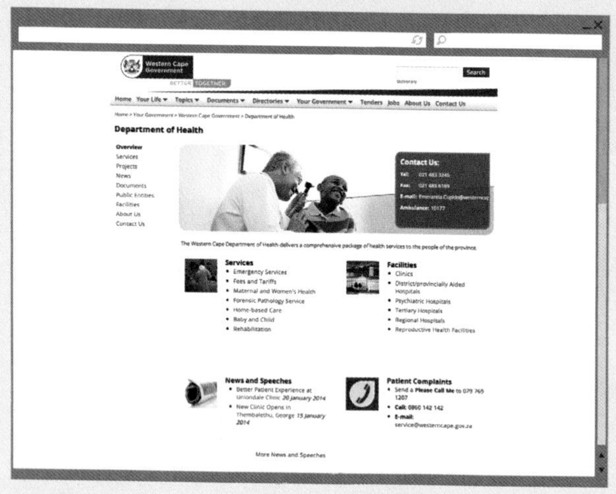

FIGURE 8.8: Western Cape Government Health

The health care solution has resulted in improved clinical and non-clinical workflow processes, more secure health records, and full compliance and accountability.

The Western Cape is a province of South Africa located in the southwestern part of the country. The core function and responsibility of Western Cape Government Health is to deliver equitable access to quality health services to the people of the province within a balanced and well-managed health system.

Western Cape Government Health had a vision to transform to a paperless work environment by reducing their reliance on physical documentation and paper-based files. Their paper-based health records were difficult to manage, needed centralized support across multiple cultures and 11 official languages, and had to be incorporated into their business processes. An e-government solution would enable Western Cape Government Health to manage documents and information with increased efficiency and effectiveness to improve service delivery.

A solution based on a framework for electronic patient records was successfully rolled out to two hospitals and is in the process of being implemented at an additional two hospitals. It includes the ingestion of paper-based patient records and their digitization in a scan center. Access permissions are controlled, and doctors can easily and efficiently access patient records for both patient care and research purposes. An additional solution for managing Forensic Pathology Services was rolled out to 18 facilities. The health care solution has resulted in improved clinical and non-clinical workflow processes, more secure health records, and full compliance and accountability.

 www.opentext.com/e-Government/WesternCapeGovernmentHealth

An increased reliance on computer usage has driven the need for computer skills in the workplace. Governments around the world must ensure that students are prepared to meet the demands of the 21st century workplace. In 1996, Bill Clinton made over $2 billion available in the Technology Literacy Challenge Fund, a program that challenged schools to make computers available to every student. Recently, there has been significant demand for computer technology in many public school systems across the globe.

Teaching that facilitates digital learning is more important than ever. Combining education and technology presents new approaches to learning that benefits students, teachers, administrators, and society as a whole. Despite the belief that digital technology can provide a powerful way to advance education, most institutions grapple with how to make this happen. The incorporation of digital learning environments are not integrated into school curriculums and most learning is still accomplished face-to-face.

Technology has the potential to transform relationships between students, teachers, and curriculum. For this to happen, top-down approaches must be replaced by participatory, engaged, and collaborative relationships made possible by e-government. For example, MOOCs (Massively Open Online Courses) are giving students access to courses and lecturers in countries that do not have an established university system.

e-Government driven education strategies deliver relevant, online, and blended courses to engage a diverse range of learners, and provide accessible materials for all learners to learn at their own pace and convenience.

FIGURE 8.9: High-Quality Online Learning Outcomes

Some of this functionality is provided by a Learning Management System (LMS) or e-learning solution. A more extensive platform is required to effectively address the broader set of needs of the complete educational community. Using an e-government solution, institutions in education are equipped to meet the expectations of students by incorporating secure network coverage, sufficient bandwidth, and access to digital infrastructure both in the classroom and remotely.

As described below, Suffolk University is using an e-government platform to update their current online presence, deliver course information, and deepen engagement and online interaction with students.

Suffolk University

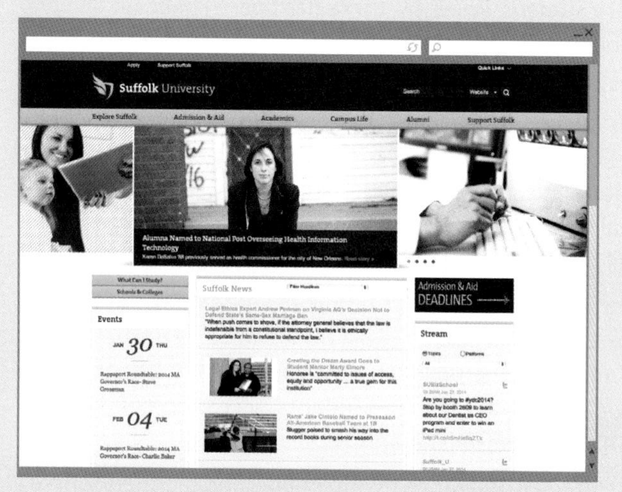

FIGURE 8.10: Suffolk University—Improving the Quality of Education

The result is a comprehensive online presence that drives more visitors to the site and offers an optimized experience.

Suffolk University is located in downtown Boston, Massachusetts. Established in 1906, the University offers degrees in more than 70 areas of study and has additional campuses in Dakar, Senegal, and Madrid, Spain.

To celebrate their centennial year, Suffolk University launched a redesigned and expanded version of their website (http://www.suffolk.edu/) using a web content management system. The new site features an improved and easily-maintainable site structure with thousands of pages of information for staff and students alike, including an online course catalog. There are now over 200 users across campus involved in maintaining the information that is posted on the site. This has created a much more dynamic system where people from all areas of the university are actively creating and editing their own, self-relevant content.

Brand identity is maintained throughout the website because the technology ensures that users only have the ability to edit content and not the appearance or layout of the site. This is achieved using templates that lock in the appearance of web pages and give users the power to make content edits, ensuring a consistent look and brand identity. The result is a comprehensive online presence that drives more visitors to the site and offers an optimized experience for those who want to learn about the University's programs and courses.

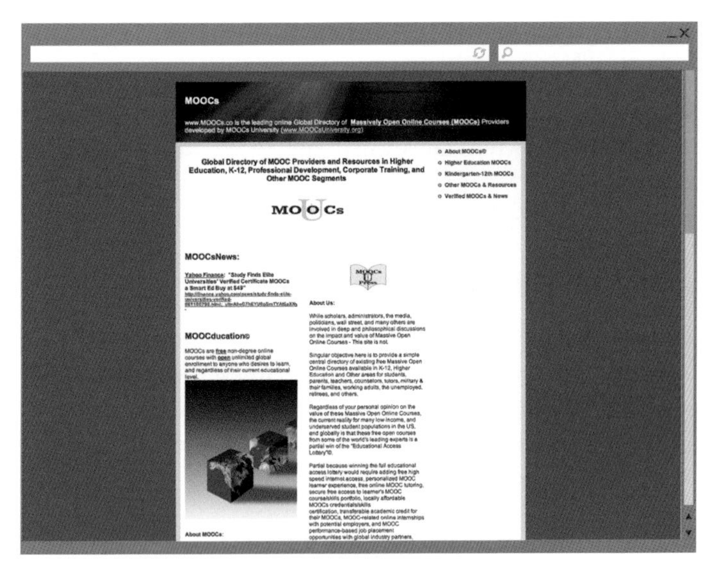

FIGURE 8.11: MOOCs Online Directory

Creating Engaging Experiences to Advance Education

Educational institutions have unique collaboration needs that are very different from the typical business organization. Teachers are spread across many different geographic locations within a school district or campus environment. Students work outside of school, after classes have ended for the day. These realities create a demand for engagement techniques that overcome distance and time restriction.

Teacher-to-Teacher Engagement: Online communities of practice create an environment in which teachers and their colleagues share experiences, reflections, and insights in a continuous dialogue, that moves beyond the physical limitations of geography and the classroom.

Research has shown that the more teachers engage with colleagues and experts, the more they contribute to their own professional development. Blended learning experiences can transform teaching. A good example of this is the Galileo Educational Network (www.galileo.org), which together with the Calgary Board of Education (CBE) has formed a learning network to advance digital learning environments.

Teacher-to-Student Engagement: Online course outlines, digital reference materials, links, assignments, and technologies like blogs, wikis, and networks extend learning beyond the classroom and supplement in-class teaching.

Student-to-Student Engagement: Collaboration engages groups of students to work together to replicate future workplace environments. Online technologies such as blogs and wikis create learning opportunities based on shared knowledge, ideas, and experience.

Teacher-to-Parent Engagement: e-Government facilitates dialogue between teachers and parents about key aspects of student progress.

Administrative Engagement: Educational institutions require support for their administrative staff. These needs are often coupled with limited IT budgets and staff. e-Government helps administrators digitize their office, consolidate information, and bring together communities of practice to advance education.

Managing Natural Resources Digitally

As in the education and health care industries, collaboration plays a key role in the management of national resources. Agencies that oversee natural resources work collaboratively with a wide variety of partners to develop and implement natural resource policies, conduct scientific research, and use technology to advance knowledge and inform decisions about how resources are best managed.

Sustainable Resource Management

In recent years, the depletion of natural resources and a shift to sustainable development has been a major focus. Sustainable development meets the needs of the present without compromising natural resources for the future. e-Government enables sustainability by giving decision makers access to accurate information and helping them work together to establish a long-term, holistic balance of economic, social, and environmental priorities.

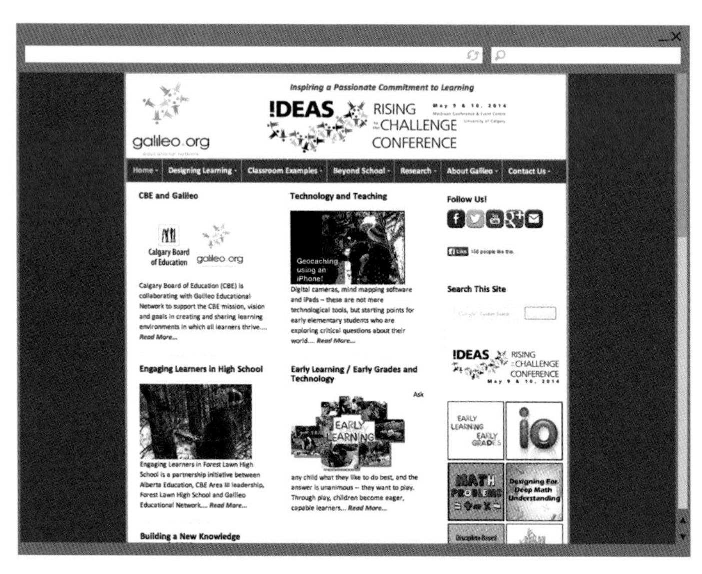

FIGURE 8.12: Galileo Educational Network

Sustainable resource development transitions from limited partnerships of the past to innovative, inclusive, and collaborative ways of working, enhanced through e-government solutions to help facilitate the following:

- **Knowledge-sharing** for building research capacity and mining data for more effective and informed analysis and decision making.
- **Collaboration** to engender mutual accountability, bring together diverse agendas, and advance natural resource development strategies.
- **Participatory government** by putting structures in place that allow citizens and stakeholders to provide input into sustainability, conservation, and preservation.
- **Transparency** based on open and available decision-making processes.
- **Innovation** through open access to information and monitoring programs to enable sustainable natural resource management.
- **Education** at all levels to deepen understanding of natural resources, biodiversity, and renewable resources.
- **Governance and compliance** through legislation, regulation, and policies to reflect priorities in sustainable natural resources.

Citizens want natural resources programs that will provide for a healthier future for their children. An integrated e-government platform supports an ecosystem approach through streamlining efforts among government departments, promoting collaboration, and facilitating mutual accountability. The Regional Government of Andalusia is using e-government to engage with citizens and stakeholders and provide access to accurate information, ensuring a natural healthy environment while achieving sound economic gains.

Effective natural resource management is based on an understanding of the environment and the impact that development has on natural resources. Adopting e-government solutions helps states and provinces compete in national and even international marketplaces by providing opportunities for entrepreneurship, job creation, and commercialization in industries such as the energy sector through the application of new technologies to natural resource management.

Junta de Andalucía

FIGURE 8.13: The Regional Government of Andalusia Website

The site is fresh, contemporary, and up-to-date—resulting in an exponential growth in the number of users visiting the portal amounting to two million visits per month.

Junta de Andalucía is the Regional Government of Andalusia, one of the largest autonomous communities in Spain in terms of population, surface area, history, culture, and biodiversity. The website of the Ministry of Environment of the Regional Government of Andalusia has established itself as one of the most advanced sites within the entire administration of Andalusia, both internally and externally.

To power the site, the Ministry selected a content management solution based on its stability for the management of volumes of content, flexible and dynamic design of the navigation trees that helps to maintain consistency and homogeneity within the site, and the extensive functionalities for role management, user permissions, and the design of specific workflows. Internally, the content manager enables editors to perform complex content management, including the tools and widgets that enable users to design text fields, content in What-You-See-Is-What-You-Get (WYSIWYG) format, dates, drop-down lists supplied from databases, and the assignment of taxonomies and metadata to content groups.

Using the system, over 10,200 cataloged pieces of content and 11,500 files can be managed and interrelated without duplication. The site is fresh, contemporary, and up-to-date—resulting in an exponential growth in the number of users visiting the portal amounting to two million visits per month.

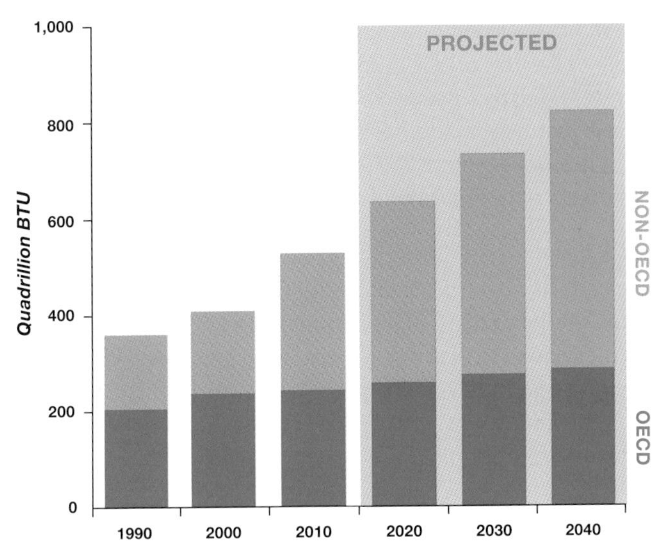

FIGURE 8.14: World's Energy Consumption from 1990 - 2040

e-Government in Energy and Utilities

The International Energy Outlook projects that world energy consumption will grow by 56 percent between 2010 and 2040, with renewable energy and nuclear power being world's fastest-growing energy sources.[2] Energy companies today are challenged to match production to demand, and they must do so despite political turmoil, regulatory requirements, and environmental impact.

Organizations in the energy sector require access to information, policies, and processes to identify reserves and to reliably produce against forecasts. They must be able to meet stringent requirements to ensure that regulatory oversight does not occur.

The energy industry is comprised of a global system of tightly integrated and highly complex relationships between corporations and government entities. Collaboration within and across projects improves the quality of decisions and minimizes rework. By enabling teams to work across facilities and time zones, energy companies can save millions of dollars annually. These savings can be attributed to improved plant efficiency, reduced downtime, and improved compliance—which works to create competitive advantage.

[2] *"International Energy Outlook 2013 (IEO2013)"*, U.S. Energy Information Administration, July 25, 2013, *http://www.eia.gov/forecasts/ieo/* (accessed February 2014).

In delivering services and developing new opportunities, companies frequently find themselves drilling in deeper water, on public lands sensitive to environmental impact, or with foreign governments interested in a portion of the profits, all of which lead to higher costs. With every new capital investment made, companies continue to search for ways to improve their rate of success. An e-government system helps organizations in the energy sector increase efficiency to offset costs and reduce risk.

The Digital Oilfield

Emerging technologies are having a profound effect on the oil and gas industries. Mobile access gives employees the immediate ability to manage information, share it, and act on it. With incidents like the Macondo disaster, mobile access to an integrated, streaming data system, for example, could potentially avert future catastrophes. The sooner organizations can react effectively to emergency situations, the less it costs in terms of dollars, environmental impact, and reputation.

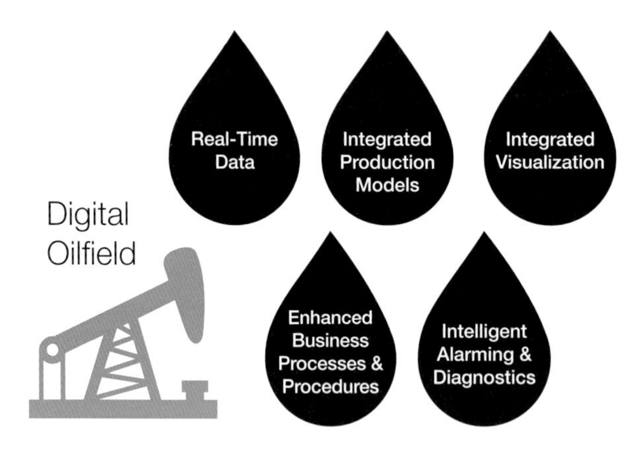

FIGURE 8.15: The Digital Oilfield

Future e-government implementations will be based on discovery technologies like content analytics and semantic navigation. Artificial intelligence involving heuristic algorithms will teach systems to recognize patterns and aggregate content appropriately. Research and development in the energy industry is already being impacted by large amounts of raw data that can be combined in new ways to reveal opportunities, spur innovation, and identify threats so that they can be minimized.

LUKOIL Overseas Holding GmbH

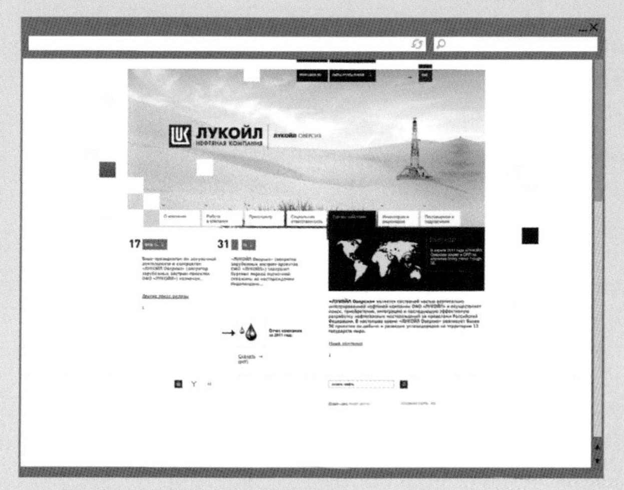

FIGURE 8.16: LUKOIL Overseas Holding Website

e-Government has unified the business processes of the company's different capital construction projects and improved productivity significantly by reducing documentation review times and quality.

LUKOIL Overseas Holding GmbH is a rapidly growing oil and gas company acting as international project operator for LUKOIL, a vertically integrated oil company. The Company has a corporate center in Moscow and subsidiaries and representative offices in 16 countries. At the present time, the holding company is managing several large oil and gas development projects in geographically scattered locations, employing outside contractors. To guarantee the integrity, relevance, reliability, and safekeeping of project documentation at all stages of the project's lifecycle, the Company needed a centralized system for managing project information.

A unified e-government solution supports 1,500 users in Russia, Uzbekistan, the Netherlands, the U.S., Iraq, and the United Arab Emirates. All holding company enterprises connected to the system use the same document base, which greatly simplifies the performance of a range of business processes involving several enterprises. The solution manages the flow of all project-related information, and includes loading and structuring all historical data and adding new projects and assets to the unified documentation management system. e-Government has unified the business processes of the company's different capital construction projects and improved productivity significantly by reducing documentation review times and quality.

Productivity in Oil and Gas

The oil and gas segment is a capital-intensive business with large-scale and expensive projects. Drilling and completion, facility design, construction, and shutdown are a few examples of the significant investments they undertake. With added investment comes the need for improved project management. Oil and gas organizations have at their disposal strong e-government tools that combine processes with the unstructured and structured information in their repositories. With these tools, companies can focus on specific tasks, increase visibility, mitigate project risks, and promote value-added collaboration.

An e-government solution brings together individuals and organizations to work together through combined processes and information to ensure the expedient and satisfactory completion of core business activities to reduce operating costs. For instance, the acquisition of large oil and gas fields has made it necessary for LUKOIL to optimize its capital construction project management system, including the preparation of large volumes of documentation and its storage.

Productivity in Utilities

According to industry experts, the top business challenge facing the energy industry today is regulatory compliance. Reducing the risk associated with storing and retrieving records is vital in achieving compliance. Paper documents require digitization, allowing for retention, retrieval, and proper security. An e-government system that incorporates content lifecycle management capabilities can help to ensure the fast retrieval of needed information for compliance and litigation purposes.

To stay competitive in a deregulated market, utility companies are recognizing the importance of customer service and the fact that satisfied customers are the direct result of effective operations, efficient processes, and responsiveness of the service provider. SWK STADTWERKE KRFELD AG is using e-government as the basis for their customer billing and information systems to improve efficiency and deliver higher quality services to citizens.

SWK STADTWERKE KRFELD AG

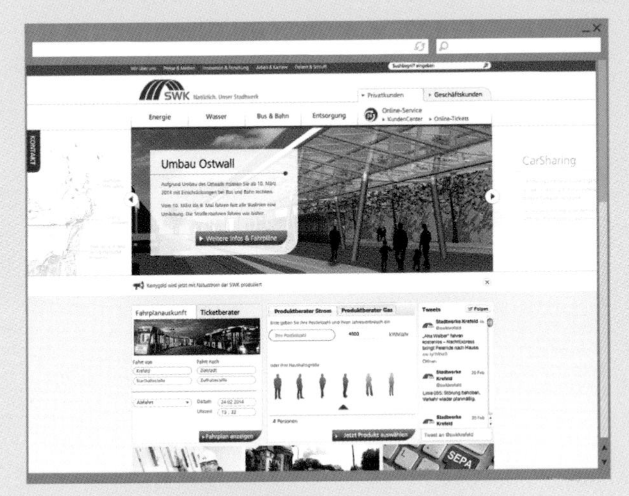

FIGURE 8.17: Stadtwerke Krefeld

"We ship around 300,000 invoices per year. The invoices generated and printed are accurate, visually appealing and intuitive. Thus we have achieved our goals of image building and quality assurance completely."

DEPARTMENT MANAGER APPLICATIONS AND PROCESSES, SWK STADTWERKE KRFELD AG

SWK STADTWERKE KRFELD AG is a municipal utility and transport company for Krefeld and for adjacent parts of the Lower Rhine in Germany. To meet new legal requirements for energy billing and improve customer satisfaction, the Company was looking for a new invoicing solution. Current billing was highly complex. The system had to support this, as well as multi-contract accounts, by providing sections for water, electricity, district heating, gas, and sewage in an automated layout format.

SWK STADTWERKE KRFELD AG implemented a new invoicing solution which generated a form that could be edited by business users and supported the integration of dynamic charts, with the sequence of data output controlled by its Enterprise Resource Planning (ERP) system. The new invoicing system has dramatically reduced the workload of the customer service center and enabled the Company to comply with regulations for energy billing. Customers are satisfied with a more intuitive bill that is easy to understand.

www.opentext.com/e-Government/SWKSTADTWERKEKRFELDAG

CHAPTER 9

E-GOVERNMENT AT THE LOCAL LEVEL

CHAPTER 9

e-Government at the Local Level

As e-government becomes prevalent around the world, policy makers and technology vendors are focusing on the effectiveness of administrative solutions at the municipal level. Local governments deliver front-line services, from basic information to transactional services, to citizens and businesses. In this chapter, we examine the benefits and example applications of e-government solutions at the local level.

FIGURE 9.1: e-Government Framework

Building Smart Cities Through e-Government

A city is designated a "smart city" when the quality of knowledge and social infrastructure contributes to urban performance and a city's competitive advantage. The concept of the smart city has been introduced to highlight the increasing importance of Information and Communication Technologies (ICTs), along with social and environmental factors in profiling the competitiveness of municipalities. Smart cities combine the innovative use of technologies with physical, social, and environmental capital to solve complex problems at the municipal level.

New business models and funding mechanisms are inherent features of the smart city. The smart city requires new partnership models between governments and businesses, which result in increased private-sector involvement. The multiple roles strategic partners play in a smart city "value chain" contribute to the complexity of the smart city. Examples of strategic partners include utility providers, technology vendors, network providers, and telecommunications operators. These organizations work with governments at the local and regional levels to create and deliver sustainable solutions.

Many cities are transitioning to new marketplaces in unique ways. e-Government technologies, such as big data analytics, cloud-based services, and mobile computing, provide integrated services as smart solutions for cities—from bus schedule apps and events apps to apps showing how much energy a city consumes. A fundamental aspect of a smart city is connecting systems and devices across all stakeholders, businesses, and institutions. Today's smart cities engage with the public through devices such as smartphones, tablets, and social media.

The Intelligent Community Forum (ICF), a think tank that studies the economic and social development of modern communities, identifies smart cities around the world and ranks them each year. They examine the ways that communities can create prosperity based on advances in communications and technology and sharing best practices for sustainable growth.[1]

FIGURE 9.2: Intelligent Community Forum

[1] Intelligent Community Forum (ICF), *http://www.intelligentcommunity.org/* (accessed February 2014).

The City of Barcelona

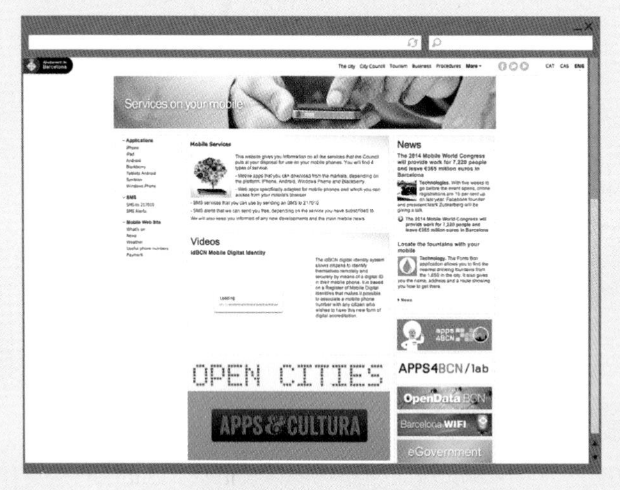

The solution, based on the principles of mobility, smart cities and administration, information systems and innovation, supports 150 portals with over 4 million user visits and more than 65 million pages generated each month.

FIGURE 9.3: The City of Barcelona—Citizen Services Are "One Tap Away"

The City of Barcelona is the second largest city in Spain, with over a million and a half inhabitants. Fulfilling its vision of transformation into a smart city, the municipal government is relying on mobile and cloud-based e-government solutions to facilitate citizen engagement with administrative processes and city services.

The goals of implementing an e-government system have been clear: to make data and services available to all citizens from any device and any location as a means to improve the quality of life for all citizens. A first step toward achieving this was making City Council and other data available in digital format, while promoting the reuse of this information to stimulate economic growth through opportunities for innovation. This approach is called open government, and it is explained in more detail in Chapter 12.

To standardize its information, the City needed to consolidate its infrastructure based on interoperable and open standards and decommission its legacy systems. The City opted to migrate its solutions to the cloud. A web content management system hosted in the cloud provides an alternative that is reliable, flexible, and produces economic gains in the long run. The result was the first Barcelona Open Data site with 510 datasets. The solution, based on the principles of mobility, smart cities and administration, information systems and innovation, supports 150 portals with over 4 million user visits and more than 65 million pages generated each month.

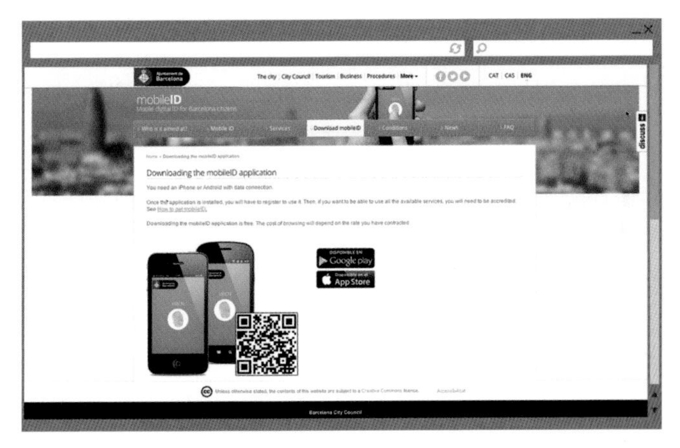

FIGURE 9.4: MobileID: an Innovative Mobile ID System

The City of Barcelona is an example of a smart city. It is using e-government solutions to transform itself into a connected hub for all city stakeholders to deliver quality services, improve its performance, and stimulate opportunities for economic development. The City markets itself as the mobile world capital, with 100 percent mobile access to services that bring the citizen closer to the city. Services are "one tap away" and include the innovative web-based mobile identification system, mobileID, supported by a secure mobile registry of users. This system enables citizens to log in to access government services using their mobile device. With their e-government system, the City of Barcelona has been able to increase citizen satisfaction and improve efficiency and productivity through the digitization and automation of internal processes.

The City of Barcelona's e-government approach is a comprehensive one that combines mobile government with e-services, e-procurement, and e-administration. Because governments around the world encounter similar administrative issues, the City is working to white-label brand its solutions. These can be replicated in a private cloud and exported for use in other implementations around the world to stimulate economic growth for the City of Barcelona. All these projects and services are included in the Barcelona Smart City strategy with the objective of facilitating citizens' needs and improving their quality of life.

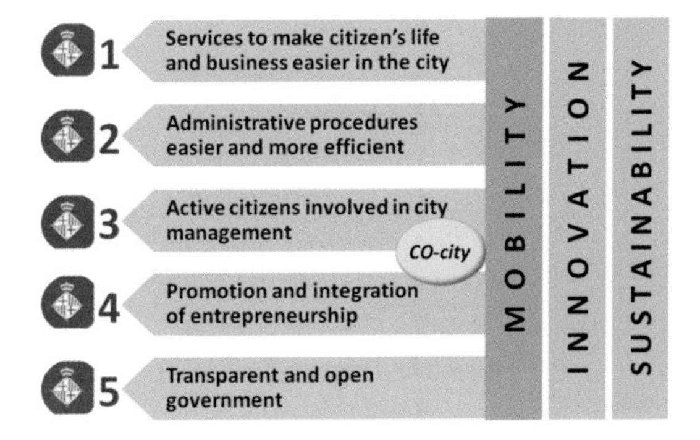

FIGURE 9.5: Barcelona's e-Government Agenda

Adoption at the Municipal Level

Although e-government solutions are deployed by many municipal governments, adoption is still in its early stages. For this reason, the benefits of e-government have not been fully realized. This is because local governments are contending with reduced budget and capacity, cultural barriers for bureaucracies and citizens, and issues of privacy and security.

As described in Chapter 3, e-government solutions are adopted on a continuum. Many municipalities have moved from bricks-and-mortar facilities to an online presence, making services available on city websites. These sites play host to information about city structure, programs and services, and minutes from council meetings. For many municipalities, keeping web content up to date and relevant is a constant challenge. A Web Content Management (WCM) or web publishing system can be used to keep information on the site accurate and accessible, supported by a designated department or automated to support multiple authors.

As citizens become more discerning and technically savvy, governments are being forced to evolve their static websites to dynamic platforms that facilitate citizen interaction and transactions. Citizen-centric experience lies at the heart of e-government. To support the transition from departmentally focused governance to citizen-centric governance, municipalities are opting for a Web Experience Management (WEM) e-government solution.

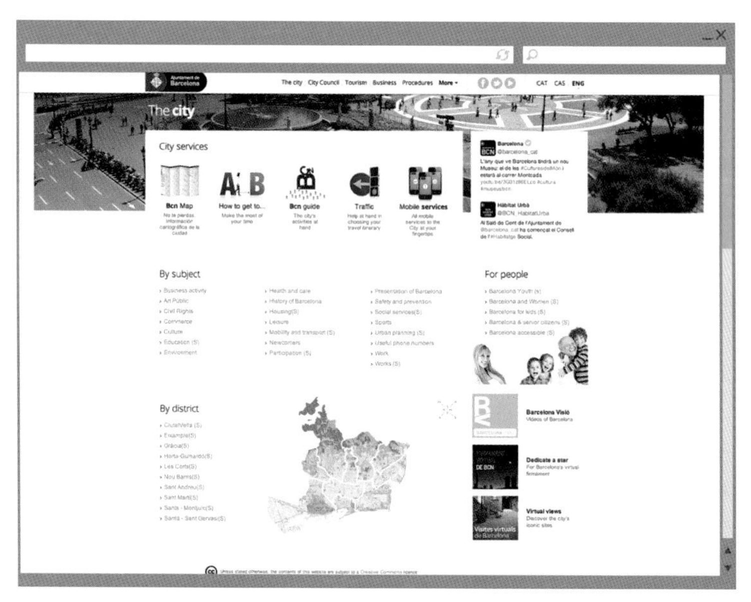

FIGURE 9.6: Citizen Experience Lies at the Heart of e-Government

A WEM solution transitions municipalities from making information available to supporting transactions with an online kiosk. Examples of services range from paying parking tickets to more complex transactions like online tax assessments. WEM delivers high-performance, scalable web applications to deliver targeted interactions across multiple channels. But citizens themselves must be comfortable using technology to engage with their government. To overcome cultural barriers, some governments offer training programs for citizens; programs to encourage computer purchases; and physical locations that combine face-to-face interaction with the online experience.

The ultimate stage of e-government adoption involves participatory levels of citizen engagement, in which citizens interact with their government to co-develop policies and programs. e-Government technologies like online communities are changing the state of citizen-to-government relationships. Ottawa, the capital of Canada, for example, enables citizens to post questions in real time to city council leaders during council meetings.

A comprehensive solution is required to support the entire citizen experience. e-Government combines responsive design, omni-channel touch-points, and the creation of compelling experiences with a platform that manages information securely, regardless of channel or device. A scalable, interactive website that facilitates day-to-day transactions results in deeper levels of engagement and allows for more meaningful connections to be made.

The Benefits of e-Government at the Local Level

Municipal governments are using e-government to do the following:

- Increase citizen engagement, trust, and satisfaction with a one-stop portal for program delivery
- Improve productivity and service quality through an integrated, centralized system for managing information within and across departments
- Increase efficiencies and time-to-delivery
- Reduce risk by managing information securely in accordance with privacy laws
- Enhance their reputation for good governance through increased transparency and accountability
- Attract economic investment through targeted business information and services
- Fine-tune resource allocation for cost savings
- Minimize technology investment with solutions that are rapidly configured and deployed

As e-government technologies evolve, the relationships between citizens and businesses and their governments will deepen and stakeholders will become more involved in governance. Municipal governments have an important role to play in government transformation as they interact with citizens on a daily basis to deliver services like police protection, transportation, and garbage collection. At the local level, the State Council in the Canton of Valais is using e-government to automate its administrative processes and modernize its services.

State Council of the Canton of Valais

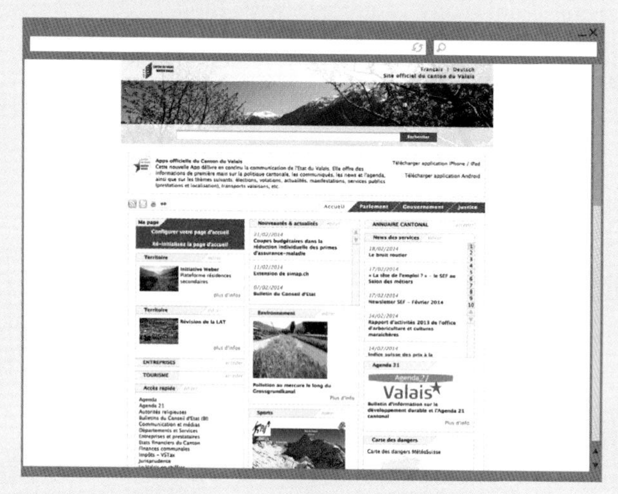

FIGURE 9.7: Official Site of the Canton du Valais

Management has a whole host of other ideas for subsequent implementations of their e-government solution. At present, the Canton of Valais is working on the automated processing of decisions of the State Council once they have been digitized and signed.

Located in the alpine region, Valais, the third largest Swiss canton, has approximately 317,000 residents. This vast, bilingual canton is renowned for its mild climate, wines, glaciers and reservoirs, and the world-famous Matterhorn.

On average, the State Council, together with the State Chancellor, discuss more than 200 cases each week. Each case contains an average of seven to eight pages, and seven copies of it must be available for the meetings. This results in up to 2,000 pages per meeting to be reviewed. These files were large, took up space, were often incomplete and, in some cases, were difficult to find due to a lack of archives. Comments by individuals before, during, and after meetings had to be inserted manually—a laborious process with periods of inactivity, ineffective use of time, and a high workload. This prompted the canton's office for information technology to evaluate various options that could provide better support with the cantonal administration deciding to adopt an e-government solution.

The Canton du Valais adopted an e-government solution to help them transition to a paper-free administration. With their new solution, documents are no longer carted around in paper format, weighing several kilograms. Up-to-date files can be accessed by authorized individuals to streamline decision-making and processes. Authenticity, integrity, and quality are guaranteed by a consolidated database that can be accessed securely at any time and from any location. This helps State Councilors access and study pertinent files before a meeting, which is important for a collegial governing body, so they can more actively intervene when processes are held up. While meetings are in session, the State Councilors can access the files, add comments to them electronically, and record the decisions made directly in the system.

Streamlining Constituent e-Services

e-Government facilitates an integrated approach to service delivery. For citizens, e-government delivers unprecedented transparency into the status of programs and services. For agencies, assembling a citizen-centric view of programs offers additional insights for streamlining, consolidating, and improving service delivery. Access to information can help to inform decisions, reduce the strain of email overload, identify new service requirements, or detect fraud or abuse.

Integration of back-end processes with front-line services requires interoperability between systems and departments. Combined information and processes allows for the simplification of administrative services, elimination of red tape, and a reduction in paperwork and duplicated efforts—all of which serve to dramatically improve program alignment.

The ability to integrate information from other business systems such as ERP, (finance or HR, for instance), Enterprise Content Management (ECM) repositories, WEM, and Customer Relationship Management (CRM), as well as core mission systems, helps to establish processes and identify situations where additional services may be advised. Underlying business process management removes the silos created by aging transactional and inflexible packaged applications to produce a consolidated view of the citizen.

e-Government delivers highly responsive services that anticipate citizen needs and connect them to the right resources at the right time. Users experience improved levels of communication and information sharing from an accountable and transparent government. The City of San Francisco is using an e-government system to digitize its processes, give caseworkers easier access to accurate information, and to provide clients with a more convenient and effective experience.

Improving Program Performance

The emphasis on performance improvement in government is growing, supported by regulations and public pressure. Government program managers are responsible for managing a portfolio of programs with limited time, resources, and budget. They are under pressure to manage projects using disparate tools, legacy systems, and paper-based systems. To do their jobs effectively, they need ways to increase visibility into projects with reporting tools to align mission and resources.

e-Government Program Management (PM) solutions enable globally dispersed teams to communicate, collaborate, report project status, and track project progress,and performance. Agencies can form teams across geographical and departmental boundaries using standard methodologies, best practices, and information from previous projects.

City of San Francisco, Human Services Agency

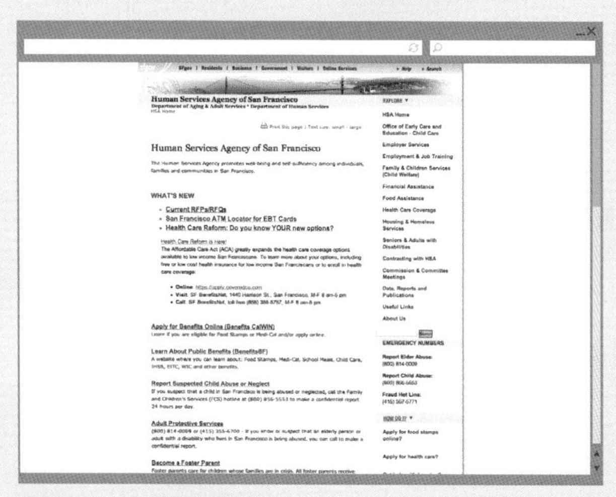

FIGURE 9.8: HSA Website

All the back files that were scanned into the system are now the official records. They are digital, password protected, and have a full audit trail as opposed to paper files that had none of these benefits.

Human Services Agency (HSA) is a department of the City and County of San Francisco and the central resource for public assistance in the city. HSA serves over 150,000 citizens each year through a range of programs and services. This involves managing more than 150,000 active case folders, each containing anywhere from 50 to 2,000 pieces of paper.

HSA needed an e-government system that enabled easy searching and filing, more efficient management of information, and automated processes to reduce the amount of physical paper being generated and stored, and to improve client service. Before implementing a solution, HSA eligibility and records staff was managing around 18,000 paper case folders for the CalFresh (Food Stamp) program. Each folder contained 50 to 60 pieces of paper, including copies of a wide variety of confidential documentation and personal data about the applicant. All the case folders were stored in a central file room on a different floor from the interview room where a social worker would meet with the clients. If a client came in without an appointment, they might have to wait two weeks before HSA could get the paper file to the right place. A tremendous amount of manual processes and inefficiency was involved in the process.

An electronic records system has allowed HSA to serve more clients without a proportional increase in staff and has been extended to MediCAL (MediCare) and CalWorks clients. They have eliminated over 100,000 paper case files. Citizens can now apply for benefits by completing an online application. Clients are happier because instead of having to make several trips to the office to meet with social workers, it can now often be done in a single day.

Inbound requests can be automatically assigned based on skills and workload. Live dashboards quantify team workload so managers can understand and monitor tasks appropriately. Improved visibility into processes and information helps all staff identify evolving issues to avoid adverse consequences and increase effectiveness. Reports summarize requests for services and the outcomes delivered in related timeframes, enabling executives to track improvements and associated savings, and compare performance over time.

An e-government solution links government programs to enable information sharing, process orchestration, and collaboration. e-Government for administration supports team effectiveness and collaboration through the following:

- Structured and unstructured processes for case handling
- Automated tracking, categorization, and routing
- Advanced knowledge sharing and management
- Dynamic, multichannel document composition, management and delivery
- Rules-based escalation supporting service level agreements and critical situations
- An up-to-date inventory of team member skill and expertise profiles

Collaborative Case Management

Case transactions rely on a mix of information types like documents, emails, meeting minutes, interview transcripts, photos, or other relevant exhibits. Case management solutions provide a centralized view of case content, no matter the type or where it is stored. An e-government solution helps to define a common process that guides case workers through tasks at each stage of a case's lifecycle—from the initial case trigger through the investigation and processing stages to resolution.

To illustrate this, let's examine the process involved when a citizen files for a change of address. To do so, they would be required to use multiple processes and tools—such as filling in an online form—and information would need to flow through all pertinent departments, including licensing, taxes, registration, and identification. All of which would benefit from having the proper processes in place to reduce the loss and duplication of information, which has frustrated citizens in the past. These needs can be addressed easily with an e-government infrastructure in place to support the flow of information through the required processes.

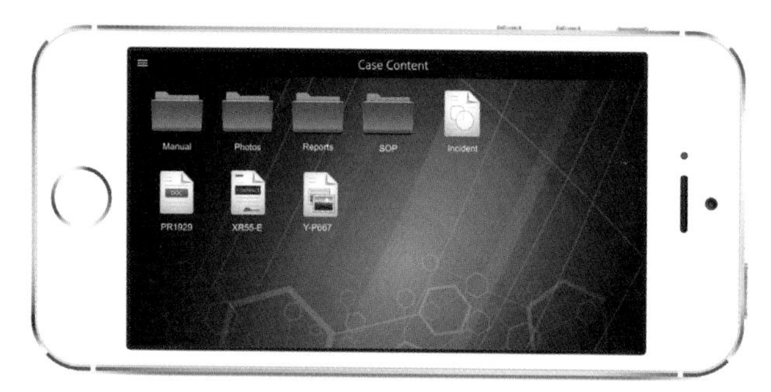

FIGURE 9.9: Case Management Content

As part of a comprehensive e-government solution, a case management application enables caseworkers to work more efficiently, resolving cases faster and with improved results. This results in a higher quality of service, while ensuring that information is classified and retained in the appropriate way. To comply with regulatory guidelines, some requests require that processes be turned into a case or lifecycle file, while others may require regulated documents to be reverse-engineered once submitted. An e-government solution can manage all these requests within a single application, demonstrating certification and accreditation of architecture, technology, and policy.

Next-Generation Processes

e-Government solutions add strategic value by facilitating the development of next-generation processes or Smart Process Applications (SPA). Governments at the local level can use them to rapidly create new processes that support customer service delivery within hours, without requiring IT support or software development skills. By combining well-structured modules with pre-built components, SPAs allow people to build new processes easily. Alternately, an existing process can be used as a template and modified to suit business needs. This means staff can be creative in anticipating service requirements and designing ways to address them. An on-demand environment supported by flexible infrastructure can dramatically improve response times. Calgary Police Service is doing just this—improving their response time by consolidating all case files in a secure e-government system.

e-Government Return on Investment

The major activities of a transformational government include sharing and publishing information, interacting with citizens and agencies, and transacting in a digital environment. To successfully carry out these activities, government organizations rely on integrated e-government solutions. The value of e-government lies in its ability to manage the processes around content more efficiently to improve performance, encourage and facilitate a culture of trusted collaboration, and control the risk and cost of content—allowing governments to focus on delivering value for taxpayer dollars.

Calgary Police Service

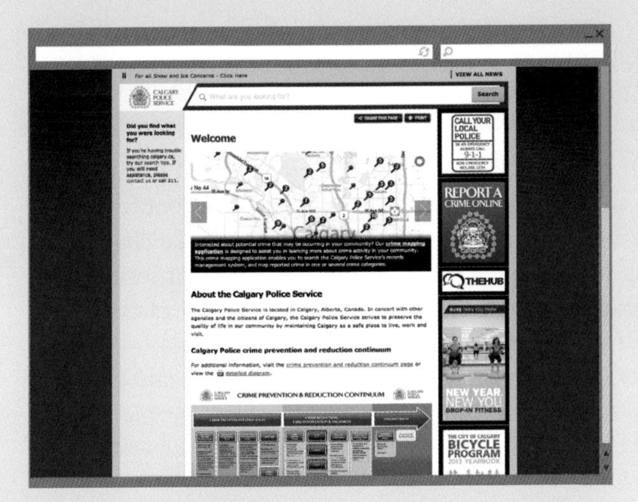

FIGURE 9.10: CPS Website

With photos and documents now uploaded to a centralized system, detectives can do a keyword search and find all related photos and documents for a case, creating a one-stop shop for case-related content.

The Calgary Police Service (CPS), located in Calgary, Alberta, Canada, is made up of more than 1,900 police officers and 700 civilian employees. Along with other agencies and the citizens of Calgary, CPS strives to preserve the quality of life in Calgary by maintaining the city as a safe place to live, work, and visit. The CPS needed a comprehensive, reliable and secure e-government system to store, manage and access their case file documents and related information. They also needed a way to enforce records management processes on their documents.

A first step in implementing a solution was to digitize hundreds of thousands of documents. The solution implemented by CPS automatically creates customized case folders designed for police case files, based on information fed in from a mainframe database. The CPS is the first police department in Canada to share digital documents with the provincial Crown Prosecutor's office. Before implementing the new solution, if detectives needed certain case documents, they would have to go downtown to the central file room to request hardcopy case files. If they needed certain case photos, they had to go to the Photo Unit to request them. With photos and documents now uploaded to a centralized system, detectives can do a keyword search and find all related photos and documents for a case, creating a one-stop shop for case-related content.

Now the CPS can access timely, accurate, and reliable information from any networked or mobile PC—a huge benefit for a workforce that is highly mobile and works 24/7. Efficiencies are further optimized by the system, which provides a complete inventory of projects that are in progress, overdue, and completed. By automating processes, the CPS has been able to improve operations after finding that certain districts had far heavier workloads in serving subpoenas, for example, than other districts.

For e-government systems to be widely adopted, they need to emulate the way people work without disrupting their daily routines. This involves creating a digital place where people can work in much the same way they would work together in departments or at office locations. For e-government to be effective, it needs to be unobtrusive.

e-Government maximizes the flow of information across an organization. How? By working on existing infrastructure and integrating processes across silos, being accessible from anywhere in the world, and leveraging a common knowledge of Internet technology. Because it is easy to use and improves the way people work together, e-government increases overall productivity, employee satisfaction, and the workplace environment.

Leading government agencies are working collaboratively across departments and jurisdictions to optimize administration, programs, and services. Regional amalgamations and the creation of mega-cities, for example, often require the consolidation of various service lines and their accompanying program knowledge. e-Government can help municipal employees exchange lessons learned to maintain continuity and manage the realignment process. Reaching beyond the public sector, governments can partner with organizations in the private sector to share best practices and refine programs. This is discussed in more detail in the following chapter.

Paperless e-Government

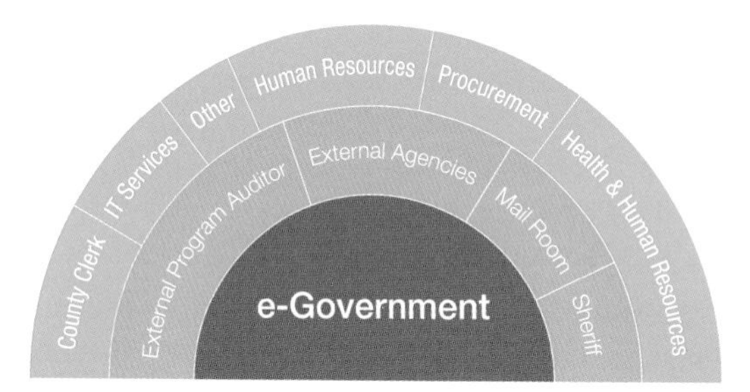

- ✔ Intranet Web 2.0 Social Workplace
- ✔ Asset Management
- ✔ Digital Mail Room
- ✔ Case Management
- ✔ Contract Management
- ✔ Procurement Processes
- ✔ Permiting and Licensing
- ✔ Automated Services Requests
- ✔ e-Learning

FIGURE 9.11: e-Government Enables the Paperless Office

Service delivery trends are emerging around the world. Governments are taking a citizen-centric approach to governance, as opposed to a programmatic one, and they are using e-government technologies to facilitate this. They are working collaboratively across departments and jurisdictions to provide services to citizens and businesses in an integrated manner, giving stakeholders self-service access at their convenience.

CHAPTER 10

REINVENTING PUBLIC-PRIVATE PARTNERSHIPS (P3S)

CHAPTER 10

Reinventing Public-Private Partnerships (P3s)

Private sector organizations are becoming key players in establishing global governance. In this chapter, we examine how e-government is modernizing public sector partnerships by transforming them from bricks-and-mortar infrastructure projects to Public-Private Partnerships (PPPs or P3s) into collaborative virtual infrastructure projects to support economic innovation and development around the world.

FIGURE 10.1: e-Government Framework

P3s play a large role in public sector development in terms of infrastructure and public-works projects. According to the Canadian Council for Public-Private Partnerships, the definition of a P3 is "a cooperative venture between the public and private sectors, built on the expertise of each partner that best meets clearly defined public needs through the appropriate allocation of resources, risks, and rewards."[1]

[1] The Canada Council for Public Private Partnerships, *http://www.pppcouncil.ca/* (accessed February 2014).

Lessons Learned from the Private Sector

In the downsized and deficit-driven environment of government, budgets are often allocated ahead of time, making efficiency and productivity more critical (and more difficult) to achieve. Government leaders must be willing to take more of an active role in implementing, adopting, and managing the use of technology to solve common challenges in the industry. A key strategic approach involves fostering collaborative relationships, including the customer-supplier relationships that exist in the private sector.

We have seen how internally complex the intergovernmental structure is. Conflicting agendas, political viewpoints, and administrative values make it difficult for a government to run like a business. Innovative approaches to management are often limited by outmoded structures and relationships. Allocating resources ahead of time can impact relationships between the public and private. Despite these obstacles to partnering, the benefits of collaborating with the private sector are clear: according to one source, the U.S. government alone has the potential to save as much as 20 percent of the $600 billion spent annually on equipment and services purchased by expanding its e-procurement systems.[2]

e-Government helps agencies overcome fragmented distribution networks by supporting relationships with private sector suppliers or contractors. As globalization continues to push the boundaries of business, market-based public-private relationships have increased over the decades. New trading models are based on e-government collaboration; can be established in weeks instead of years; and are highly efficient, agile, and cost-effective.

e-Procurement and Streamlined Efficiencies

With the fast pace of government today, private contractors are under pressure to have projects up and running quickly, while controlling costs and meeting compliance requirements. Government-to-Business (G2B) relationships are based on commercial interactions between government and the business sector. e-Government facilitates the development of G2B networks by providing a platform for private sector organizations to bid on government opportunities. Many organizations, made up of contractors and subcontractors and public sector entities, are involved in these trading communities.

Procurement is a multi-party collaboration process that spans multiple stakeholders in purchasing, financial accounting, inventory management, and other external vendors. e-Procurement replaces manual, paper-based processes with electronic processes and information management to improve efficiencies across all touch-points in the supply (or value) chain. It eliminates inefficient processes by capturing and managing content in digital format and providing immediate visibility in an optimized, collaborative workflow.

[2] United States Government Accountability Office, "*Strategic Sourcing: Improved and Expanded Use Could Save Billions in Annual Procurement Costs*", GAO, September 20, 2012.

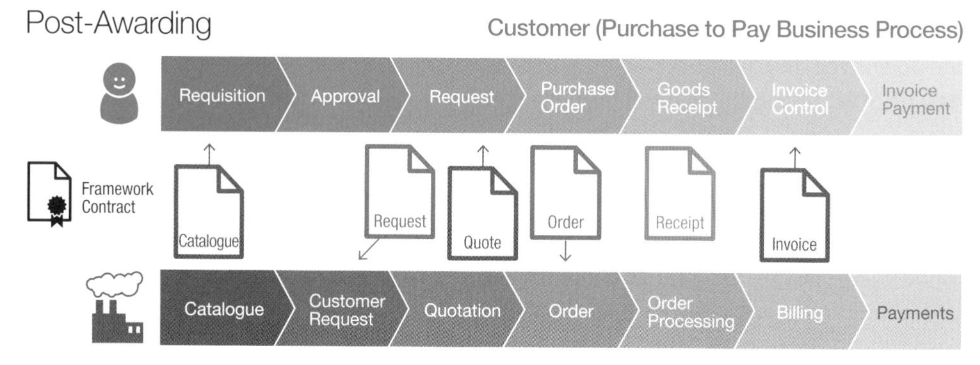

FIGURE 10.2: Multi-Part Collaboration in Government and Business

e-Procurement describes the G2B purchase and sale of supplies or services using Internet-based technologies like Supply Chain Management (SCM) or Enterprise Resource Planning (ERP). Public sector organizations use e-procurement to increase efficiencies, improve transparency, and save time and money in government procurement. e-Procurement has seen rapid growth in the public sector in recent years.

e-Government promotes the efficient, secure, and compliant flow of information across the entire G2B value chain, facilitating an increasing volume of transactional and conversational data through a host of mediums—from faxes and cloud services to file sharing, Electronic Data Interchange (EDI), and Managed File Transfer (MFT). Government organizations can significantly reduce the administrative burden of G2B information exchange by moving the management of systems to the cloud.

Agencies can rely on e-government to help them migrate from ad-hoc manual processes, multiple vendors, or single fixed solutions to a streamlined, virtual trading community that can be up and running quickly and efficiently. An integrated e-government platform improves the reach, reliability, and efficiency of G2B processes. As illustrated in the feature below, Alabama Gas is using e-government to streamline its procure-to-pay process.

What Are Public-Private Partnerships?

Public-Private Partnerships (P3s) can improve the delivery of public infrastructure and provide better value for taxpayer dollars. Under P3 arrangements, governments continue to own infrastructure assets while the private sector plays a larger role in their design, construction, operation, and maintenance. In doing so, the private sector assumes a share of the project risks.

Alabama Gas

FIGURE 10.3: Alagasco

Using Vendor Invoice Management (VIM) software, users can code invoices and submit requestor approvals in a matter of minutes, a task that once took an hour or more to complete.

Alabama Gas Corporation (Alagasco) is the largest natural gas distribution company in Alabama serving more than 425,000 customers, businesses, and industries. It is the largest natural gas utility in the state of Alabama and is regulated by the Alabama Public Service Commission. With roots dating back more than 160 years, Alagasco today has operation divisions in Anniston, Birmingham, Gadsden, Montgomery, Opelika, Selma, and Tuscaloosa.

Alagasco is automating and optimizing its procure-to-pay process using an e-government solution. It integrates easily with the Company's ERP solution, and effectively manages a large volume of invoices and purchase orders in its Procure-to-Pay process in accordance with its internal controls. The solution is used by all departments to make its procurement process more efficient and to help improve internal controls for compliance.

The solution allows Alagasco employees to work seamlessly between an e-government platform, Optical Character Recognition (OCR), Microsoft Office® Outlook,® and SAP. Using Vendor Invoice Management (VIM) software, users can code invoices and submit requestor approvals in a matter of minutes, a task that once took an hour or more to complete. Additionally, users have the ability to identify accrued liabilities; view all critical documents for a vendor electronically; and take advantage of special terms and discounting. Using the system, Alagasco has seen a reduction in the number of calls taken from vendors. With an e-government solution, Alagasco has improved its internal processes, allowing the company to increase productivity, reduce risk, and garner a better relationship with vendors.

Ideally, all stakeholders can benefit from a P3-based project, including the government, the private company, and the general public. The public sector leverages P3s to allow for domestic infrastructure or international development to be completed cost effectively. For the private sector, the partnership provides revenue by putting projects into production. In a P3, the public's interests are protected through guaranteed oversight of and transparency into the operation. If outcomes are on target, citizens benefit from quality infrastructure and the promotion of economic development.

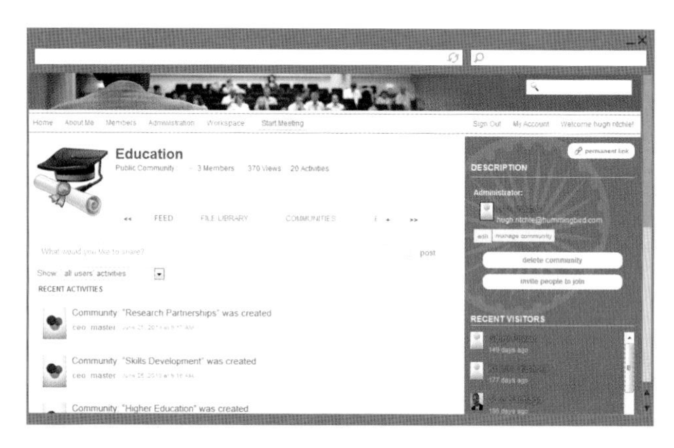

FIGURE 10.4: The India-Canada CEO (ICCEO) Forum Promotes Bilateral Engagement

The public stands to lose some degree of control when a private sector company is involved in the development of public facilities or services. In the areas of health care and education, for example, P3s are criticized for placing commercial goals above the public interest. Governments have been accused of selecting P3s over traditional publicly-designed, owned, and operated infrastructure projects. Despite potential drawbacks, P3s are widely used in the U.K., Europe, Canada, the U.S., and Australia.

Each level of government can be involved with P3 projects, with provinces and municipalities being the most active to date. P3 projects can be built and operated by public and private companies ranging from domestic, foreign, or transnational, and may involve a large number of subcontractors. A government owned or managed company may also be involved in the financing, construction, and operation of a P3 project.

A Brief History of P3s

Facing today's worldwide economic downturn and globalization, government organizations have recognized that it is critical to streamline infrastructure development for economic prosperity and higher standards of living. This can be accomplished by adopting new approaches to partnership with the private sector.

Traditional P3s span a scale of engagement models that run from straightforward contracting to partnerships that are based on an agreement for financing, building, operation, and ownership. When most or all of the control of assets is retained by the private sector, the term "privatization" is used to describe the situation. Types of partnerships come in many different formats and typically, no two partnerships are exactly alike.

Relationships include Operations and Maintenance (O&M), Build-Operate-Transfer (BOT), Build-Own-Operate (BOO), Design-Build-Maintain (DBM), Design-Build-Finance-Operate-Maintain (DBFOM), and Enhanced Use Leasing or Underutilized Asset (EUL). More recently, a new model has been introduced: the Public-Private Community Partnership (PPCP), which involves public and private sectors partnering to focus on social welfare endeavors.

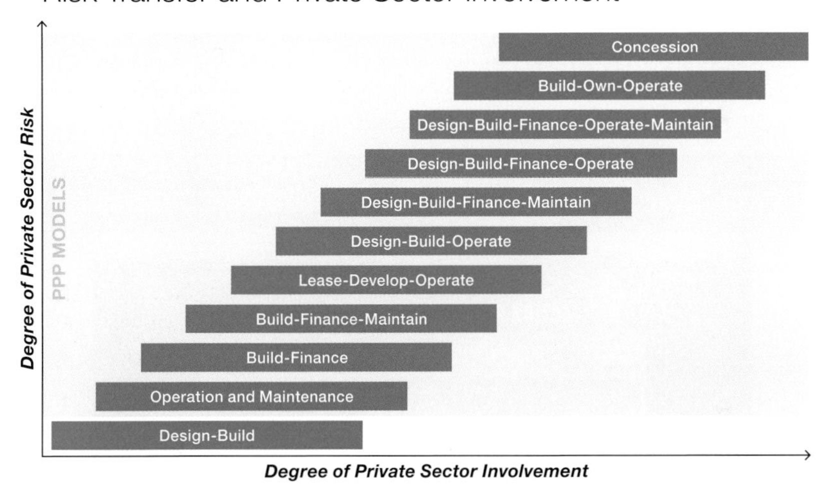

FIGURE 10.5: The Scale of Public-Private Partnerships[3]

Typical P3s have been based on large infrastructure and international development projects that warrant alternative approaches to partnership—construction projects like building new schools and hospitals for local municipalities are good examples. At the international level, P3s have been used in connection with the development of the Panama Canal, the Channel Tunnel (or "Chunnel"), U.S. oil exploration in the 1930s, and the bulk of nineteenth- and early twentieth-century railroads.

[3] The Canada Council for Public Private Partnerships, *http://www.pppcouncil.ca/* (accessed February 2014).

Large-scale infrastructure projects have a long history in Canada. The construction of railroads is an early form of P3 (using a privately-funded model for implementing public projects), combining both public and private capital with financing from foreign investors in the U.S., Britain, France, and Germany. These projects were typically long and took years to complete at great social, labor, and financial cost. Since the late 1990s, tens of billions of dollars have been spent on 180 P3 projects, including such essential infrastructures as Prince Edward Island's Confederation Bridge and Toronto's Highway 407.[4]

The U.S. has been using Public-Private Partnerships for more than a century, with thousands in operation today for the delivery of services or facilities in water/wastewater, transportation, urban development, and the delivery of social services. According to the National Council of Public-Private Partnerships, the average U.S. city works with private partners to perform 23 out of 65 basic municipal services.

Government Program Support

At the federal level, governments are being called on to support P3 development by building business cases around the most effective financing model for projects at the regional or municipal level. Governments are working to ensure that P3s can be effectively managed and deliver investments and outcomes in a timely manner.

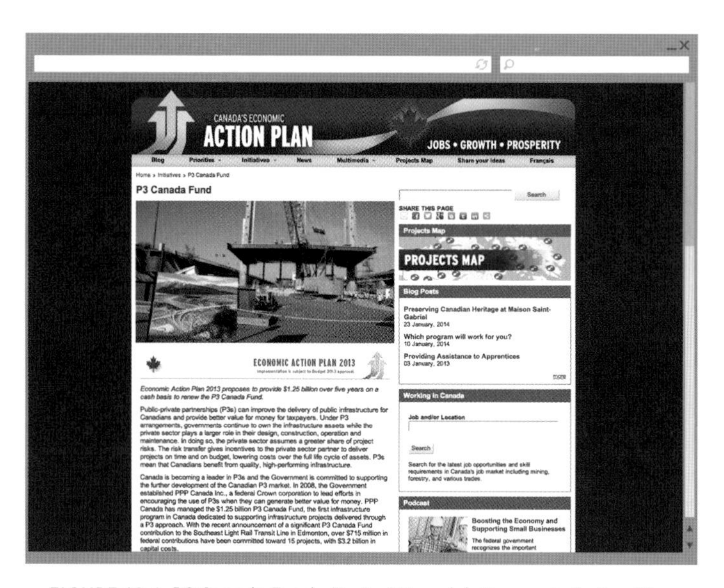

FIGURE 10.6: P3 Canada Fund—Part of Canada's Economic Action Plan

[4] Barrie McKenna, *"The hidden price of public-private partnerships"*, The Globe and Mail, October 14, 2102, *http://www.theglobeandmail.com/report-on-business/economy/the-hidden-price-of-public-private-partnerships/article4611798/* (accessed February 2014).

Many government programs are available to support P3s:

- In 1992, John Major's Conservative Government in the U.K. introduced the Private Finance Initiative (PFI), the first program aimed at encouraging public-private partnerships. In 1997, Tony Blair's Labour Government expanded the PFI initiative with a focus on value for money.
- Australian state governments have programs in place based on the PFI, including Partnerships Victoria.
- Over the past 20 years, more than 1,400 PPP deals were signed in the European Union, representing a capital value of approximately €260 billion.[5]
- In the U.S., President Barrack Obama has made public works a crucial part of his economic agenda for 2013, proposing to spend $40 billion on them. He has also renewed a proposal to create a $100 billion national infrastructure bank focused on fostering P3 project development.
- In 2008, the Canadian Government, under Conservative Prime Minister Stephen Harper, established PPP Canada Inc., a federal Crown Corporation to lead efforts to encourage the use of P3s when they can generate better value for money.

To date, PPP Canada has managed the $1.25 billion P3 Canada Fund, the first infrastructure program in Canada dedicated to supporting projects delivered through a P3 approach.[6] The Economic Action Plan 2013 will provide $1.25 billion over five years to renew the P3 Canada Fund. The Fund will continue to focus on supporting P3 projects that deliver value for citizens and further develop the Canadian P3 market.

Government program support for P3s is also available from Export Development Canada (EDC), Canadian Commercial Corporation (CCC), Industry Canada, and the Department of Foreign Affairs, Trade and Development (DFATD). American counterparts include the U.S. Department of Commerce, the International Trade Administration, the U.S. Department of Foreign Affairs, and the National Council for Public-Private Partnerships (NCPPP).

The Evolution of P3s

As multi-sector innovative models of collaboration, P3s help to modernize government operations by applying the expertise, efficiencies, and digital solutions implemented in the private sector. By combining Information and Communications Technologies (ICTs) with new approaches to partnerships, P3s are expanding their application beyond bricks-and-mortar infrastructure development to facilitate virtual infrastructure on a global scale.

[5] Andreas Kappeler and Mathieu Nemoz, "*Public Private Partnerships in Europe - Before and During the Recent Financial Crisis,*" European Investment Bank, July 2010, *http://www.bei.europa.eu/attachments/efs/efr_2010_v04_en.pdf* (accessed February 2014).

[6] Canada's Economic Action Plan, *http://actionplan.gc.ca/* (accessed February 2014).

As we have illustrated throughout this book, public and private sector organizations are working together to promote service transformation by implementing back-office information and payment systems, citizen portals, e-procurement systems, integrated communications, and more. Many of the solutions described in this book are the result of innovative P3 collaboration. More recent P3 models engage governments at the international level.

These technology-based partnerships facilitate innovative P3 models of engagement to:

- Fund virtual investments that would not otherwise receive financing
- Use public funds more cost-effectively
- Get projects up and running more quickly compared to traditional delivery methods—hosting solutions in the cloud, for example, as excellent alternatives that save on initial capital investments and offer faster time-to-implementation
- Stimulate innovation and economic development at all levels of government
- Promote sustainability
- Create competitive advantage to stimulate new market growth

Collaboration across sectors is implemented based on requirements, time constraints, and the challenges being solved or services offered. The result is a joint development of public-private governance structures and processes. The partnering of these sectors, facilitated by an integrated e-government infrastructure, can improve economic development, innovation, and the successful transformation of programs and services.

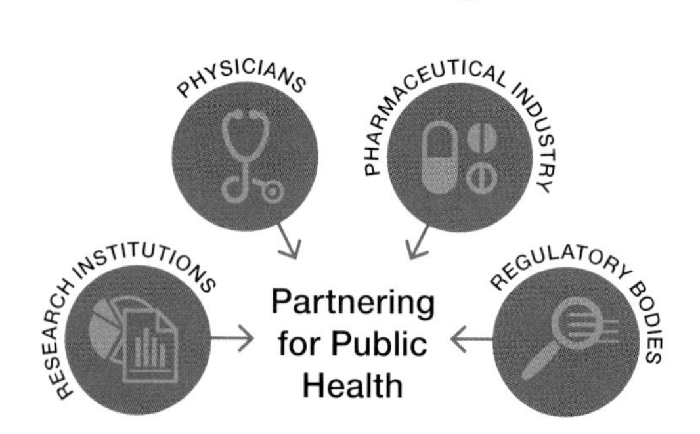

FIGURE 10.7: A P3 Model for the Health Care Industry

Health care is currently an active sector for P3s. This is because the costs to deliver health care services are increasing exponentially. Governments around the world are searching for alternative mechanisms to reduce costs and increase capacity with investments in infrastructure. A number of countries have begun to use P3s as a means to achieving these objectives. An example of a P3 in health care might involve partnerships between the public and private sector to establish an electronic patient record system and other e-health services to maximize resources and improve quality of care.

One of the major benefits a P3 has to offer is the creativity and innovation that private sector organizations bring to the relationship. On a daily basis, private companies must consistently innovate to bring sustainable solutions, new technologies, and smart business practices—all of which can be applied to P3 infrastructure projects. Often, they can run projects more quickly and with less bureaucracy that a government agency can.

A crucial element for successful innovation-led development is quick and easy access to information, expertise, and resources. Governments have realized this and are opening up access to data to encourage innovation and development. In 2009, the White House unveiled a new Open Data initiative that called for government data to be more open and accessible, allowing entrepreneurs to use it to create new products and services.

Adding P3s to the open data equation results in the development of fast, mobile solutions and partnerships formed between governments and a consortium of private sector companies. These innovative partnerships bring together intellectual and human capital alongside technology to drive innovation and create the conditions for economic growth. Open data initiatives are discussed in more detail in Chapter 12.

The G20 Summit social network is an example of a virtual infrastructure project that was the result of a public-private partnership between the G20 and G8 organizations, the Department of Foreign Affairs, Trade, and Development Canada (DFATD), and a private software vendor. The effective collaboration between representatives of states illustrated in the following example was based on a secure e-government solution to facilitate collaboration, interaction, and dialogue with global levels of security.

e-Government: Powering Public-Private Partnerships

Ironically, the Internet itself exemplifies a P3: developed by the Department of Defense, it is software based on the ARPANET that has been appropriated by a private company (Mosaic Communications Corporation) and made available to the public.

In a digital economy, digital media needs to be a part of everything we do. The first step a government can take to effectively serve a digital society is to make an investment in a long-term vision to build a culture around economic development and innovation. This happens through expanding its infrastructure and developing new models of engagement. As a collaborative, social, and secure platform, e-government is a key enabler for effective public-private partnerships.

G20 Summit—Secure International Engagement

FIGURE 10.8:
Mobile Access to the Social Network

The Group of Twenty (G20) is the premier forum for international cooperation on the most important issues of the global economic and financial agenda. Its mandate includes policy coordination between members, the promotion of financial regulations, and modernizing international financial architecture. During the G8 and G20 Summits in Canada in 2010, for the first time in history, a mobile social network facilitated collaboration for finance ministers and central bank governors from 19 countries.

The Organization was looking for a platform that would support constructive dialogue and collaboration before, during, and after the Summit. The system had to be secure, mobile and globally accessible. A social community provided the G20 with a collaborative workplace for delegates and attendees, presenting a streamlined and consistent experience—from the social networking interface to complex records management rules, functionality, and integrated back-end databases and technologies.

The interface emulated a Facebook-like experience, giving users a profile and the ability to post status updates, share photos and videos, blog, and hold discussions with other users. Air-tight security was achieved through authentication and permissioned access to information in a highly collaborative system. The interface was easy to use and consistent between laptop, desktop, mobile device, and tablet. For the duration of Summit meetings, the social network was used successfully without requiring any training, enabling delegates to focus on building a future of sustainable and balanced economic growth. The network was so effective it was used subsequently in Seoul, Korea, and Australia.

 www.opentext.com/e-Government/G20Summit

P3s provide a unique perspective of the collaborative aspects of the public sector. Through P3s, government organizations can more readily implement e-government solutions to deliver higher quality services at lower costs. According to some sources, governments traditionally realize cost savings of 20 to 50 percent when the private sector is involved in providing services.[7] Time-to-value can be realized more quickly; more innovative solutions can be developed; performance and efficiency improvements can be realized at the operational level; and programs, activities, and budgets can be better coordinated.

P3s connect public and private stakeholders, helping entrepreneurs, academic groups, research institutes, intermediary companies, and governments collaborate to accelerate the commercialization of a nation's digital talent, solutions, and companies. As a facilitator of new models of collaboration, e-government enables deeper P3 connections to bring more public sector solutions to market and create a higher standard of living, expand on business and investment opportunities, and jumpstart a more prosperous economy.

"In our relationship with IT companies we don't aim to have a customer-supplier relationship, but a technology partner with knowledge that is able to help us expand our e-government strategy for the City and innovate with us. In working with multinational companies, it's important that they understand our philosophy and approach for the future, which includes applying e-government technology internally to Public Administration, as well as the concept and scope of Barcelona as a Smart City, based on a close relationship with our citizens, businesses, and the different industrial sectors in the City of Barcelona."

JOSEP RAMON FERRER I ESCODA,
DIRECTOR OF SMART CITY DEPUTY CIO,
AJUNTAMENT DE BARCELONA,
CITY OF BARCELONA

[7] Richard Dobbs et al, *"Infrastructure productivity: How to save $1 trillion a year"*. McKinsey Global Institute, January 2013.

CHAPTER 11

E-GOVERNMENT AND THE FUTURE

CHAPTER 11

e-Government and the Future

FIGURE 11.1: Dr. Egerton Ryerson

We have been through technological transformations before. In the 1840s and '50s, Dr. Egerton Ryerson (1803 -1882) earned lasting gratitude for his inspired efforts to create a modern, province-wide educational system in Ontario. His vision of a coordinated system was based on a standardized curriculum, common textbooks, well-designed schools, and trained teachers. Today, one of Canada's most innovative universities proudly bears his name. Making his vision a reality required a commitment to the importance of education and a sustained effort, but it also required a reliable communication system.

Ryerson's reforms depended on the transformation of communication technology in Toronto in the early 1840s. The steam-driven printing press, advances in paper-making, and a reliable postal system connected Toronto and scattered school boards. Printed questionnaires provided detail on local conditions and supported evidence-based decision-making. Newspapers supported this progressive initiative, while the province was able to develop and monitor educational standards.

Modern bureaucracy, analyzing facts and trends from across a growing society, creating policy and tracking implementation emerged from this technological revolution. Local and regional government transformed as society's means of information storage and communication were modernized. Today, society is driving an information revolution as profound and meaningful as that of the 1840s. Governments must adapt.

The digital revolution is transforming politics and the nature of government. From education improvement and tax collection to better health care systems and job creation, technology is putting pressure on governments to make all aspects of government more accessible. Citizens' voices are "present" in public policymaking and their demands for an always-on, connected government are intensifying through social media. Governments are realizing that technology can act as an enabler to transform government processes, enhancing the provision of public services and increasing productivity.

The challenge for modern government is complex but two key trends emerge:

1) **Society is being profoundly transformed by new Information and Communication Technologies (ICTs).** Entire commercial sectors and old business models have already been swept away as consumers find new ways to access news media, music, films, books, and entertainment and satisfy daily needs. Governments, imprisoned by decades of regulation and bureaucratic habit, are challenged to become more responsive, citizen-centered, and flexible organizations.
2) **Governments are experiencing financial constraint with increased demand for services.** Productivity is the key to the future and to public support. To achieve this, governments need to manage their information assets more collaboratively and effectively. Information is the life-blood of public service. While the imperative of change has been recognized by leaders in government, the extent of change required is challenged by laws, regulations, and a public service culture inherited from an analog world.

In government, traditional models of hierarchy define (and confine) how information flows. Accountability and performance management regimes inherent in these models work to reinforce hierarchy and inhibit collaboration and teamwork. But the issues of a modern society require open information sharing and collaboration across the organization. Digital natives coming to the public service today encounter a fossilized culture that is adapting too slowly to address today's issues. Many agencies are recognizing the cultural shift that is taking place in the public sector, as illustrated in the excerpt below from an interview with the Head of Data Management at NAVSEA.

2020: e-Government or Out of Government

While there are many possible scenarios for e-government over the coming decade, the challenge will be to achieve the productivity and service quality that new information technologies offer while remaining true to the fundamental values of a professional public service.

The emergence of technologies like big data, mobile apps, and cloud computing could be used for extensive social control, eavesdropping, and monitoring all communications—tracking the locations, shopping and entertainment preferences of all citizens, and intruding into all aspects of life. This is the scenario envisioned by novelists and film producers as they contemplate the future. These technologies are simultaneously liberating and can be used to encourage individual expression and participation in society's issues. Social media played a major role in the Arab Spring, the rash of demonstrations and protests, riots, and civil wars in the Arab world that began in December 2010. Social media enables NGOs and interest groups to mobilize faster than governments can respond. The issue facing all governments and societies is to determine where they want to be on the continuum of state-control and individual freedom. This will determine the fundamental values and characters of their societies in the coming decades.

Naval Sea Systems Command

Naval Sea Systems Command (NAVSEA) is the largest of the Navy's five system commands. With a team of 60,000 civilians, military, and contracted employees, the mission at NAVSEA is to "design, build, deliver, and maintain ships and systems on time and on cost for the U.S. Navy".

What follows is an excerpt from an interview with Dr. Lawrence Totimeh, Head of Data Management for NAVSEA and Tom Jenkins, Executive Chairman of OpenText.

DR. LAWRENCE TOTIMEH: *In 2000 we adopted a data management system called CDMS to help us move files digitally from Crystal City to the Washington Naval Yard. At the time, there were no DoD [Department of Defense] regulations in place governing electronic record keeping. The Paper Reduction Act had not yet come into effect. From this exercise, and incidents that followed, we learned how important it is for us to digitize and securely store our information in a single repository.*

TOM JENKINS: It must have been a challenge for you to rely on a secure cloud to get to your information. What are some of the lessons you've learned from accessing content in the cloud?

From a change management perspective you have to be very patient with your users. They come from a culture based on holding onto assets. We change the system and say, "Now you can move your information into this trusted repository for 24/7 access". I have to communicate to them that this is a benefit because information is in the cloud, and when certain incidents take place we can still access our content. And we have to make sure the system is secure. Accreditation has to be up to date.

The newer generations entering the workforce have a different view of security based on their use of technologies like social networks. How does this impact NAVSEA?

There is a cultural shift happening. If you look at the generation that is coming into the workforce, they are used to having technology available to them all the time. So how do we work with younger generations to make them more productive? That's the issue I think about. They are very savvy. When it comes to security, they don't care as much about it; it's the responsibility of the designers to build it into the system when it is being developed.

They're used to using Google or Bing® where they have permission to see everything.

Technology is exciting, but we have to emphasize that security is important. I work in a classified and unclassified environment, so you just can't have open access to records. There are personal records in databases and we have to be careful that we don't compromise confidential information.

You have built up an enormous archive. Have you thought about big data and how to leverage this data using analytics or predictive analysis?

I have developers trying to figure out what kind of reports the system should generate, but the answers lie in the future rather than in the reports being generated today. We figured out parameters by demonstrating what reports the system could generate and then gathering feedback from experienced users. Now we can figure out what kind of business intelligence we need to look for in the future.

FIGURE 11.2
NAVSEA Website

> There is a cultural shift happening. If you look at the generation that is coming into the workforce, they are used to having technology available to them all the time.

Many governments are in crisis, torn by conflicting interests and faced with insurmountable challenges that span national borders and require resources to be mobilized on a scale that often exceeds capacity. These governments are criticized for their failure to respond to market conditions and citizen demands. This is because theory and policy are rooted in approaches, solutions, principles, and technologies that have become obsolete.

Outmoded approaches to governing are based on traditional values about organizational structure, processes, and performance. The table below illustrates the evolution of values from the 19th through to the 21st century. The path of the future is clear, with the focus shifting to empowerment and a state of transformation that is only really beginning now.

1. **Liberal Values** *(18th Century):* covering constitutional and subsidiarity structures; the legal framework: law, regulations and rules; law enforcement, defence and security; personal justice; and individual rights.
2. **Democratic Values** *(19th Century):* covering citizenship; democratic participation through representation; democratic participation through direct engagement; engaging private interests; and developing the plural society.
3. **Social Values** *(20th Century):* covering how needs for and responses to socio-economic support are determined; service design and production; service delivery; inclusion of all; environmental sustainability; place development and quality of life.
4. **Empowerment Values** *(21st Century):* covering how citizens, communities, groups and interests in society can be empowered to further their own as well as collective benefits; extending subsidiarity and reciprocity; governance coherence and balance; transparency and openness; ethics and accountability; trust; empowering the public sector as an individual actor; empowering the private sector for individual users; and empowering the individual service user.

FIGURE 11.3: The Evolution of Values[1]

Transformation is the way forward for government today. As a strategy, e-government is already helping public sector organizations master change. To be effective in today's complex, connected, and fast-paced world, governments need to redesign their structures and processes to capitalize on a new set of actors and tools. The approach, strategies, standards, and technologies can all be defined as e-government.

e-Government can enable a better government. But what does the future model of government look like? How will we be governed in 2020?

The Transformative Promise of e-Government

What we have illustrated throughout this book is that e-government innovations play a pivotal role in the evolution of government programs and services. Change runs the gamut from new technical infrastructure to reconstructed internal processes to redefined relationships and new solutions.

[1] Valerie Frissen and Jeremy Millard, et al, *"The Future of eGovernment: An exploration of ICT-driven models of eGovernment for the EU in 2020"*, European Commission Joint Research Center (JRC) Scientific and Technical Reports, 2007.

Future models of government are suggested by current trends. Many of the trends examined in this book pertain to those in ICTs. This is because the effective management of information is a key player in government transformation. In the context of e-government, a range of solutions—from content lifecycle management to contract or case management, records management, e-discovery, digital rights management, and web experience management—function to help inform citizens in their roles at work, in the family, and in society.

Digitization improves access to information and enhances engagement with government. Able to connect with their governments across a myriad of interfaces, citizens are inclined to participate—and even co-create programs and services (using mobile apps)—and, ideally, deepen their relationship with their governments based on trust. Many governments are in the early stages of digitization and managing their digital information assets—an important first step toward true e-government.

e-Government 2020

In the year 2020, models of e-governments will be:

- Mobile and connected
- Open and transparent
- Intelligent
- Participatory

e-Governments Are Mobile and Connected

The use of mobile and cloud technologies have made citizen access to government more direct and immediate. Governments can capitalize on this and apply these technologies to streamline service delivery through personalized access. Programs and services can be accessed through the use of digital IDs, such as mobileID, a web-based identification system that the City of Barcelona is using to give citizens mobile access to services, discussed in Chapter 9.

A digital identity is the starting point for access to government services, benefits, and entitlements. By 2020, citizens will be assigned a unique digital identity to access services and complete government transactions online. Interfacing with government will be portable and personalized. Paper documents will no longer be required to complete government transactions. Governments will maintain a secure digital space where each citizen can access and update all their data, including their electronic health records.

The majority of government administrative interactions will be digital. Our reliance on paper-based transactions and documents will be minimized. This is already mandated in many countries. The Australian government, for example, has set the goal to have more than 50,000 interactions per year available online by 2017, with Internet as the default option for most services.

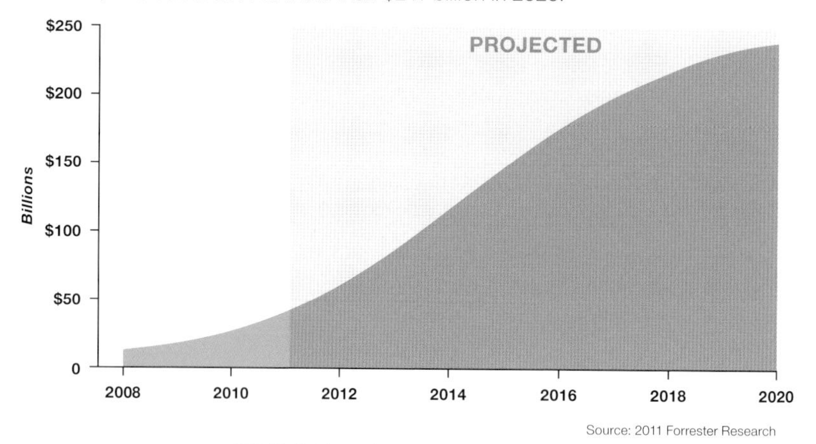

FIGURE 11.4: Cloud Market Takes Off[2]

As accessibility and bandwidth increases, the economy will also become digitally based. Governments will be required to support access across many channels. Their focus will be on creating a responsive experience for their users—both internally with public servants and externally with citizens. A common e-government infrastructure will provide users with a seamless interface and integrate underlying processes and programs.

Alignment on the back end will integrate different government departments to offer shared services. Networked government projects will replace today's bureaucracies, making governments more flexible and anticipatory in their approach. As they turn to private sector organizations to outsource solutions, many government services will be wholly privatized. As the world becomes smaller due to globalization, international dialogues will form in a global, competitive marketplace. Laws, regulations, and policies that impede public/private cooperation will have to be remodeled so that projects take less cycles to complete and are more cost-effective in the long run.

The City of Surrey in Canada is using a combined e-government solution to digitize services and create a responsive, mobile experience for its citizens.

[2] Stefan Ried and Holger Kisker, *"Sizing the Cloud"*, Forrester Research, April 21, 2011.

City of Surrey

FIGURE 11.5: City of Surrey's Citizen-Centric Website

"Whether it's an internal customer or an external customer isn't important. Citizen-centric is important whether you're a youth, a kid, a future investor, a developer, or you're just a parent who wants to know how to register your child for swimming. No matter what your perspectives are, all of those viewpoints matter. And how they use technology and consume technology or content matters."

PROJECT AND RELATIONSHIP MANAGER, CITY OF SURREY

With a population of 472,000, the City of Surrey needed a website that was reflective of one of the fastest growing major cities in Canada. Despite being a truly unique place in which to live, work, and play in British Columbia, the website was not adequately communicating the value and strengths of the City to its public. Site navigation was difficult, search was ineffective, and visitors found it difficult to find contacts and city council information. The City needed to give its citizens multiple ways to interact with content.

The City of Surrey redesigned their website (www.surrey.ca) making it more citizen-centric by using social media tools to ensure a two-way dialogue with constituents. Community consultation was conducted through each phase of the launch to engage with people who had strong opinions and to ensure customer centricity, connectedness, and transparency. The site's design reflects the City's broad community culture; visitors to the new website are offered a compelling, interactive online experience; and the City is using rich images and video to showcase the stories of the businesses and people who live there.

On the new site, navigation is straightforward so that information is available and easy to find. Online transactions are conducted effectively and efficiently. Citizens can report a problem or submit an inquiry using an online form. All council information, whether it is the Surrey bylaws or council minutes, agendas, corporate reports, or planning, is organized and easy to find. Citizens connect directly with their government in a variety of ways, including mobile apps that showcase things to do in the City and live-streaming council meetings. With the new site, the City delivers a targeted experience to visitors, pushing information they care about to the web and mobile devices.

www.opentext.com/e-Government/CityofSurrey

e-Governments Are Intelligent

As transactions move online across all industries, citizen engagement with governments will increase. In 2020, governments will have to find a fine balance between collecting volumes of personal data and protecting the privacy of this information.

The mining of personal data is already a highly charged issue. In 2006, *Wired Magazine* blew the whistle on AT&T and Verizon for giving the National Security Council (NSC) access to network traffic without a warrant.[3] With Google's March 1, 2012 privacy modification that permits the company to share data across various services and third-party websites, there are growing concerns about organizations storing millions of user-based Internet searches and information in a cloud-based data warehouse.[4] What would prevent organizations from sharing information like this with any party, including the government? At the moment, private sector policies on data protection and law enforcement are not consistent or clearly articulated.

The USA PATRIOT Act, created to prevent terrorism post-9/11, gives the U.S. government broad powers to access personal data. With provisions extended by the President, the PATRIOT Act has become a trade issue in selling cloud computing services to governments due to fears that providers could be forced to hand over data to U.S. authorities. This means essentially that any company that deals with a company in the U.S. can have its records and data accessed by the U.S. government. Ironically, the U.S. government will not allow their own data to be stored in foreign clouds. Fears about security of information caused governments in Europe to consider banning U.S. based cloud firms from competing for government contracts.[5] So who owns information in the cloud and who protects the data? And, in the wake of big data—with many different data points amassed, examined, compared, and analyzed—how will this impact privacy for the 2020 citizen?

On the other side of the coin, capturing, combining, and transforming data across silos will provide deeper insight into how performance can be improved. Technologies like data-mining, artificial intelligence, gaming technologies, geospatial technologies, sentiment analysis, and discovery technologies will help governments respond in a more timely fashion to natural disasters, protect citizens from crime in real time, and deliver more targeted services. Governments will be empowered to make critical decisions based on real-time insights leading to transparency and predictability—and the ability to improve services and save lives.

[3] Ryan Singel, *"Whistle-Blower Outs NSA Spy Room"*, Wired Magazine, July 2006, *http://www.wired.com/science/discoveries/news/2006/04/70619* (accessed February 2014).

[4] Bob Brown, *"Google previews new privacy policy"*, Network World, January 31, 2012, *http://www.networkworld.com/news/2012/013112-google-privacy-policy-255529.html* (accessed February 2014).

[5] David Saleh Rauf, *"PATRIOT Act clouds picture for tech"*, Politico, November 2009, *http://www.politico.com/news/stories/1111/69366.html* (accessed February 2014).

FIGURE 11.6: Big Data Analytics Produce a Heatmap of Protest Activity Worldwide January-June 2013[6]

Governments will be responsible for ensuring the security and authenticity of these volumes of information. They will have to manage information effectively and transparently on an enterprise-wide basis to ensure the accuracy and authenticity of sensitive data. To do this, they will need to manage the delicate relationship between transparency and privacy. Large-scale data mining will be strongly regulated. Record-keeping processes will be streamlined on a common e-government infrastructure to simplify and secure the processing of information. Standard metadata will be agreed upon and implemented, and technologies that allow permissioned access to information will become increasingly important in preventing infringements of privacy. As society becomes digital and the Internet engenders a faster pace of crime, governments will need to focus on the development of interoperable policies, standards, and systems to prevent identity theft and online fraud.

e-Governments Are Open and Transparent

Open Government will be the new norm in 2020. Governments are already opening up public access to datasets, such as the Data.gov initiative from the Obama administration and Open Data in Canada. These initiatives are aimed at increasing public access to high-value and machine-readable datasets. The application and uses of this information will stimulate economic growth by creating opportunities for innovation. External organizations and entrepreneurs are already crowdsourcing solutions for improved government service delivery.

[6] John Beieler, *"Mapping Protest Data"*, John Beieler Blog, July 17, 2013, *http://johnbeieler.org/blog/2013/07/03/mapping-protest-data/* (accessed February 2014).

FIGURE 11.7: The Canadian Government's Open Data Initiative

In 2020, new media tools and technologies will continue to increase the transparency and accountability of governments through exposed government operations. These data sharing directives will be required to comply with privacy standards, regulations, and licenses.

Accountability will be shouldered as a joint responsibility as governments increasingly partner with citizens, businesses, government agencies, and even international governments to produce innovative solutions and services. New challenges will emerge from new business models as governments strive to balance security and privacy with innovation, based on open access to information.

> "With regards to open government, we have launched an initiative on transparency, citizen collaboration, and open data where two aspects co-exist: data is the new raw material in the information society and applying it to push industry growth and business development. As a reference in the public sector, we are obliged to position Barcelona as the leading IT city in transparency and collaboration."

SERGI JEREZ, DIRECTOR OF MOBILE, EGOVERNMENT Y DATA, AJUNTAMENT DE BARCELONA, CITY OF BARCELONA

e-Governments are Participatory

As President Abraham Lincoln stated in his famous *Gettysburg Address*, the ideal democratic government is a "government of the people, **by the people, for the people**." In the democracies of the future, citizens will have a range of channels available to influence the outcomes of governance policies and programs. They will monitor the performance of governments on their mobile devices and tablets—watching council meetings, attending a court ruling, or viewing a government debate. Interactive tools will include Internet Protocol television (IPTV), mobile e-voting, and online forums. Citizens and governments will unite in communities of practice where feedback will be collected, stored, and accessed for reuse to create guidelines and policies for more effective governance.

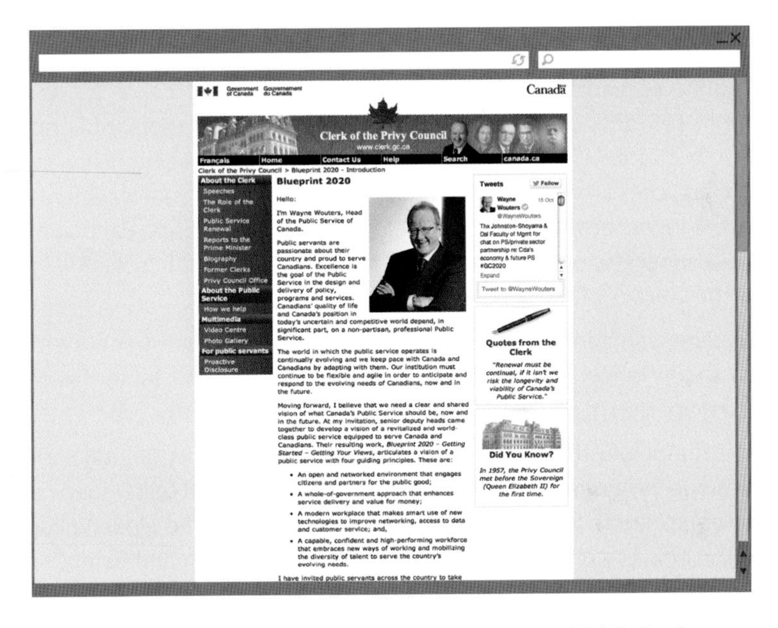

FIGURE 11.8: Blueprint 2020—Redefining the Future of Public Service

The participatory approach of the future is outlined in the Government of Canada's "Blueprint 2020: Building Tomorrow's Public Service Together"—a dialogue about the future of public service launched in June 2013. This engagement exercise was launched in a first-time-ever coast-to-coast webcast to give voice to public servants in reshaping the future of Canada's government.

The multi-channel, bottom-up initiative resulted in conversations hosted on over 120 group discussions, webinars, face-to-face meetings, townhalls, and hundreds of events organized across the country. A groundswell of ideas provided the Government of Canada with a vision of the government's future. The government has made these available to the public as part of an ongoing dialogue.

In the future, governments will rely more heavily on citizen participation to guide mission and policymaking. Based on new partnership models, the roles of government, business, and society will shift. New legislation will help to regulate accountability of governments in joint citizen and business initiatives.

The adoption of e-government moves beyond using Internet technologies to make services available to citizens. There are many government activities that fall outside of the realm of delivering programs to the public. Based on the examples that appear throughout this book, we can see that improvements in efficiency and service delivery are a culmination of processes that come together behind the scenes. These internal processes are essential to every aspect of government. Successful government transformation can only be achieved from the ground up, through the empowerment of public servants.

As governments become central information gathering, processing, and sharing entities, the role of public servants is evolving. When implemented correctly, e-government empowers public servants by giving them access to the information, tools, and processes they need to do their jobs effectively. Approaches have to be user centric, not just citizen centric. Improved access to information is critical. Participatory government is a bottom-up approach that incorporates all users—including public servants. Participation leads to an engaged and impactful cultural shift. This theory is outlined in practice in the feature below, about the Library of Parliament in Canada.

Like public servants, citizens are likewise empowered by e-governments through access to services of their choice at their convenience. e-Government increases transparency and citizen participation in the public sector decision-making process.

e-Governments empower their nations to become digital nations. Digital nations strive to develop educational programs, encourage entrepreneurship, and foster innovation in order to commercialize products and services. Governments across the globe encounter similar challenges in the delivery of their mission activities. Developing and patenting repeatable solutions, and making them available stimulates economic development and transforms nations into players on an international stage.

But how does a government transform itself into an e-government? The following chapters provide examples of transformation through e-government, detailing agencies and organizations that have adopted open, mobile, and data-centric approaches to governing. The final chapter in the book, *Strategies for Change Management in Government*, outlines effective approaches to transformation with a focus on change management.

The Library of Parliament, Canada

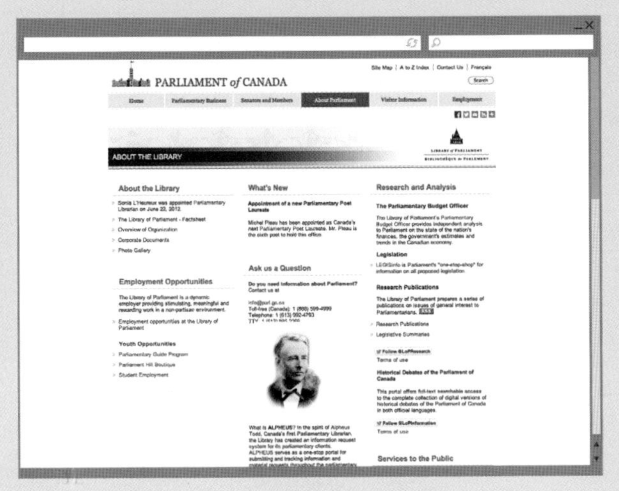

FIGURE 11.9: Library of the Parliament of Canada

While the main benefit is a streamlined workflow, a second benefit is the centralization of information in a single repository where it can be easily searched for and accessed.

The Library of Parliament is the main information repository and research resource for the Parliament of Canada. An organization of about 350 people, the Library's team of knowledge professionals includes lawyers, economists, librarians, social science experts and scientists. Together they provide expert research and analyses on any issue related to the duties of parliamentarians in the Chambers, in committee, in caucus, in the constituency or as a member of a parliamentary association or delegation.

The Library provides research services to parliamentarians, working on very tight deadlines and schedules. In the past, the process of taking a request from clients was manually based—from intake to research response, the request was handed off in a docket or file folder with all the challenges inherent in manually tracking a document. Management never knew with any precision what stage the process was at and the manual process created a duplication of effort and information. The Library was looking to automate this process and improve transparency by replacing paper forms and static logs for tracking workload.

The Library's digital solution is now completely automated, giving researchers time to focus on areas of their expertise rather than managing the process. It is more transparent, providing visibility into every piece of work or document in the Library. It also provides the Library with metrics. Managers can easily track requests and see and adjust bottlenecks. While the main benefit is a streamlined workflow, a second benefit is the centralization of information in a single repository where it can be easily searched for and accessed. Documents are automatically classified according to an underlying records management system as part of the solution, and the Library is now compliant with the Government of Canada's Record Management Plan for 2014.

CHAPTER 12

OPEN GOVERNMENT AND CROWDSOURCING

CHAPTER 12

Open Government and Crowdsourcing

Governments produce huge amounts of information that are only now being recognized as national assets. Public Sector Information (PSI) plays a fundamental role in the provision of public services. Over the past decade, governments have launched policy initiatives to promote the reuse of PSI—from developing open license models to establishing regulatory frameworks and making "open data" available on government websites. Companies that tap into this information can apply newfound knowledge to better understand customers, create products and services to meet demand, and discover new markets. Governments have the opportunity to use this information to improve transparency, efficiency, and service delivery to citizens.

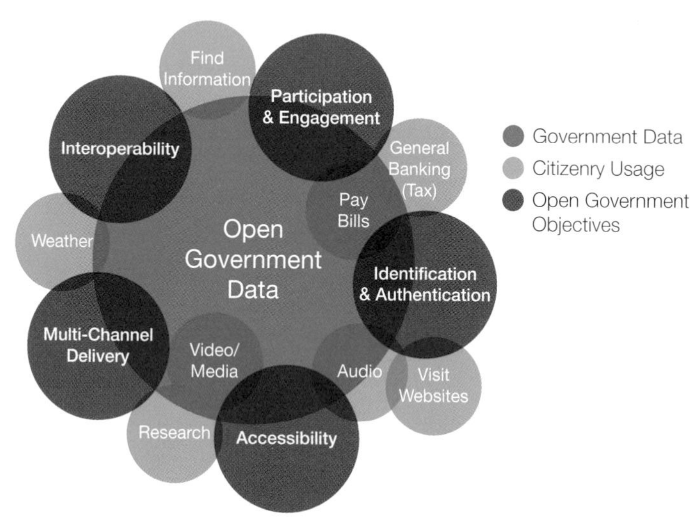

FIGURE 12.1: Open Government: Empowerment Through Information Access

This chapter describes the convergence of PSI and technology, and examines the role that e-government plays in driving the open data phenomenon.

What Is Open Government?

Open government is a principle that gives citizens the right to access the documents, data, and proceedings of government to allow for greater transparency. It reflects the necessary balance between freedom of information and protection of privacy legislation in many jurisdictions.

In an information economy, data is the raw material for new products and services. Governments around the world have articulated their commitment to facilitating a more open approach to governing.

> "My Administration is committed to creating an unprecedented level of openness in Government. We will work together to ensure the public trust and establish a system of transparency, public participation, and collaboration. Openness will strengthen our democracy and promote efficiency and effectiveness in Government."

U.S. PRESIDENT BARACK OBAMA ,
MEMORANDUM FOR THE HEADS OF EXECUTIVE DEPARTMENTS AND AGENCIES, THE WHITE HOUSE

Canada's commitment to open government is part of the federal government's efforts to foster greater openness and accountability, to provide Canadians with more opportunities to learn about and participate in government, to drive innovation and economic opportunities for all Canadians and, at the same time, to create a more cost-effective, efficient, and responsive government.[1]

Canada's approach to open government is described as a "three-legged stool" based on Open Data, Open Information, and Open Dialogue. Open Dialogue leverages tools like social media to engage citizens in policy development. Open Information makes access to online information requests faster and easier. The third leg in the stool is Open Data, which we will discuss below in more detail.

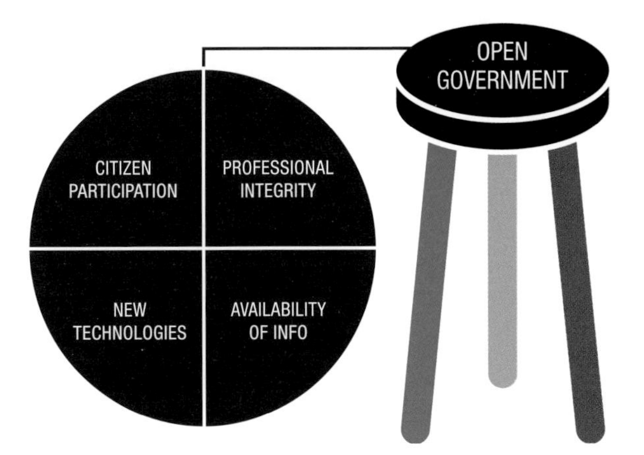

OPEN INFORMATION
- Modernizing the Administration of ATI
- Virtual Library
- International Aid Transparency Initiative
- Opening Government of Canada Records
- Advancing Recordkeeping in GCDOCS
- User-Centric Web Services – GCWeb

OPEN DATA
- Open Data (data.gc.ca)
- GC Resource Management Data

OPEN DIALOGUE
- Consulting Canadians
- Open Regulation

FIGURE 12.2: Canada's Commitment to Open Data[2]

[1] Government of Canada, *"Canada's Action Plan on Open Government", data.gc.ca, http://data.gc.ca/eng/canadas-action-plan-open-government* (accessed February 2014).

[2] *Ibid*

The Open Government Partnership (OGP)

The Open Government Partnership (OGP) was launched in September 2011, when the eight founding governments (Brazil, Indonesia, Mexico, Norway, Philippines, South Africa, United Kingdom, and the United States) endorsed an Open Government Declaration. The declaration outlines a voluntary, multilateral mandate to "promote transparency, empower citizens, fight corruption, and harness new technologies to strengthen governance."[3]

The OGP is a dynamic global movement that promotes open government, free dialogue, and sharing among governments, civil society, and private sector organizations. Since its inception, the OGP has grown to include 62 participating countries (as indicated on the map below) in a worldwide movement that goes beyond strengthening accountability to connecting data across governments on a global spectrum.

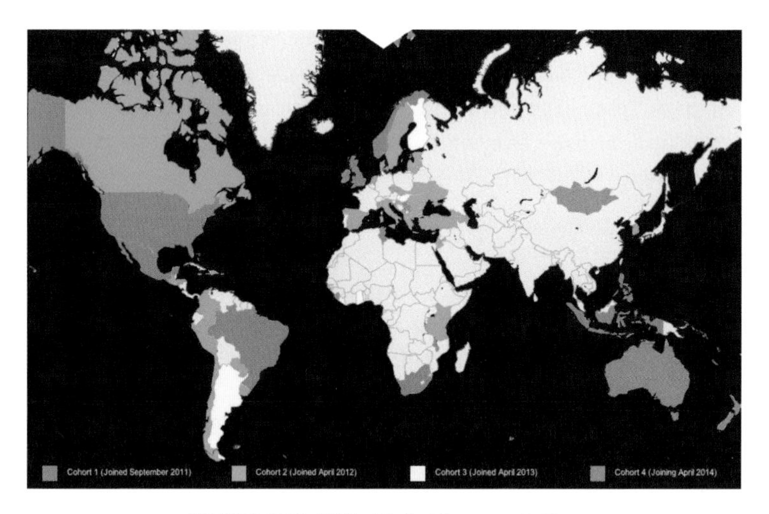

FIGURE 12.3: OGP—Global Representation

"Africa needs open government: on a daily basis, ordinary citizens face the challenge of a lack of transparency and accountability. The Open Government Partnership presents a real opportunity to build a new trustful relationship between African citizens and their governments."

GILBERT SENDUGWA, HEAD SECRETARIAT AFRICAN FREEDOM OF INFORMATION CENTRE

[3] Open Government Partnership, *http://www.opengovpartnership.org/* (accessed February, 2014).

To become a member of the OGP, a nation's government must support its high-level Open Government Declaration, deliver an action plan developed with citizen input, and provide progress reports against the plan. The U.S., for example, has achieved 24 of the 26 steps it outlined in its open government action plan to encourage public participation in government, increase transparency, and manage public resources efficiently. Part of this involved its launch of the "We the People" petition platform, which is used by more than 10 million people, has opened up thousands of government data resources on Data.gov, and expanded the transparency of federal records by improving Freedom of Information Act (FOIA) records processing and declassifying more documents.[4]

To date, almost 1,000 commitments have been made by OGP countries to make their governments more open and accountable.

Open Government Standards

The Open Government Standards were initiated in 2012 to coincide with the presentation of OGP National Action Plans. The initiative aims to define open government based on open government policy measures. In other words: what constitutes an open government and how can new technologies advance transparency?

FIGURE 12.4: Open Government Standards

[4] Gayle Smith and Nick Sinai, *"Open Government Progress"* The White House: Open Government Initiative Blog, October 31, 2013, *http://www.whitehouse.gov/blog/2013/10/31/open-government-progress* (accessed February 2014).

What Is Open Data?

Open data is information that is accessible, available in digital machine-readable format, and reusable under open license terms.

The full Open Definition breaks this down into the following characteristics:[5]

- **Availability and access:** Data should be available as a whole in readable format, preferably by download over the Internet.
- **Reuse and redistribution:** Data should be available under terms that permit reuse and redistribution.
- **Universal participation:** Everyone should be able to use, reuse, and redistribute data without discrimination.

Interoperability is essential to achieving the benefits of open data. Interoperability refers to the ability of diverse systems and organizations to work together to combine datasets.

The focus of open data is on non-personally identifiable data (information contained in maps, genomes, chemical compounds, mathematical formulae, and medical data, to name just a few) that can be aggregated into context for value. Access to government information is made available via an Open Government License (OGL). Proponents of open data insist that access be opened up without restrictions like copyright, patents, etc., including the development of derivative works. Open data is inexorably tied to technology and is part of a larger movement that incorporates open source software, open hardware, open content, and open access.

There are many areas where the analysis of large datasets can be of tremendous value. Along with increasing transparency and accountability, the high-level benefits of open data include creating a more participatory government through approaches like crowdsourcing, citizen empowerment, innovation and business development, improved efficiency and productivity, and new meanings based on context and combined sets of data.

Why Is Open Data Important?

Open data is good for the economy. The European Commission predicts that the open data revolution could bring as much as $55 billion in economic benefit a year to the continent alone.[6] Once opened up, information based on water quality, border wait times, health trends, flight tracking, and crime statistics can be accessed and transformed into user-friendly applications to improve the lives of citizens.

[5] Open Definition, *http://opendefinition.org/* (accessed February 2014).

[6] McKinsey Global Institute, "*Open data: Unlocking innovation and performance with liquid information*", MGI, October 2013.

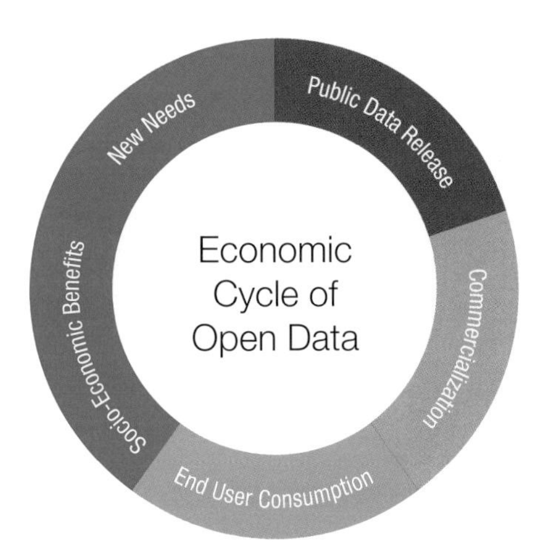

FIGURE 12.5: Economic Cycle of Open Data

In 2013, geospatial data was estimated to generate $270 billion in global revenue.[7] Geospatial data is the foundation of many map- and weather-based applications. Recognizing the importance of reliable data for this growing industry, the Government of Canada has established a Federal Geospatial Platform.[8] Unlocking the government's geospatial information and combining this with data across departments, for example, will affect decisions made about natural resource development, renewable energy, environmental management, and regulations. Consolidating data from many sources with clear analysis enables evidence-based decision making. Government itself can become better informed and more effective in responding to emerging trends.

Open data promises unlimited potential in its combinations and applications of information. New combinations create new applications of knowledge, which lead to innovations that have yet to be conceived. To fully capitalize on this resource, governments must commit to making their data available. The development and consensus of standards is also critical so that datasets can be easily accessed and combined in similar formats.

Applications built on open data have exploded. Google Maps® is based on public transit data made available on websites around the world. Danish website husetsweb.dk offers ways to help citizens increase the energy efficiency of their homes, based on surveys and government subsidy data.[9] FixMyCity is another app that enables citizens to report issues via mobile devices with GPS directly to their municipality. Some of these applications are being crowdsourced and are based solely on the availability of open data.

[7] *"Recap 2013: Most discussed Geospatial News"*, Geospatial World, December 2013, *http://geospatialworld.net/Paper/Business/ArticleView.aspx?aid=30791* (accessed February 2014).

[8] *"The Federal Geospatial Platform"*, Natural Resources Canada, *http://www.nrcan.gc.ca/earth-sciences/geomatics/canadas-spatial-data-infrastructure/geospatial-communities/federal* (accessed February 2014).

[9] *"Why Open Data?"*, Open Data Handbook, 2012, *http://opendatahandbook.org/en/why-open-data/index.html*, (accessed February 2014).

FIGURE 12.6: Open Data Benefits Home Owners in Denmark

Open Data and Crowdsourcing

Crowdsourcing is a great example of democracy in action, as enabled by e-government technologies. The use of crowdsourcing has created new opportunities for citizens to engage with governments at all levels. It gives governments the ability to solve complex and dynamic challenges by outsourcing solutions to citizens. When properly implemented, crowdsourcing solutions are a cost-effective and innovative way for governments to overcome challenges, engage with the community for unique insights, and build trust with citizens.

The term "crowdsourcing" was coined by editors Jeff Howe and Mark Robinson at *Wired Magazine* in 2005. It means essentially "outsourcing to the crowd". According to their definition, it is "the act of a company or institution taking a function once performed by employees and outsourcing it to an undefined (and generally large) network of people in the form of an open call... The crucial prerequisite is the use of the open call format and the large network of potential laborers."[10]

[10] Jeff Howe, "*Crowdsourcing: A Definition*", Crowdsourcing Blog, June 2, 2006, *http://crowdsourcing.typepad.com/cs/2006/06/crowdsourcing_a.html* (accessed February 2014) .

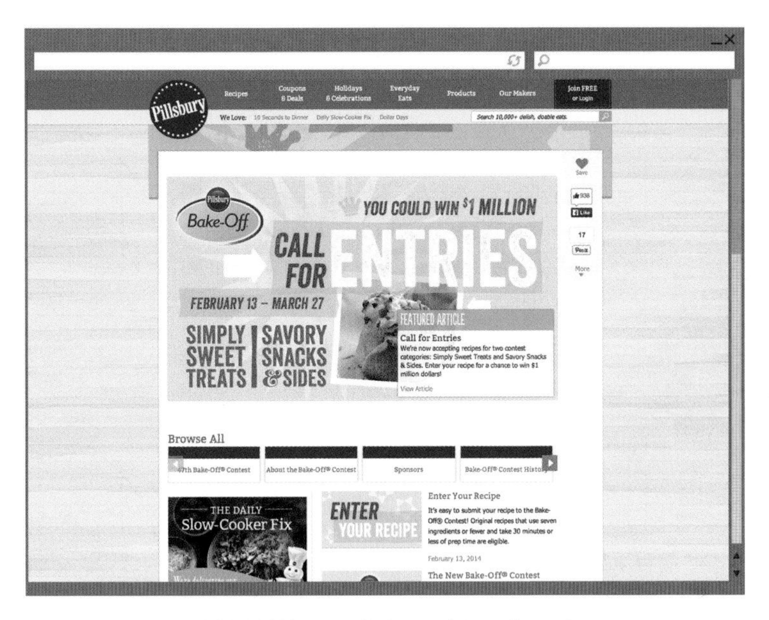

FIGURE 12.7: An Early Form of Crowdsourcing

Early forms of crowdsourcing go back as far as 1858 with projects like the Oxford English Dictionary (OED), which involved volunteers looking through books for every instance of a word and sending this information to editors compiling the OED. Many examples take the form of contests issued to the public by consumer companies, such as the Pillsbury Bake-off in 1949. The bake-off was so popular that it is still held today, with prizes awarded for the best recipes and inclusion in a cookbook full of "crowdsourced cooking tips."[11]

Today, crowdsourcing is an online, distributed problem-solving approach that has become more widespread, fueled by easy access to web, social, and mobile technologies as enablers for collaboration and ideation.

> "I think the most exciting thing…is that we don't know the coolest things that are going to come out of it. With open data, the best thing about it is that other people find these amazing ways to use it."
>
> **GARETH MACLEOD OF TINKERCOIN**

[11] *"Top 5: Oldest Examples of Crowdsourcing"*, Article One Partners, September 16, 2011, *http://info.articleonepartners.com/top-5-oldest-examples-of-crowdsourcing/* (accessed February 2014).

The Wisdom of the Crowd

Crowdsourcing capitalizes on collective intelligence or the "wisdom of the crowd." It is being applied by governments and not-for-profits as a problem-solving tool for community building, civic engagement, and funding.

Crowdsourcing occurs at the grassroots level with governments maintaining a presence but handing control of the evolution of an idea or approach to governing or planning over to citizens. Once open data is available, the network effect takes hold and data becomes increasingly more valuable as more people contribute and participate.

FIGURE 12.8: Wikipedia—Available in 287 Languages

Wikipedia is the modern-day equivalent to the centuries-old OED crowdsourced project. The approach is similar but the collaborative tools have evolved. Wikipedia is a collaboratively edited, multilingual, free online encyclopedia that currently ranks fifth among globally visited websites.[12] Volunteers from around the world collaborate to write and submit 30 million articles in 287 languages in this massive online wiki. Studies that have been completed to assess the reliability of Wikipedia have found the content to be of a high standard, with a level of accuracy in places comparable to *Encyclopædia Britannica*.[13]

[12] *"Wikipedia"*, Wikipedia, *http://en.wikipedia.org/wiki/Wikipedia* (accessed February 2014)

[13] *"Wikipedia survives research test"*, BBC News, December 15, 2005, *http://news.bbc.co.uk/2/hi/technology/4530930.stm* (accessed February 2014)..

In the public sector, evidence suggests that civic co-creation of programs and services can lead to improved outcomes, especially in the areas of health services, crime prevention, education, neighborhood services, and social programs. The previously mentioned FixMyCity is a good example of this. People are given a fast and easy way to report non-emergency issues in their neighborhood, such as potholes, blocked storm drains, and downed street signs through direct engagement with the municipal government. Public works departments can use the information to allocate resources and address issues, making government more responsive, effective, and efficient.

Crowdsourcing has shown that a community is more likely to come together to solve issues when they are directly impacted and their participation is making a difference. As digital citizens, the public is crowdsourcing at a global level to save lives—from Ushahidi, the online mapping platform that saved lives in the Haiti earthquake to using Twitter to track diseases.

FIGURE 12.9: FixMyCity

Internally, both the U.S. and Canadian governments are crowdsourcing to improve engagement and performance. The SAVE Award (Securing Americans Value and Efficiency) recognizes U.S. Federal employees for thinking outside the box to make government more efficient and bring value for taxpayer dollars. To date, Federal employees have submitted more than 85,000 ideas, with the most promising ideas included in the President's Budget.[14]

[14] *"The President's SAVE Award"*, The White House, *http://www.whitehouse.gov/save-award* (accessed February 2014).

In Canada, the Head of the Public Service in Canada invited government employees across the country to take part in a dialogue about the future of the public service. Based on a vision of governing in the future called "Blueprint 2020," employees can use an online form or template, an email address, and private, collaborative spaces to participate, share, and provide feedback on the strategic vision.

The Benefits Outweigh the Challenges

Using technology to tap into collective intelligence and create solutions does present challenges. Legal issues around copyright and intellectual property can arise for participants involved and businesses that sponsor crowdsourced ventures. These can be avoided by having policies in place to protect intellectual property and prevent copyright violations. One example is the Digital Millennium Copyright Act (DMCA) that describes terms of use for websites.

Crowdsourcing is an extension of democracy. It brings new insights and innovation to issues of governance. Despite the inherent challenges, governments should look to the wisdom of the crowd to address challenges that cross jurisdictions, like transportation and the environment. Many governments can use crowdsourcing to deliver services cost-effectively in the wake of budget cuts and financial recession. Capital investment can be minimized by using existing e-government infrastructure and technologies as key facilitators. Often, crowdsourced solutions are created at a faster pace, bypassing the bureaucratic red tape traditionally associated with government projects.

Cost is not always a factor in a project's success. Benefits can also be measured in terms of social value. The co-delivery of government services by citizens makes for a more engaging democratic process, involving citizens directly in government. Throughout the process, citizens have the opportunity to connect more deeply with their government and build trust. Joint initiatives, developed using e-government technologies, can make a government more responsive and relevant to its public.

> "Blueprint 2020 is engaging public servants in an unprecedented variety of ways... We are seeing groups of employees self organize to crowdsource solutions using new tools. On the web, the Blueprint 2020 vision document has been consulted over 125,000 times. The dialogue resulted in more than 13,000 tweets from June to November using the #GC2020 hashtag. Blueprint 2020 continues to be about public servants taking ownership of the process."

WAYNE WOUTERS, CLERK OF THE PRIVY COUNCIL AND HEAD OF THE PUBLIC SERVICE, GOVERNMENT OF CANADA

Open Data Global Initiatives

Canada: www.data.gc.ca

The Government of Canada (GOC) has committed to implement five open data principles and best practices by 2015. As part of this exercise, the GOC recently launched its Open Data Portal from which federal data can be downloaded free of charge. The portal is based on an open source software platform and features targeted search and Web 2.0 capabilities such as blogs, comments, and social feedback.

FIGURE 12.10: Data.gc.ca

There are currently over 265,000 datasets compiled by over 20 departments and agencies on the portal. While this information helps to inform Canadian citizens, who can, for example, compare year-over-year federal budgets, there is also great opportunity to mine and combine this data to develop apps. A Developer's Corner offers software tools such as APIs, open data file formats, and an open data metadata element set. Access to information is based on a new Open Government Licence which offers unrestricted re-use of government data and information for commercial and non-commercial use.

Many departments are aligning open data initiatives with the GOC's Action Plan on Open Government. As part of the International Aid Transparency Initiative (IATI), for example, information on international assistance through former Canadian International Development Agency (CIDA) is available to help donors publish information and increase the transparency of aid throughout the world.

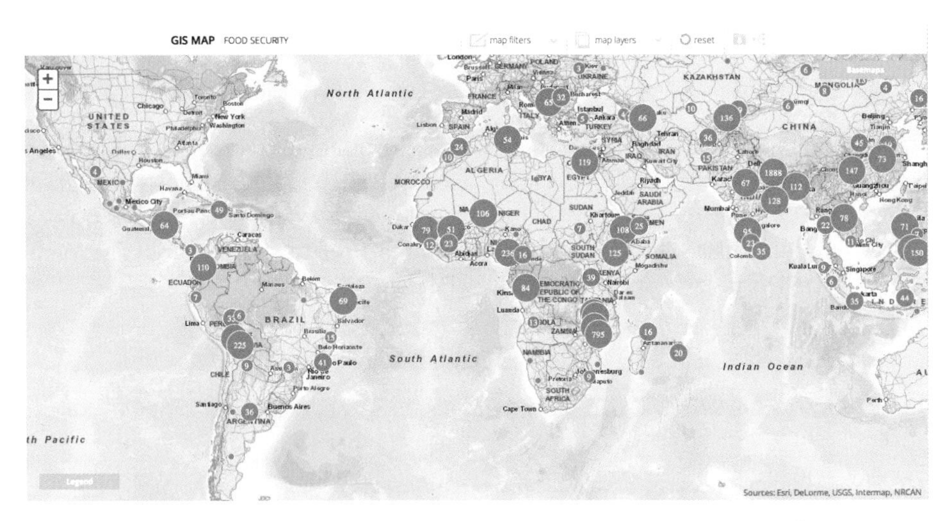

FIGURE 12.11: Geo-Enabling Aid Information Through the IATI Standard[15]

To further demonstrate its commitment to open data, the Canadian Federal government has allocated funding towards creating an Open Data Institute in Waterloo, Ontario, Canada. A mix of public, private, and academic organizations are involved in the endeavor, including the Canadian Digital Media Network (CDMN), the University of Waterloo, Communitech, OpenText Corporation, and Desire2Learn, Inc. A key objective is the development of a common framework for open data to establish a standard that businesses can use when accessing data sources.

President of the Treasury Board, Government of Canada, Tony Clement is the country's strongest political proponent of open data. What follows are excerpts from an interview between Tony Clement and Mark Barrenechea, President and CEO of OpenText.

"With increased access to government data repositories, developers will be able to create applications, advance the digital economy, and expand the boundaries of the possible."

MARK J. BARRENECHEA, OPENTEXT PRESIDENT AND CEO

[15] *"Geo-enabling aid information through the IATI standard"*, International Aid Transparency Initiative (IATI) *http://www.aidtransparency.net/news/geo-enabling-aid-information-through-the-iati-standard* (accessed February 2014).

Open Data: The Natural Resource of the 21st Century

MARK BARRENECHEA: What is the Canadian Government's position on open data and open government?

TONY CLEMENT: *You can't have big data without open data. You can't have all of the applications, all of the innovations that are the result of data being available, without having open data from government sources.*

Do you think this will change the way government operates in terms of efficiencies and effectiveness?

It's going to be revolutionary and in some cases disruptive, but disruptive in a positive, entrepreneurial way. We have a border app, which tells people which border sites are congested and which are open. That's valuable information. [Open data] will revolutionize the flow of information and the way government operates with its citizenry. We'll have much more of a two-way flow of information.

"[Open data] will revolutionize the flow of information and the way government operates with its citizenry."

TONY CLEMENT,
PRESIDENT OF THE TREASURY BOARD,
GOVERNMENT OF CANADA

You called open data the "natural resource of the 21st century" and you see it as improving not only government, but the economy as well.

This is a natural resource that unlocks the door to many things, and it makes the government more accountable. One of the sites that I opened up this year was for real-time compare-and-contrast on budgetary items within the federal government. You used to need a Master's thesis to understand how to unlock the budgetary cycle of the Canadian government. Now it's a lot easier to keep the government accountable, which is of course, an element of our democracy.

I'm a developer at heart; I like to say that developers make all things possible. You need a few ingredients: you need data, you need APIs, and you need a long-term commitment to attract the community. Is the government committed to this for the long term?

Absolutely, we're one of the original signatories for the Open Government Partnership (OGP), which is a worldwide movement. You can't just sign up; you have to commit yourself to meeting certain goals. They are common goals in the sense that we want more open government and we want more open data. It requires us to have a process by which we interact with civil society on an ongoing basis.

United States: data.gov

The U.S. Government is making data more accessible and useful for citizens and government more accountable through its commitment to treat federal information as a strategic asset. Data.gov is the flagship Open Government Initiative from the U.S. Executive Office of the President and supports the principles of open government: transparency, participation, and collaboration. Information has been uploaded from 176 agencies and sub-agencies, with 88,137 datasets available on the site for download. From this data, 349 applications have been developed by citizens, of which 137 are mobile apps.

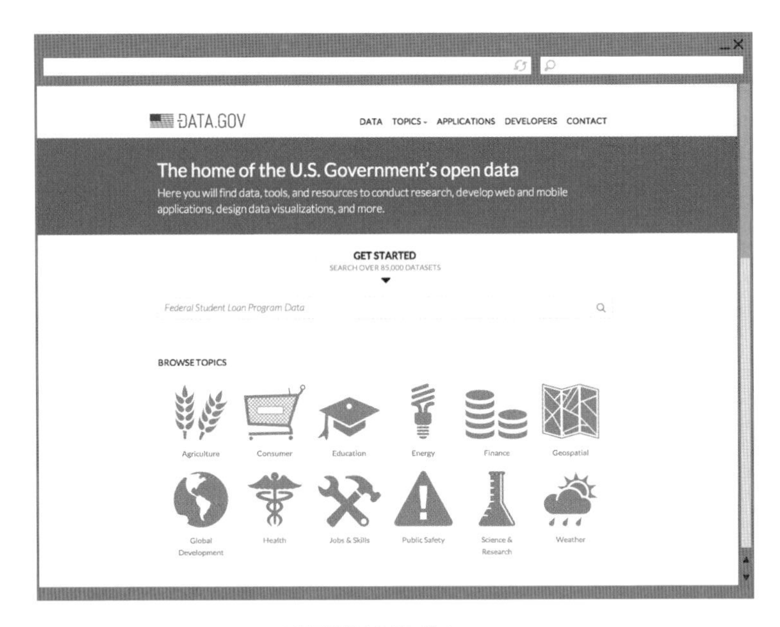

FIGURE 12.12: Data.gov

An Innovator Toolkit is available, along with 409 government APIs and access to open source code. The site promotes participation and interaction using blogs, feedback mechanisms, and a community page that organizes datasets based on industries or areas of interest.

FIGURE 12.13: Open Data—Helping U.S. Farmers Manage Crops

The lens of the open government movement is focused on how society benefits from free access to information. In the U.S., federal data has been used to help the media expose inconsistency in hospital billings, to educate citizens about social services, to aid farmers in the management of their crops, and to help educators develop curriculum. Space agency NASA, for example, has released data on 50 years of space exploration, making over 200 datasets available. My NASA Data (MND) gives the public access to satellite data, which can be generated into charts, plots, and graphs. These can then be incorporated into lesson plans to enhance curriculum and advance education and research.

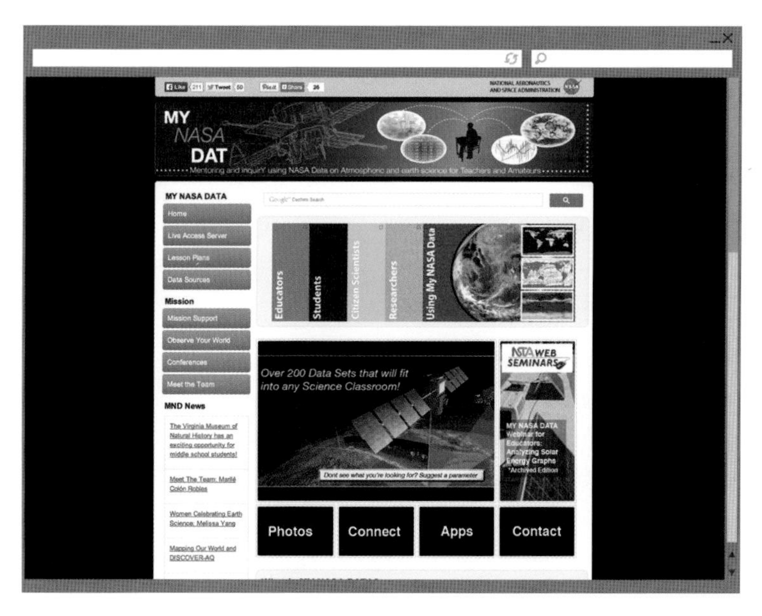

FIGURE 12.14: Opening Up 50 Years of Space Exploration to the Public

United Kingdom: data.gov.uk

As a founding member and co-chair of the Open Government Partnership (OGP), the UK Government has continued to develop policies that promote the re-use of public sector information. In 2010, the UK Government launched data.gov.uk, a searchable portal to release public data. Over 9,000 datasets are currently available on the website, from all central government departments and government bodies.

To maximize the benefits of public sector information, the U.K. has established the Open Government Licence (OGL) as its default license for public sector information. The Open Data Institute (ODI), chaired by Sir Tim Berners Lee and Professor Sir Nigel Shadbolt, was established to demonstrate the commercial value of open data through the mentorship of new ideas and innovation. Other UK initiatives, such as the Open Data User Group (ODUG), legislation.gov.uk, and the UK Regulatory Framework have influenced open government activities in other jurisdictions.

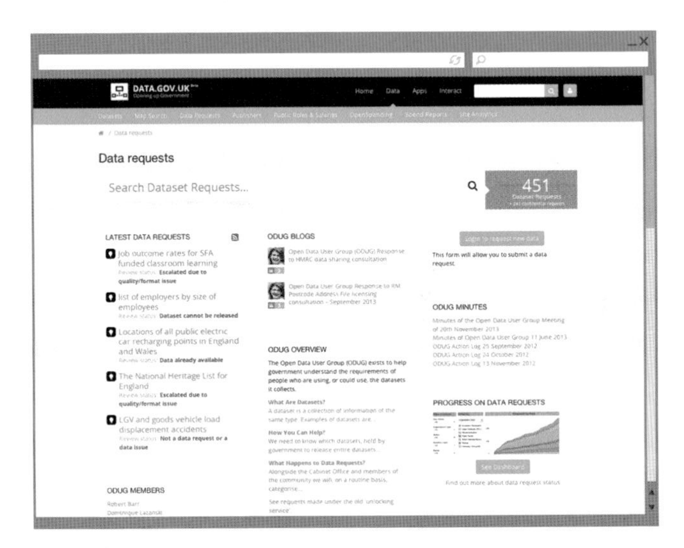

FIGURE 12.15: Data.gov.uk

> "...the [OGL] gives principles for what we mean by 'open' in 'open data' or 'open content'. This means that open material can be used and shared by anyone for any purpose, and—crucially—that open material can be freely combined without legal issues. This relatively short bit of text helps to keep the digital commons interoperable, serving as a green light for reuse and remixing. The fact that the UK government's new default licence is now compliant with the definition, formally makes good on official commitments to make open the new default for public sector data."

JONATHAN GRAY, DIRECTOR OF POLICY AND IDEAS, THE OPEN KNOWLEDGE FOUNDATION

Germany: govdata.de

As of 2013, the latest coalition government in power in Germany stated their intention to join the ODP, making a commitment to open government a part of their legislative agenda. Germany's current open data portal, GovData.de, is based on a custom license model, which potentially excludes Germany from a larger, global data pool.[16] Joining the ODP paves the way for Germany to implement a common license to allow for greater interoperability and combinations of datasets. Additional open data initiatives are underway in Germany, including the Open Data Network, The Government 2.0 Network Germany, The Internet & Society Collaboratory, and *Apps für Deutschland.*

Conceived at Government 2.0 Camp Berlin 2009, the Government 2.0 Network Germany is made up of volunteers interested in advancing the cause of Government 2.0—a more participatory and engaged government based on emerging web technologies.

> "We welcome Germany joining that race, for Germany's sake but also because we know that as more countries provide data about more things, so we all will get a picture of the state of the whole world, a picture which is very important in this crucial era."

TIM BERNERS LEE, W3C CONSORTIUM AND ADVISOR OF THE UK GOVERNMENT ON LINKED OPEN DATA

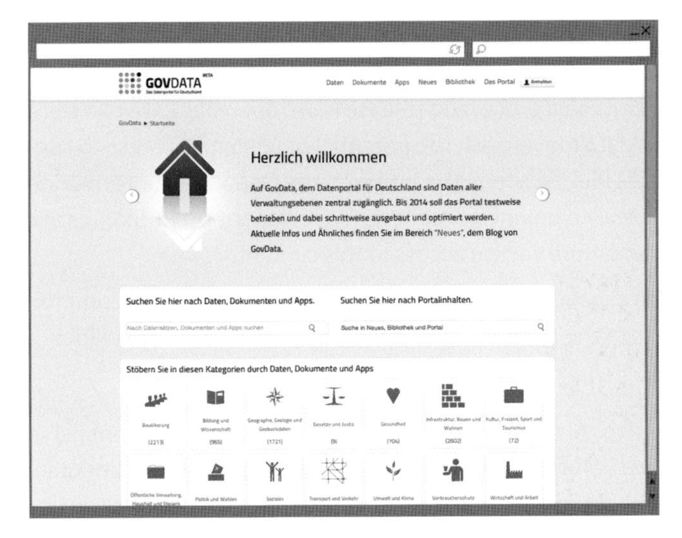

FIGURE 12.16: GovData.de

[16] Maria Schroder and Christian Heise, "*From OpenGovData to GovData: Why Germany needs the OGP (and the OGP needs Germany)*", Open Gov Blog, February 15, 2013, *http://blog.opengovpartnership.org/2013/02/from-opengovdata-to-govdata-why-germany-needs-the-ogp-and-the-ogp-needs-germany/* (accessed January 2014).

e-Government: A Platform for Open Data and Crowdsourcing

Governments around the world are establishing more consistent information management structures, standardizing the way this data is stored and presented, and endorsing the publication of federal data in machine-readable formats. What is the role that e-government plays in all of this?

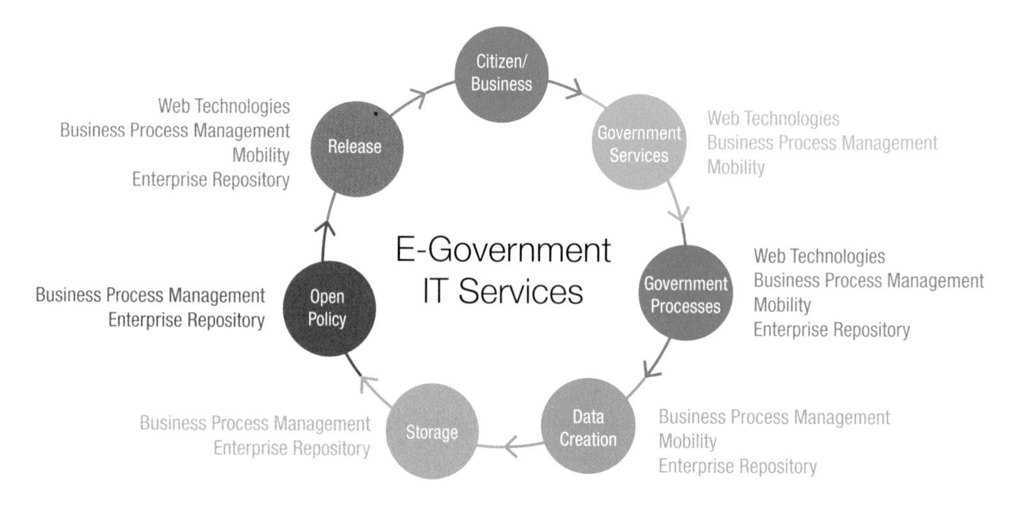

FIGURE 12.17: The Open Data Lifecycle

As nations, organizations, and citizens share, use, and release more open data, we can see a new web emerging. With the open data movement, the potential of unlimited access to content is becoming clear as boundaries blur between the Internet, the Deep Web (information behind firewalls), open data, and search engine content. e-Government technologies are being developed to deliver faster and more secure access to this content.

As part of a complete solution, an e-government system standardizes data on a common infrastructure and opens up access to this content through search and archive capabilities.

The Importance of Archiving to Open Data

Open data requires a robust archive. Archiving delivers a multi-faceted, comprehensive solution that can handle massive volumes of data—tens and millions of documents—increasingly common in government organizations today. Government organizations can use archiving to capture digital information and make it more accessible. For open government, effective archiving ensures that the analysis of trends over time remains possible.

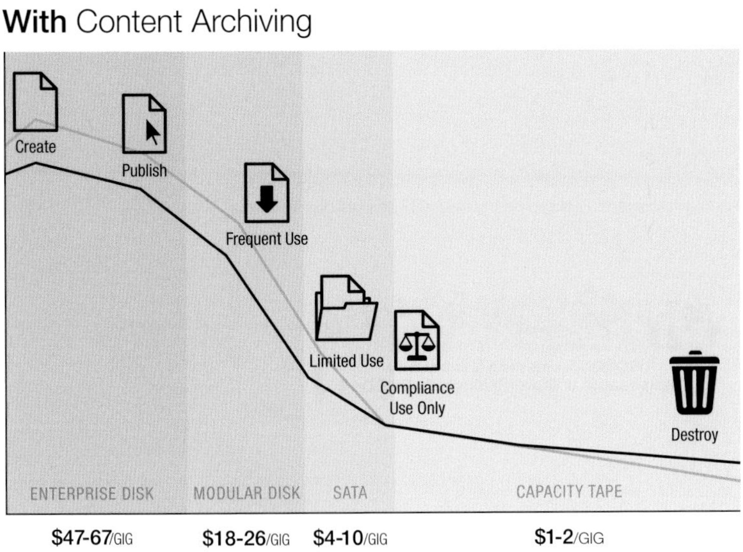

FIGURE 12.18: Open Data Needs a Robust Archive

Archiving is a critical component of sound governance practices. Information can be stored and managed in a single repository, making it easier to manage and less costly to operate. Tiered storage allows for content to be stored where appropriate, at different stages in its lifecycle. Information is easier to find, improving efficiency and response times, and reducing the time and cost involved in processing legal e-discovery requests.

The lifecycle of federal content and information starts with the business applications used most in agencies and associated data, documents, and records. Keeping a separate archive for each of these applications is proving to be too costly and complex. e-Government provides a single archiving backbone for all types of information.

Fully integrated e-government solutions deliver an automated system that removes the complexities of information lifecycle management, records management, process automation, storage, and archiving. Cross-repository functionality such as federated records management and enterprise search, along with collection tools are also important components of open data.

The Government of Canada has standardized its approach to data and records management across the public service with GCDOCS, a hosted, government-wide information management system. GCDOCS supports the Open Information stream of the GOC's Open Government Initiative and is currently being implemented in a number of departments and agencies.

GCDOCS

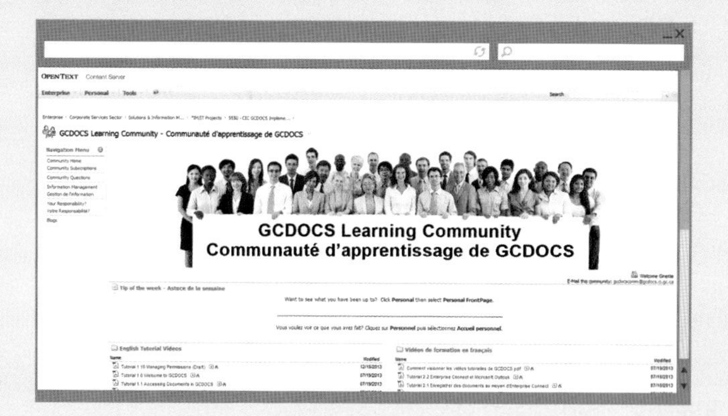

FIGURE 12.19:
GCDOCs

To meet directives for effective recordkeeping practices and information management, as well as the mandate to retain any data created after 2017 in digital format only, the Government of Canada (GOC) adopted a hosted, government-wide solution for archiving and records management. GCDOCS is an e-government system that is currently helping departments create, acquire, capture, manage and protect the integrity of information resources of business value in the delivery of Government of Canada programs and services.

The move to GCDOCS was an exciting opportunity for government departments to start comprehensively managing their digital information resources. The e-government solution is more than just a records management tool: GCDOCS embraces an enterprise-wide design that effectively manages all of its information in a consistent manner. The solution is also being used as the central repository for storing structured and unstructured information.

With GCDOCS, the government is considering information management transformation from a much higher and broader perspective. As a full information lifecycle management system, GCDOCS manages information in the background, placing no burden on the end user beyond the needs of regular document management best practices and departmental standards. The focus is on usability to leverage the value of information. Today, GCDOCS is making it easier for 90,000 civil servants to do their jobs and provide Canadians with information on programs and services more efficiently. Dozens of line departments are using GCDOCs to work consistently with central agencies. Long-term plans are to roll out the solution to the entire federal government to help the GOC achieve its vision to function as a fully digital government by 2017.

e-Governnment provides the national infrastructure required to promote open government. Open government strengthens the relationships between governments, industry, academia, and citizens for improved efficiencies in service delivery, advances in education and research, increased innovation and entrepreneurship, and economic gains and prosperity.

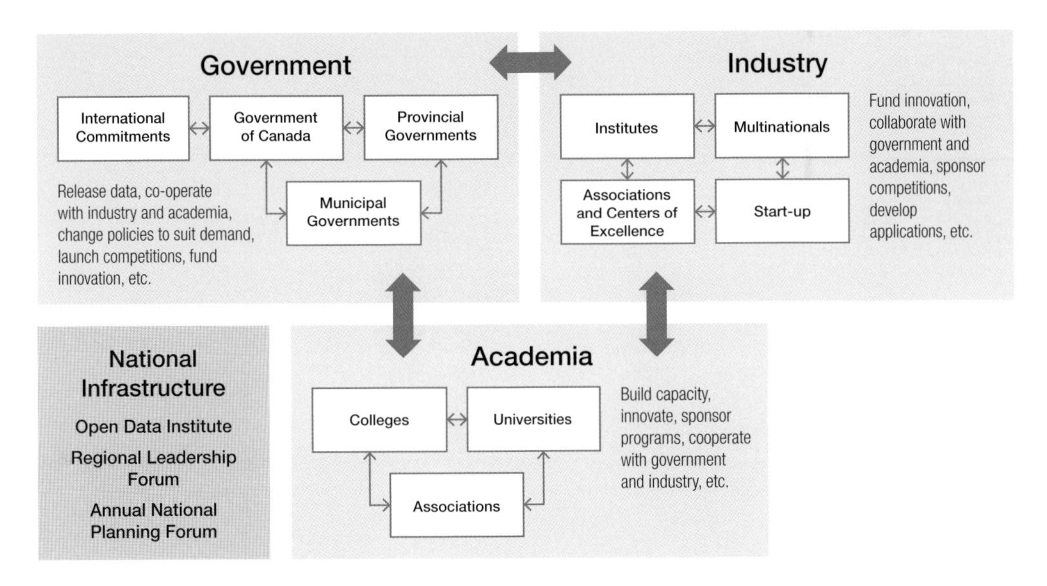

FIGURE 12.20: Powering an Open Government Platform

CHAPTER 13

E-GOVERNMENT AND BIG DATA

CHAPTER 13

e-Government and Big Data

Big data has received a lot of hype lately—for both the challenges and the opportunities it presents across all industries. For most organizations, big data is not a trend but the reality of doing business. It describes the increasing volume, velocity, and variety of information that organizations face every day. This deluge of data consists of both structured and unstructured information and is fueled by emerging technologies and devices that provide immediate access and exchange of information.

In a recent report, McKinsey Group identifies big data as the next frontier for innovation, competition, and productivity.[1] What potential does it bring to the public sector? This chapter discusses the impact of big data on the public sector and explores how e-government can help organizations unleash the power of their information in new and innovative ways.

How Much Data?

IDC predicts that by 2020 the world will generate 50 times the amount of information it does currently.[2] New technologies, skills, and analysis will be required to mitigate the cost of creating, capturing, managing, and storing information.

Organizations are collecting increasingly detailed amounts of information. Consumers are adding to this data volume as the ability to create and share data has been revolutionized by the number of people, devices, and sensors connected to digital networks. Multimedia is the most popular format of data shared on the Internet. Over six billion hours of video are watched each month on YouTube—that's almost an hour for every person on Earth and 50 percent more than last year.[3] As far a social media is concerned, 1,310,000,000 active Facebook users per month share over one million links and three million messages[4] and upload 350 million photos a day.[5]

Finally, the devices, sensors, RFID tags, meters, and smart appliances that make up the Internet of Things are also contributing to the growth of big data. According to Gartner there will be nearly 26 billion devices on the Internet of Things by 2020.[6]

[1] McKinsey Global Institute, *"Big data: The next frontier for innovation, competition, and productivity"*, McKinsey & Company, 2011.

[2] John Gantz and David Reinsel, *"The Digital Universe in 2020: Big Data, Bigger Digital Shadows, and Biggest Growth in the Far East"*, IDC, December, 2012.

[3] *"YouTube Statistics"*, YouTube, *http://www.youtube.com/yt/press/statistics.html* (accessed February 2014).

[4] *"Facebook Statistics"*, Statistics Brain, January 1, 2014, *http://www.statisticbrain.com/facebook-statistics/* (accessed February 2014).

[5] Craig Smith. *"By the Numbers: 64 Amazing Facebook User Statistics"*, Digital Marketing Ramblings, December, 2013, *http://expandedramblings.com/index.php/by-the-numbers-17-amazing-facebook-stats/#.UtMD3_v5OXM* (accessed February 2014).

[6] *"Gartner Says the Internet of Things Installed Base Will Grow to 26 Billion Units By 2020"*, Gartner Inc., December 12, 2013.

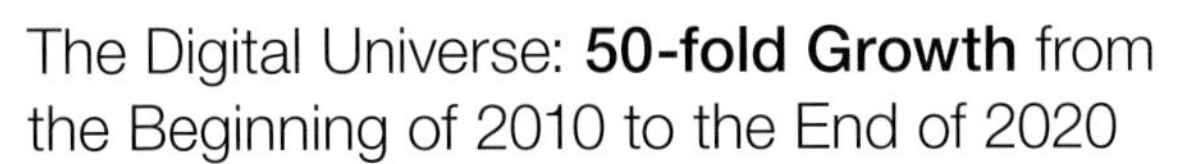

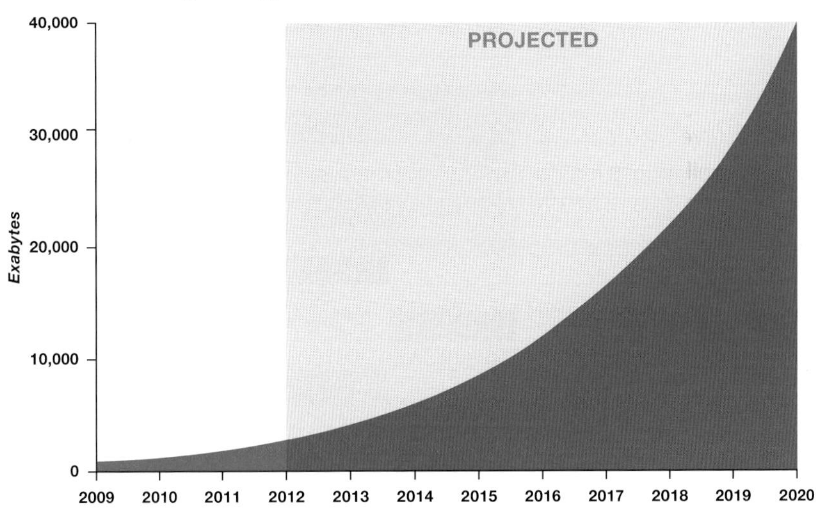

FIGURE 13.1: Growth of Information by Exabytes[7]

Big Data in the Public Sector

Government agencies collect massive amounts of information from web logs, citizen transactions, medical files, satellite images, weather sensors, research programs, disease tracking, anti-crime activities, and more. This information holds great potential for analysis, insight, and innovation.

Despite all this information, governments are leveraging its potential. In a survey of state and local government CIOs and IT managers, 79 percent predicted that it would be three years before they could take advantage of big data. The same survey participants recognized the advantages of using big data—for gains in efficiency (57 percent); speed and accuracy of decision making (54 percent); and providing a deeper understanding of citizens' needs (37 percent). Of those surveyed, only two percent have developed a big data strategy.[8]

Agencies are grappling with managing and digitizing their data. Even in countries with advanced e-government programs, agencies still fail to make information available across organizational silos and disparate systems. Much of the information is duplicated and stored numerous times. IT budgets are allocated to modernizing legacy systems, consolidation, mobile apps, security, and connectivity, rather than to big data processing.

[7] *Ibid.*

[8] MeriTalk, *"State and Local Agencies Expect Data to Double in Next Four Years; Show Little Adoption of Big Data"*, MeriTalk Press Release, April 29, 2013.

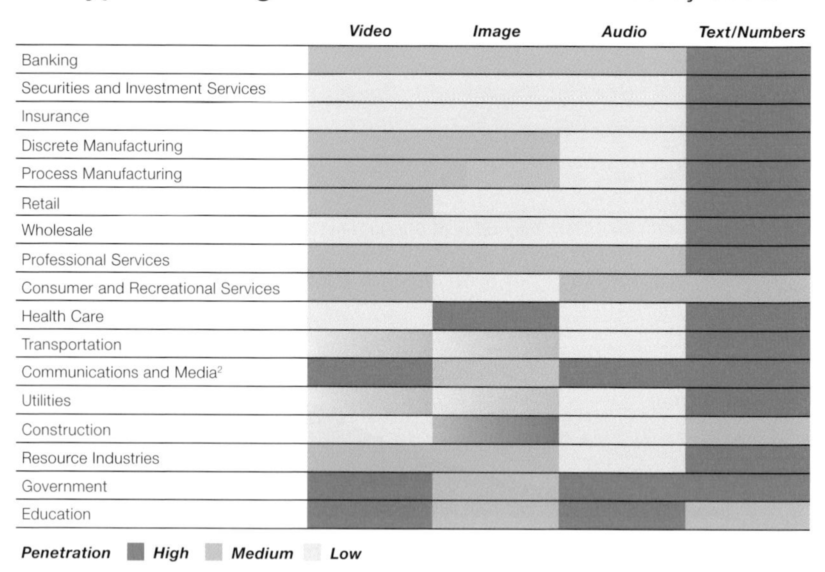

[1]We compiled this heat map using units of data (in files or minutes of video) rather than bytes. [2]Video and audio are high in some subsectors.
Source: McKinsey Global Institute analysis

FIGURE 13.2: Types of Data Generated and Stored by Sector[9]

Despite conflicting priorities, there is widespread recognition that big data must be unlocked to realize its true value. In March 2012, the Obama administration launched a $200 million big data initiative to promote the use of big data for scientific discovery, environmental and biomedical research, education, and national security.[10] As described in Chapter 12, governments around the world are making big data sets available as part of the open data initiatives.

Big data creates big value. In the same study referred to above, 69 percent of federal IT professionals expect big data to help the government work more efficiently, with cost-savings of $500 billion.[11]

In a separate study on big data in the public sector, McKinsey assessed its value at $300 billion a year for the health care sector alone, based in part on reduced national expenditures.[12] The same report concludes that government administration in Europe could save more than €100 billion ($149 billion USD) in operational efficiency by using big data.[13]

[9] McKinsey Global Institute, *"Big data: The next frontier for innovation, competition, and productivity"*, McKinsey & Company, 2011.

[10] *"Obama Administration Unveils 'Big Data' Initiative: Announces $200 Million in New R&D Investments,"* The White House, March 29, 2012, *http://www.whitehouse.gov/sites/default/files/microsites/ostp/big_data_press_release.pdf* (accessed January 2014).

[11] MeriTalk, *"Smarter Uncle Sam: The Big Data Forecast"*, MeriTalk Press Release, 2013, *http://www.meritalk.com/pdfs/emc-big-data/Smarter_Uncle_Sam_Press_Release.pdf* (accessed February 2012).

[12] McKinsey Global Institute, *"Big data: The next frontier for innovation, competition, and productivity"*, McKinsey & Company, 2011.

[13] *Ibid.*

Figure 13.3: The Value of Big Data in the Public Sector

When managed effectively, big data can create significant value by increasing transparency, measuring performance, enabling more accurate and informed decision making, personalizing citizen services, and advancing innovation to contribute to economic growth and competitive advantage.

The Hidden Value of Big Data

Data held by government agencies is an asset. When big data is unlocked, it has the potential to enhance public sector performance in administration, health care, science and research, transportation, infrastructure, education, security, and social sciences. Benefits are already being realized by applying predictive modeling to clinical trials, advanced analytics to test the effectiveness of patient treatments, and the analysis of public health surveillance to detect the outbreak of disease—as illustrated in the following story about Global Public Health Intelligence Network (GPHIN).

With e-government solutions, organizations like GPHIN gain leading-edge capabilities, including progressive search, semantic analytics and navigation, and categorization, all designed to mine, extract, and present the true value of big data.

The ability to store, aggregate, combine, and analyze big data has become easier as technology trends have reduced associated costs and technology barriers. For agencies to realize the hidden value of big data, they must effectively manage big data and derive insights from this information. e-Government helps agencies find the hidden knowledge locked within big data.

e-Government solutions can be used to capture, combine, and transform data across information silos into formats that can be analyzed for deeper business insight. The first step toward extracting value from data is managing the data. e-Government solutions integrate data on a common platform where it can be secured, accessed, exchanged, and archived.

Global Public Health Intelligence Network (GPHIN)

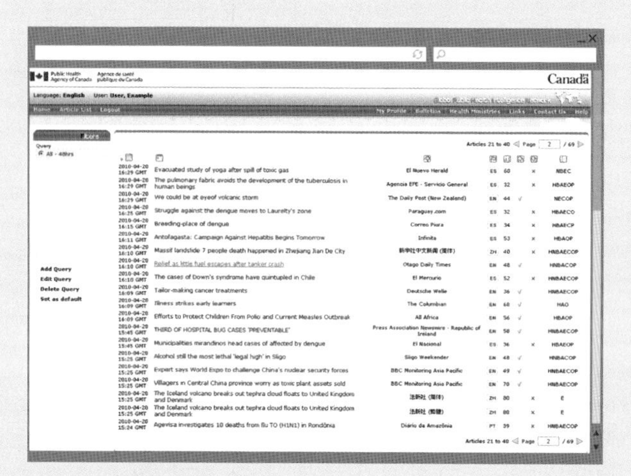

FIGURE 13.4: Translingual Text Mining Results

Processing up to 20,000 articles a day, it would be impossible to track this volume without having the right technology in place.

The Global Public Health Intelligence Network (GPHIN) Centre for Emergency Preparedness and Response Public Health Agency of Canada uses the latest technology to spot threats to human life. The GPHIN system uses translingual text mining to assign relevancy scores to numerous articles coming from worldwide sources, helping analysts count and track instances of possible threats.

Unlike its American counterpart ProMed, GPHIN does not just track diseases. The group monitors any threat to human life—natural or man-made—for example, bush fires in California, pestilence outbreaks in Africa, even theft of nuclear material. As such, the Canadian team and its technology are continuously monitoring over 1,000 potential threats around the globe. The team publishes eight different reports, three times a day. It is precisely this monitoring by organizations like GPHIN that triggers responses—such as the World Health Organization (WHO) declaring H1N1 a pandemic, which in turn accelerates the development of vaccines.

Processing up to 20,000 articles a day, it would be impossible to track this volume without having the right technology in place.

Increase Transparency

Greater transparency into information and performance improves accountability. Agencies can make use of advanced analytics like predictive analysis to identify costs savings and to detect fraud, waste, and error. Anomalies in the receipt of benefits can be revealed, for example, to reduce instances of fraud. Data from different sources and departments can be combined to identify productivity gaps. Greater levels of transparency save time and money and help to optimize resources for maximum efficiency.

Improve Productivity

Analyzing big data improves productivity. Making data available and searchable frees up valuable time so resources can be allocated to focus on priorities. Information is combined across departmental systems and processes, making it easier to access and reduce the duplication of both data and effort. Automated solutions eliminate the need for business users to sort and classify growing amounts content. Big data can be analyzed to identify costs savings and opportunities to increase overall productivity.

Monitor Performance

Many managers feel they do not have all the information they need to effectively run their departments. e-Government helps agencies determine how information is analyzed to support the decision-making process at each step in a business process. Data sets can be combined into management dashboards and comparative engines can be used to measure the effectiveness of programs and policies. Variability in performance can be revealed. Through big data, government organizations are able to improve decision making through visualization techniques and greater visibility. e-Government adds value to big data by continually measuring impact. The following feature on the State Lotteries of Spain demonstrates how insight can fuel continual performance improvements, learning, and growth.

Optimize Citizen Engagement

Analyzing big data in new ways surfaces relevant topics, summaries, sentiments, and relationships to deliver more enriched information. Through predictive and sentiment analysis, agencies can better understand their citizens and tailor their services to meet their needs. Trends can be revealed by monitoring system logs, web clicks, communications, news channels, and social media content. Insight into citizen personas and behavior gives agencies the ability to make faster and more accurate and cost-effective business decisions.

State Lotteries of Spain

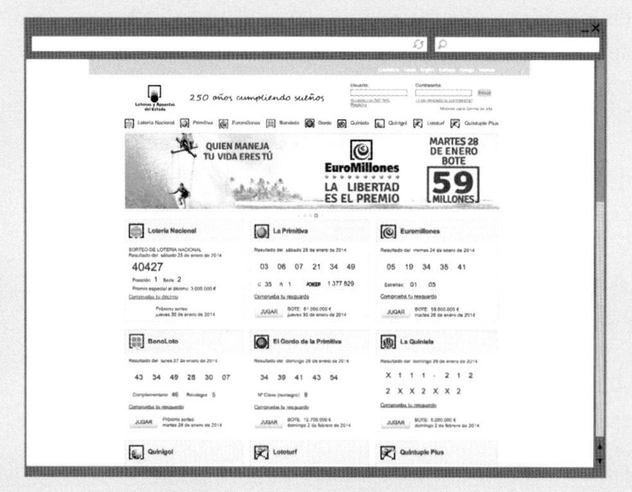

FIGURE 13.5: SELAE's Award-Winning Website

A key benefit of the system is the ability to update content quickly and easily for delivery across multiple channels, including mobile devices or social networks.

The State Lotteries of Spain (officially the *Sociedad Estatal Loterías y Apuestas del Estado* or SELAE) is a public company that was created in December 2010 by the Spanish Ministry of Finance and Public Administrations to administer a variety of lotteries in Spain. The SELAE network consists of 12,000 outlets, 700 employees, and 55 sales offices required to manage the State Lotteries and Gambling Society. The IT infrastructure that supports this network is a complex one, made up of gaming terminals that connect to a central system via satellite network and over 200 servers that range from media servers to small systems.

The SELAE gaming platform supports an annual turnover of 10,000 million euro. The National Lottery constitutes approximately 55 percent of this total, and the remaining 45 percent comes from other active games. In January of 2012, the online site reached 200,000 registered and verified users. To support growing volumes of hits and visits to the site, the SELAE implemented a solution that could integrate with existing applications, scale, and provide audit and usage analysis so that the SELAE could continually monitor and improve the performance of the site.

A combined social media, web experience management, analytics, and portal solution was selected to replace the SELAE's ad hoc content management system and integrate with its online gaming platform. On the back end, the solution provides an agile development environment that permits users to modify content. It scales to support traffic greater than 80 million page views per month. A key benefit of the system is the ability to update content quickly for delivery across multiple channels, including mobile devices or social networks. The site, which was recently awarded the most popular site in its category, has proven itself through the efficient handling of volumes of traffic—cost-effectively scaling to support a growing membership.

Advance Collaboration and Innovation

With e-government, agencies can exploit new ways to manage and analyze big data to ignite innovation, form new partnerships, and drive business outcomes to create competitive advantage. Public and private sector organizations are already collaborating around big data sets and creating opportunities for partnership. As we have described in the chapters on open data and mobile e-government, access to big data sets has inspired the development of new products and services. Governments are working with educational institutions, Non-Government Organizations (NGOs), and private companies to exchange knowledge, develop research, and innovate with big data. In the following excerpt, the IQ Business Group is using e-government to manage and analyze vast amounts of big data in the cloud.

The Challenges of Big Data

Big data creates big headaches for CIOs and IT managers—from management to infrastructure, storage, resourcing, and security. Based on its sheer volume, extracting value from big data is a daunting task. Current technologies and architectures are not equipped to handle massive volumes of data. Security and privacy are important issues associated with big data. To benefit from big data, agencies will need to rethink their data management strategies, invest in solutions, and acquire the skills needed to maximize the value of their information.

Technology

The right resources have to be in place to analyze big data effectively. For many organizations, big data accumulates so quickly that it outruns an organization's ability to use it to their advantage. Fifty-seven percent of state and local agencies in the U.S. admit that their current enterprise architecture is unable to support big data projects. Their data storage and access falls short (at 47 percent of what is required), as does their computational power (at 42 percent) and personnel (at 35 percent), putting them in a position where they have data sets too big to manage and analyze.[14]

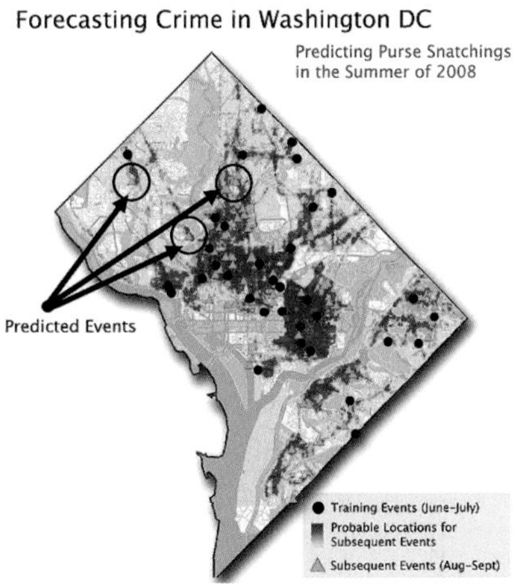

FIGURE 13.6: Geospatial Predictive Modeling Used to Forecast Crime[15]

[14] MeriTalk, *"State and Local Agencies Expect Data to Double in Next Four Years; Show Little Adoption of Big Data"*, MeriTalk Press Release, April 29, 2013.

[15] Peter Borissow *"Forecasting Crime in Washington D.C.,"* Wikipedia, *http://en.wikipedia.org/wiki/File:Signature_Analyst_Assessment_of_DC.jpg* (accessed February 2014).

IQ Business Group

For more than 10 years, the IQ Business Group (IQBG) has helped hundreds of clients manage mission-critical information while reducing costs. IQBG is an implementation partner for deployments at the Department of Interior, Virginia State Bar, Philadelphia's DA's Office, and at the Courts of Puerto Rico.

What follows is an excerpt from an interview between Mike Beck, President and CEO of IQBG and Tom Jenkins, Executive Chairman of OpenText.

MIKE BECK: *We run our own cloud: it's called the IQBG Cloud. It is FISMA-certified (a government standard for only the most secure technology) and is soon to be FedRAMP-certified for cloud security controls. We host over 100,000 users, capture over 66 million emails a month, and have 200 terabytes of storage, and we manage all that data with auto classification, records management, and e-discovery support. A major U.S. federal agency is our primary customer in that cloud.*

TOM JENKINS: How do you handle data at such a huge scale?

We process credit card-type volumes that, typically, enterprise content systems don't support. In order to achieve this, we made modifications to the technology's infrastructure, particularly to the mechanism that allows the application to "talk" to the database. We also made some changes to the standard search capabilities, allowing for high volume search results to be returned within seconds. Because we had a fully functional cloud environment already in place, we were up and live in just 45 days.

How big do you think your cloud is going to get?

There could be hundreds and millions of terabytes of data in our cloud. Disposition, and deciding what to keep and what to dispose of, will play a large role in determining capacity.

So far, our struggle has been to get our arms around the data. How do you see that playing out?

Chapter one is about putting everything where it should be. Chapter two is about learning from the information. It's through the content analysis and the predictive analytics that we can extract value from the databases and the archives.

How do you leverage big data in a strongly permissioned, large-scale environment?

In one instance, an agency had 19 organizational silos operating in their permissioned environment. We found that there were replicated business processes among many of these divisions because we're collecting, auto-classifying, and analyzing this data in the cloud. So, we were able to save the government more money by identifying and removing these redundancies.

What about the distribution of information on social sites or mobile devices?

Social media occurs in real-time more than e-mail, so that changes the breadth and depth of the information that must be captured and analyzed. More volumes of data will require more speed to process, and that's a challenge with today's technologies.

How do you find the tradeoff between openness and security?

It's about ease-of-use and minimizing cost, so if you agree to abide by security standards, like the FedRAMP standard, information stays encrypted as long as it's meant to be. Information that's meant for internal consumption can only be used in a permissions-based model. Ultimately, it will be up to our clients to decide which information should be open and which information should remain secured.

> More volumes of data will require more speed to process, and that's a challenge with today's technologies.

FIGURE 13.7 IQ Business Group

To meet the demands of big data, organizations must meet processing and storage requirements. The size and scale of these systems makes them costly to manage. Cloud computing offers an affordable solution for storage and analysis of large data sets. While CIOs are focused on minimizing the cost of storage, backups, and security, cloud computing offers affordability, flexibility, and scalability.

Many technologies have been designed specifically to analyze big data. These include data mining, crowdsourcing, pattern recognition, semantic analysis, predictive modeling, sentiment analysis, spatial analysis, visualization, and more. Data must be accessible and usable for it to have value. Having the right technology in place to capture, manage, and secure data is a good first step. e-Government integrates information from multiple and fragmented data sources to allow for advanced analytics.

Within an e-government system, data can be managed according to regulations and governance policies and procedures—ensuring that analysis and release happens in a secure manner. Features like version control, permissions, and audit history increase the accuracy and security of information.

Privacy and Security

Governments collect an inordinate amount of information from citizens. Much of this highly sensitive information is digitized and exchanged across firewalls. At the same time, citizens as consumers leave "digital shadows"— personal data left by transactions and interactions on the Internet, applications, and across other connected devices and sensors. From time spent on Facebook to purchases made, texts sent, video surveillance footage, and energy metered—big data draws on all aspects of our lives.

The information about you is much greater than the information you create yourself. This is called your **digital shadow.** And it's growing continually...

Source: IDC's Digital Universe Study, sponsored by EMC, June 2011

FIGURE 13.8: Your Digital Shadow

FIGURE 13.9: Total Government Requests for Facebook Data[16]

The U.S. Government, for example, requests data from web properties like Facebook, Google, Microsoft, and Twitter.® The map above charts the saturation of requests (in dark green), showing the density by location of data requests. In Canada, the Federal Government has put restrictions on the amount of data it collects from Canadians. For the first time in 20 years, new rules have been put in place governing the use of data gathered when Canadians visit government websites.[17] These rules, however, do not apply to data that's available on social media and other sites.

Citizens are suspicious about the ways that governments make use of their personal information. Governments will need to communicate the potential value of big data and ensure the privacy and security of personal information to build trust.

In their collection of citizen data, governments must comply with a number of privacy acts and regulations, including the Freedom of Information Acts or laws, which help to protect the privacy of citizens while building public confidence in the government as a protector of privacy. Big data will force governments to manage additional complexities in security to avoid risks like cyber-security breaches, hackers, and identity theft.

> The Utah Data Center is a data storage facility that houses extremely large amounts of data, (estimated to be as high as 12 exabytes) to support the Comprehensive National Cybersecurity Initiative (CNCI). The National Security Agency (NSA) leads operations at the facility.

[16] Derrick Harris. *"Take a look at how much the U.S. government loves requesting user data"*, Gigaom, August 27, 2013: *http://gigaom.com/2013/08/27/take-a-look-at-how-much-the-u-s-government-loves-requesting-data/* (accessed January 2014).

[17] *"Ottawa restricts use of data collected through government websites"*, CBC News, March 13, 2013: *http://www.cbc.ca/news/technology/ottawa-restricts-use-of-data-collected-through-government-websites-1.1307853* (accessed January 2014).

Alongside privacy and security, intellectual property rights are another legal issue that will need to be closely managed, especially in the case of data that is managed in the cloud. Questions about property rights and fair use will need to be addressed as data is increasingly duplicated and used in combination with other data.

The Skills Gap

The right people with the right skills are required to run big data initiatives. Due to its diversity, big data requires people with diverse skill sets to manage it. Groups that have formed for analysis bring together researchers from many disciplines, including the sciences, statistics, mathematics, medicine, astronomy, and technology. In many cases, such as the Genome Project, these skills sets come from the combined efforts of specialists in many fields.

The world's largest set of data on human genetic variation was produced by the international 1,000 Genomes Project. The data set is 200 terabytes, which is equal to 16 million file cabinets filled with text or more than 30,000 standard DVDs—a prime example of big data, where data sets become so comprehensive that few have the required skill sets or computing power to make best use of them.

There is currently a skills gap in expertise for the analysis of big data. The demand is there, and according to Gartner, it will reach 4.4 million jobs globally by 2015.[18] Strategies around big data will be developed as agencies partner with organizations in the private sector, research organizations, and educational institutions to attract and train expertise. Government culture will shift to one that rewards knowledge sharing and innovation.

Big Data in Action: Crime Prevention and Protection

While big data poses security threats, it also presents opportunities for security agencies, law enforcement, and militaries to accomplish their missions more efficiently.

FIGURE 13.10: Big Data—Highly Beneficial to Security Agencies[19]

[18] *"Gartner Reveals Top Predictions for IT Organisations and Users for 2013 and Beyond"*, Gartner Inc., October 24, 2012, *http://www.gartner.com/it/page.jsp?id=2211115* (accessed January 2014).

[19] Erin Leahy, *"The State and Local Big Data Gap"*, MeriTalk, April 29, 2013.

Big data drives intelligence-led policing, giving law enforcement agencies more effective ways of fighting and preventing crime. Law enforcement officers are using devices to collect data—from close-circuit television to cameras in police cars, surveillance cameras, and sensors—that can be analyzed to reveal patterns and threats. As criminals move their efforts online, law enforcement is better able to analyze information from a number of sources. This information can be combined and processed to expose and relate criminal activities in specific areas. Suspicious individuals or entities can be identified and tracked. Predictions can then be made based on these activities to prevent criminal activities from taking place.

e-Government combines critical data, such as criminal records and complaints, on a fully integrated platform where it can be more readily accessed, managed, and processed. Information can be shared at national and international levels to investigate and prevent terrorist activities. Being able to immediately access up-to-date information in the short term and collaborate to fight crime in the long term arms agencies with the ability to protect citizens.

> The FBI's Law Enforcement National Data Exchange (N-DEx) is a 10-terabyte data warehouse that serves 4,100 law enforcement agencies across the U.S. Their mission is to promote the national sharing of data for increased levels of collaboration to expedite crime fighting. At the same time, the data set is stored, saved, and processed for close analysis. It is a cloud service, capable of processing criminal information and returning results in fractions of a second over secure Internet links. It is also a big data application, comprised of 200 million law enforcement records and more than 1.5 billion data points.

Big Data in Action: Visualization

Visualization is one of the most valuable ways to make sense of big data. Visualization is an analytical approach that results in histograms, scatter plots, infographics, dashboards, maps, and more. It brings together disparate data and communicates complex findings in a visual format. As an approach, visualization is popular because it does not require sophisticated interpretation for understanding.

The visualization of big data gives us the ability to process, visualize, and synthesize data in highly accessible ways. One of the most popular sets of data visualization today is Google Maps. It is highly interactive, continually updated, available on any platform, and even a platform itself. Numerous geographic representations can be created using its API (see figure below).

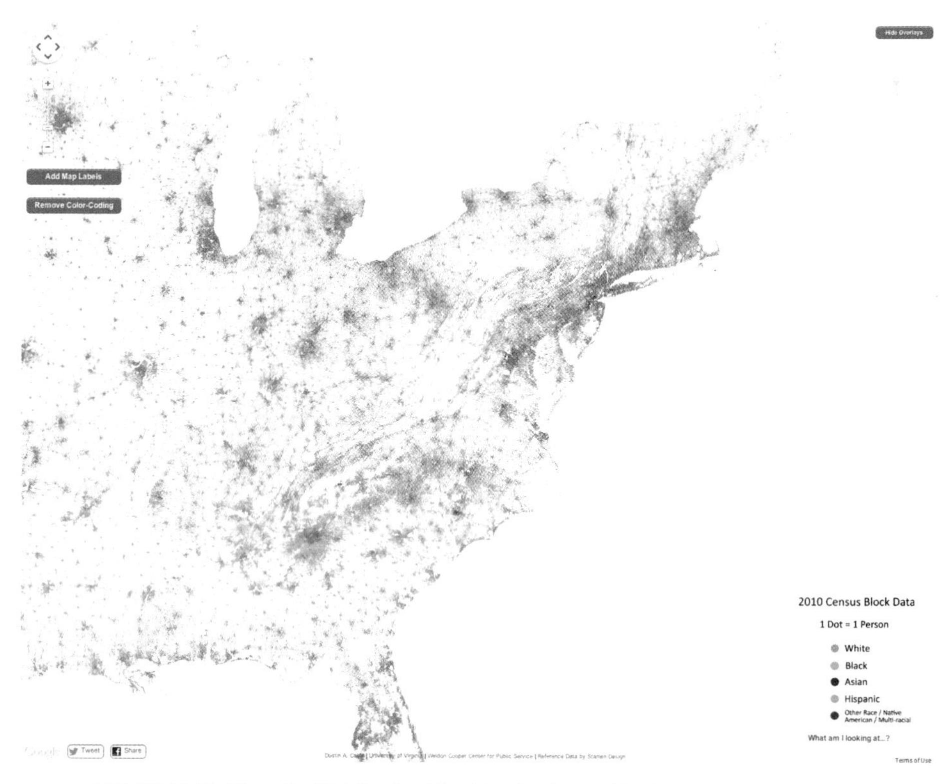

FIGURE 13.11: Diversity Distribution (One Dot Per Person) Built Using the Google Maps API[20]

Robust tools are needed to make visual sense of big data. e-Government provides access to data and management tools, and facilitates the collaborative, multidisciplinary approach needed to bring expertise together for analysis. In the following feature, Penn State University is advancing research through the interactive visualization of data.

Big Data in Action: Geospatial Data

As discussed in Chapter 12, new types of personal and location-based data will continue to grow, fueling the geospatial revolution well into the next decade and beyond. Technologies like Global Positioning System (GPS) and WiFi networks are making geospatial data more accurate and available. GPS is a global satellite navigations system, owned and operated by the Department of Defense (DoD) for the U.S. Government. As an open resource, it provides reliable positioning services to users for any place that has an unobstructed view of four or more GPS satellites. WiFi adds additional data by combining network identification with location.

[20] Dustin Cable, *"The Racial Dot Map"*, Demographics Research Group, July 2013, *http://www.coopercenter.org/demographics/Racial-Dot-Map* (accessed February 2014).

Pennsylvania State University

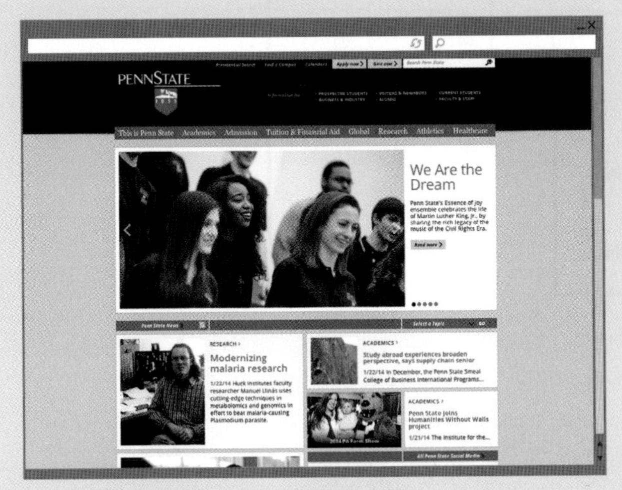

FIGURE 13.12: Penn State—A Public Research University

"[The solution] has enabled our researchers in engineering and other data intensive sciences to become much more productive when using and manipulating three dimensional representations of large datasets."

SYSTEMS ADMINISTRATOR, PENN STATE UNIVERSITY

Founded in 1855, Pennsylvania State University (Penn State) has a long and distinguished history of pursuing their tripartite mission of teaching, research, and service in the finest way possible. Today, Penn State continues this tradition with 24 locations and more than 95,000 students worldwide.

As part of Penn State's Research Computing and Cyberinfrastructure (RCC) group, close to 3,000 users visually interact with their research data through modeling applications or visualizations tools. Penn State wanted a solution that performed better than existing solutions in terms of rendering either two-dimensional (2D) or three-dimensional (3D) user interfaces. The system had to be easy to manage and operate on Penn State's current system, supporting sets of several terabytes in size. They chose a managed application solution to provide remote access to graphical applications. The solution is able to deliver complex 2D and 3D applications to users from any location, along with low cost scalability and trusted secure access over any network connection.

Offering innovative ways to approach research, the solution has enabled Penn State researchers to produce more high-quality quantity papers. The more scholarly output that researchers deliver, the higher Penn State climbs in stature as a preeminent research institution.

www.opentext.com/e-Government/PennState

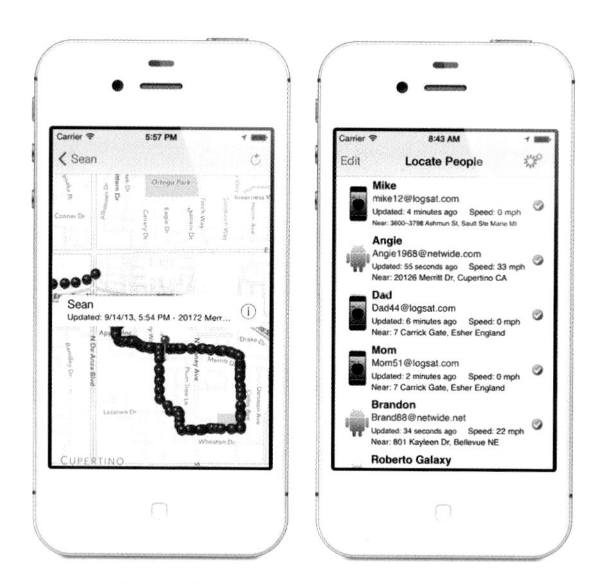

FIGURE 13.13: Family Tracker—Available on iTunes[21]

As a powerful example of visualization, geospatial data is adding new meaning to citizen interactions and transactions. Geospatial data brings context to citizen demographics, city infrastructure, physical assets, and the distribution of government programs and services. Analyzing geospatial data helps governments become more responsive. Gaps between supply and demand can be identified and resources allocated to fill these gaps. Governments can use data-driven insights to better plan and manage services, such as the transport system. For example, bus routes can be analyzed to improve public transportation and traffic congestion can be mapped in real time.

FIGURE 13.14: Streamlining Bus Routes in Africa[22]

[21] *"Family Tracker"* App, iTunes, *https://itunes.apple.com/ca/app/family-tracker/id349880412?mt=8* (accessed February 2014).

[22] Simnikiwe Mzekandaba, *"Big data may help streamline Abidjan bus routes"*, Web Africa, May 7, 2013, *http://www.itwebafrica.com/ict-and-governance/379-ivory-coast/231010-big-data-could-help-streamline-abidjan-bus-routes* (accessed February 2014).

In developing countries like Africa, cloud-based geospatial information has the potential to improve the quality of life for its citizens. Cloud-based mobile apps are game changers, making programs and services much more accessible. When data is hosted in the cloud, it can be combined with other data sets and information from social media sites to provide deeper insights. Chapter 14 explores how mobile and cloud computing are impacting governments, businesses, and citizens around the world.

As governments follow the digital shadows left by citizens, concerns about privacy and security become more pressing. Citizens need to be assured that access to their personal location data will not be collected and shared without their permission and for the wrong reasons. It is the government's mandate to protect the privacy of citizens and their personal data. For policymakers, this extends to ensuring that intellectual property rights are protected.

Budget is a big issue for any agency, but big data, if used effectively has the potential to save governments money. Applications of big data are in the nascent stage; this is an exciting time for the public sector, with increasing opportunities to collaborate with citizens and private companies to introduce new and innovative services. Investments should be made in areas of research and development to promote innovation and stimulate economic growth. Likewise, governments can add big data to school curriculums to build skill sets and human capital.

CHAPTER 14

MOBILE E-GOVERNMENT IN THE CLOUD

CHAPTER 14

Mobile e-Government in the Cloud

Mobile computing and the cloud are two of the most important new trends in IT to impact government services. When they are combined, these technologies represent a tremendous opportunity to increase civic engagement; cross boundaries, organizational silos, and constituencies; and deliver highly targeted solutions at a lower cost. This chapter examines these opportunities through examples of agencies that are applying mobile and cloud technologies as part of an e-government strategy.

A New APPtitude

The mobile industry is the fastest growing industry on the planet.[1] The personal computer has fallen of the cliff as smartphones and tablets have risen in popularity.[2] Devices like Androids,® BlackBerrys,® iPhones, iPads, and Nokia® smartphones have had a profound effect on the way people access information, resources, and each other.

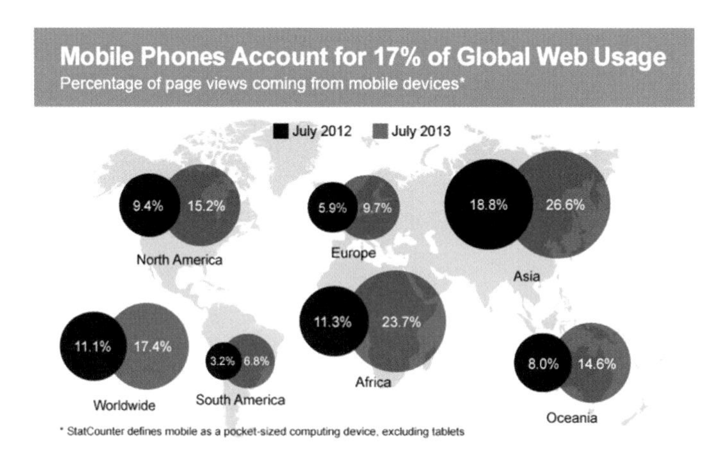

FIGURE 14.1: The Mobile Internet: Mobile Phones Account for 17% of Global Web Usage[3]

[1] Mobile Marketing Watch, *"Major Mobile Trends Show Global Mobile Industry is now the Fastest Growing Market in the World"*, MobileMarketingWatch.com, *http://www.mobilemarketingwatch.com/major-mobile-trends-show-global-mobile-industry-is-now-thefastest-growing-market-in-the-world-16840/* (accessed 3 Jun. 2013).

[2] Chetan Sharma,*"2013 Mobile Industry Predictions Survey"*, Chetan Sharma Consulting, January 2013, *http://www.chetansharma.com/MobilePredictions2013.htm* (accessed May 2013).

[3] Felix Richter, *"Mobile Phones Account for 17% of Global Web Usage"*, Statista, August 20, 2013, *http://www.statista.com/topics/779/mobile-internet/chart/1380/mobile-web-usage/* (accessed February 2014).

Currently, 91 percent of all people on the planet have a mobile phone and 50 percent of these people use mobile as their primary Internet source.[4] IDC predicts that in 2015, for the first time ever, there will be more people accessing the Internet on mobile devices than on personal computers.[5]

The mobile market is being dominated by the rapid-fire development of mobile apps. Mobile apps, discrete programs designed to solve a specific problem, have made our lives easier as well as more dynamic, social, and fun. According to research, 82 billion apps worldwide were downloaded in 2013 and by 2017 there will be more than 200 billion downloads per year.[6] Cloud computing makes access to mobile apps as straightforward as a series of finger taps.

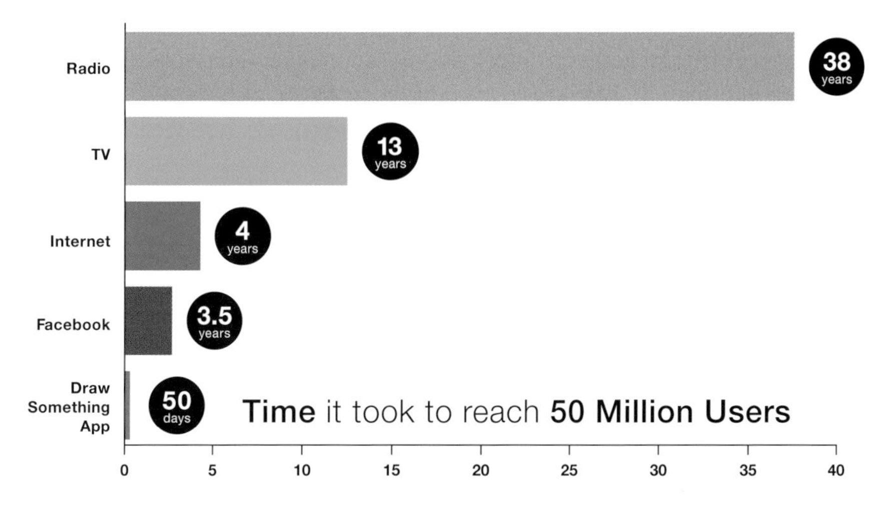

FIGURE 14.2: The Agility of Mobile App Development

The combination of cloud and mobile computing has dramatically changed market dynamics in all sectors. Disruptive technologies are transformative. Pioneers in government like the City of Barcelona are capitalizing on the opportunities that mobility presents. The U.S. federal government directed each major federal agency to make two key customer services available on mobile devices by 2013. Looking ahead at worldwide government IT spending priorities, mobile technologies, IT modernization, and cloud computing are the top three areas of focus for investment.[7]

[4] *"Infographic: 2013 Mobile Growth Statistics"*, Digital Buzz Blog, Tuesday Oct 1, 2013, *http://www.digitalbuzzblog.com/infographic-2013-mobile-growth-statistics/* (accessed January 2014)

[5] Frank Gens, *"IDC Predictions 2013: Competing on the 3rd Platform,"* IDC, 2012, *http://www.idc.com/research/Predictions13/downloadable/238044.pdf* (accessed February 2014).

[6] Karl Whitfield, *"Fast growth of apps user base in booming Asia Pacific market"*, Portio Research, March 2013, *http://www.portioresearch.com/en/blog/2013/fast-growth-of-apps-user-base-in-booming-asia-pacific-market.aspx* (accessed February 2014).

[7] Christine Arcaris and Rishi Sood, *"User Survey Analysis: IT Spending Priorities in Government, Worldwide, 2013"*, Gartner, Inc., January 25, 2013.

"The "e" in "e-government" stands for "empowerment". Mobile technology has achieved this. With only a few taps on a smartphone screen, magical things happen—laws, services, records, and processes turn into something very simple and user friendly, making life easier for everyone. For governments to be most effective, services should be 100 percent mobile-focused from the outset."

SERGI JEREZ, DIRECTOR OF MOBILE, EGOVERNMENT Y DATA, AJUNTAMENT DE BARCELONA (CITY OF BARCELONA)

Hyper-mobile connectivity is now affordable and widespread. The key question now is how this new social, mobile, and cloud-based culture will influence the public sector. Mobile technology promises more efficient access to information, resources, and services. The explosion of access points to information that mobile introduces, however, also serves to complicate programs and policymaking. Mobile information in all its formats needs to be securely managed.

Mobile Government

Mobility makes government more accessible, affordable, agile, collaborative, and convenient. As we have illustrated throughout this book, governments can drive efficiency and productivity internally, while increasing the effectiveness of their services externally. The case for mobile government is driven by the ubiquity of mobile use, opportunities to improve service delivery, improved transparency through increased access to information, and new products and services that can be co-created with citizens.

Workforce Productivity

Mobility enhances productivity. Using mobile devices to access work-related applications and information employees can stay productive, even on the go. In a Forrester Consulting survey of IT decision-makers, 76 percent cited increased employee responsiveness and decision-making speed as observed benefits of mobile access, while 47 percent believe they have increased productivity.[8] In another report, mobile-related increases in productivity were calculated to potentially offset retirements, resulting in $25 billion in salary and pension savings.[9]

Mobile technology empowers civil servants to perform their jobs more effectively. Mobile combines remote location and preferences in a time-relevant manner to create targeted decision-making opportunities. It makes these abilities available to a much larger set of users than ever before possible. In the feature below, Belgian Railways is exploring new models for delivering public services, using mobile devices to keep employees and customers better informed in real time.

[8] *"The Expanding Role of Mobility in the Workplace,"* Forrester Research and Cisco Systems, February 2012.

[9] William D. Eggers and Joshua Jaffe, *"Gov on the go: Boosting public sector productivity by going mobile,"* Deloitte University Press, Feb 2013, *http://dupress.com/articles/gov-on-the-go/?id=us:el:dc:govgo:crosspromo_mobilemicro:fed:021913* (accessed Feb 2013).

Belgian Railways

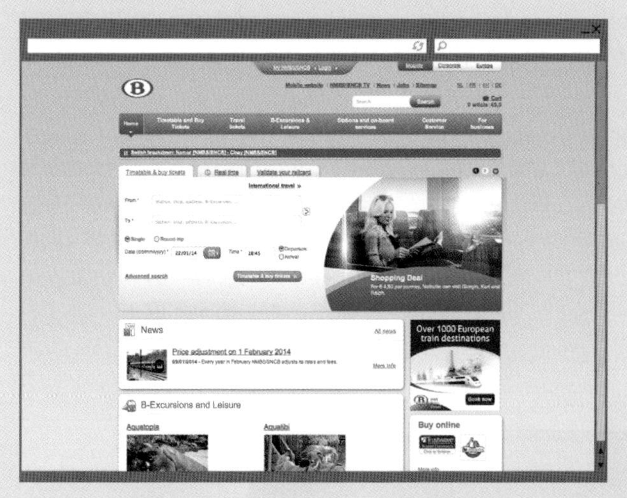

FIGURE 14.3: Belgian Railways

"Based on centralized information, more than 5,000 drivers are able to access the latest bulletins and record service information on their mobile devices in real time. So this means that information can be pushed directly to our drivers' devices based on their profile, significantly improving our efficiency and response rates."

STÉPHANE HAELTERMAN, PROGRAM MANAGER, BELGIAN RAILWAYS

Belgian Railways, headquartered in Brussels, employs more than 21,000 staff, providing transportation for more than 200 million passengers and handling over 60 million tons of freight each year. In total, they operate over 550 stations and stops, using around 1,500 locomotives and numerous other pieces of rolling stock and infrastructure. With operations and maintenance taking place around the clock, not only do Belgian Railways provide services based on their own fleet, track, and other infrastructure, they also provide services and maintenance for high-speed, international services, including Eurostar™ and Thalys.

Belgian Railways faces a complex set of business drivers that range from cost optimization while delivering customer service through to punctuality with uncompromising safety, against a backdrop of a maturing workforce and a new generation of employees coming on board. To satisfy its directives, Belgian Railways set out a vision for its digital future where all business processes would be content-enabled, removing much of the paper that flowed through the organization.

Belgian Railways has standardized its processes and information across the organization on an e-government platform, with expected savings of €30 million per year (close to $41 million USD). Around 2.5 million documents were added to the system in the first year, growing by some 1.3 million each year to over 7.5 million after five years. With the foundational platform now established and providing fast, accurate information access—in context—staff have the confidence that information accessed is the single source of the truth. This has led to the possibility to grow the use and application of the technology. As Belgian Railways deals with more information, program manager Stéphane Haelterman is building the vision for their enterprise information management journey to achieve a single version of the truth.

www.opentext.com/e-Government/BelgianRailways

Mobile Case Management

Applications represent the customer-facing component of e-government. Although terminology in this area varies, Forrester Research Inc. defines them as Smart Process Applications (SPA). SPAs are designed to support business activities that are people intensive, highly variable, loosely structured, and subject to frequent change.[10] Delivered in the cloud, SPAs give mobile users the ability to access processes under consideration from mobile devices.

SPAs enable the launch of integrated service apps to support government workers in the field. Government caseworkers are often burdened with managing hundreds of clients and spending a good portion of their time on the road, visiting clients. They need current information, drawing on every piece of content related to a client's case. Mobility supports remote offices or work, which increases productivity and efficiency in the field. Response times are increased while project cycle, travel costs, and equipment expenses are reduced.

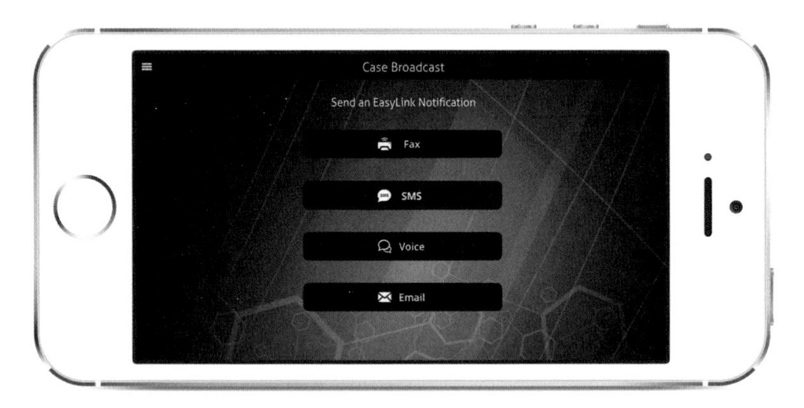

FIGURE 14.4: Mobile Case Management

With Mobile Case Management, public servants can quickly create cases, track progress, and use built-in features like the camera and Global Positioning System (GPS) to support the process. Integrated service apps for workflow, content management, portals, and social collaboration are combined to collectively process the completion of a case or unit of work. Issues can be dealt with as they arise and information about a case updated on the fly. Case-related information is centralized and secured on an e-government system. Costs are reduced when caseworkers are more responsive and information is accurate.

[10] Andrew Bartels and Connie Moore, et al., *"Smart Process Applications Fill A Big Business Gap"*, Forrester Research, November 2012.

Citizen Engagement

Governments will always be required to give citizens access to information. As mobile adoption increases, governments will have to give citizens access to content in every format across every kind of device. This is the defining characteristic of digital content today—it is fragmented, mashed up, delivered across many channels, and accessible at any time in any place. Mobility feeds the pace and complexity of content that is created and shared.

As we have seen in previous chapters, mobile technology increases opportunities for civic engagement. With the convergence of geospatial technologies and location data, government can deliver information and services directly to citizens. Forward-thinking governments have developed mobile apps that provide direct and personalized access to information and services.

Mobile Industry

As discussed previously, many functions of government could be provided through partnerships with the private sector. New engagement models include government partnership with citizens to co-create and produce solutions. We introduced this in the chapter on *Open Government and Crowdsourcing* using examples of citizens accessing datasets made available by governments to develop applications and improve the lives of citizens in a multitude of ways. FlightAware makes use of government information to provide services for citizens.

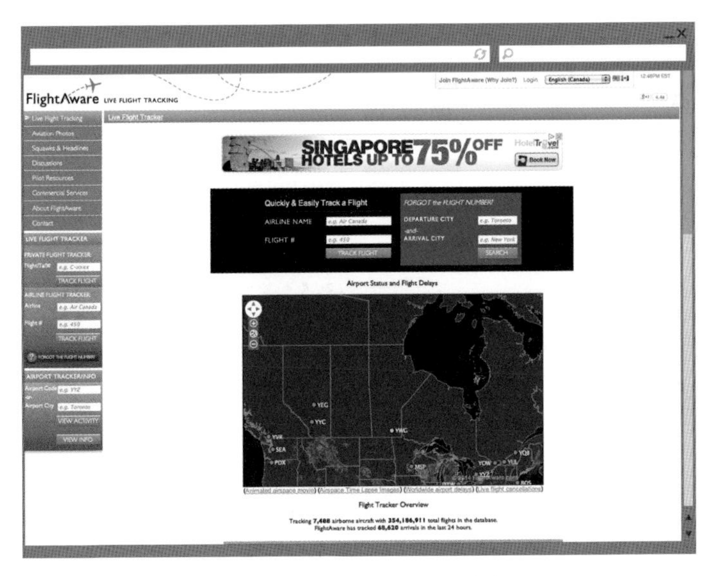

FIGURE 14.5: FlightAware Website

FlightAware is a service based on processing live flight data and airport status from publicly available Federal Aviation Administration (FAA) information. It provides live flight data, airport delays, fuel prices, weather maps, flight planning, routes, navigation charts, as well as aviation news to over three million users.

Mobile technologies are key enablers for citizen-to-government collaboration. Many governments understand this and are hosting contests, hackathons, and appethons to engage citizens, foster innovation and creativity, and reap the rewards of getting closer to their citizens.

Hackathons and appethons are contests in which government agencies, developers, computer programmers, designers, students, statisticians, and librarians (and anyone else who might be interested in software development) collaborate to create applications within a designated period of time. These events are incredibly effective at building community and deepening relationships between citizens, communities, and private organizations.

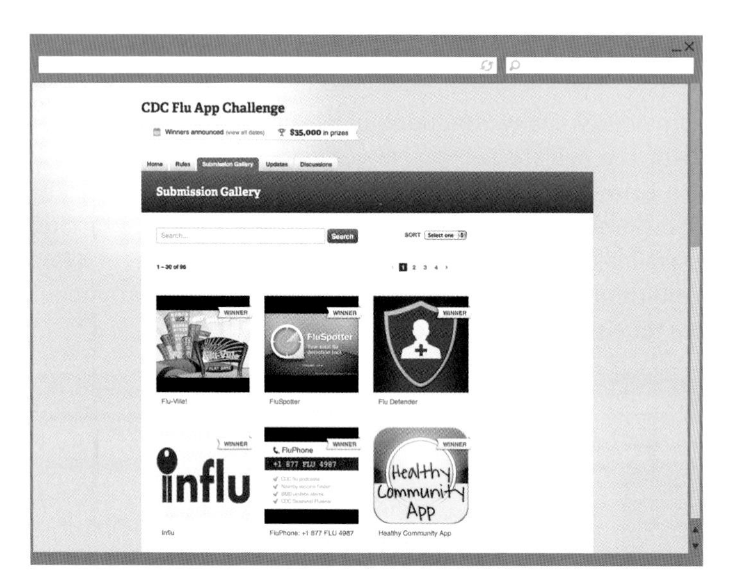

FIGURE 14.6: CDC Flu App Challenge Winners

Appethons are happening at local and national levels. The U.S. Center for Disease Control and Prevention (CDC), for example, sponsored a *Flu App Challenge* based on flu data that was available to the public. The outcome was the app "Flu-Ville!" which leverages the CDC's influenza activity report and has players manage outbreaks of the flu in their own fictional cities. Likewise, NASA hosts an *International Space Apps Challenge*. The event encourages younger generations to help governments solve key challenges with collectively developed, future-based solutions. In both cases, the traditional structures of government are infused with new ideas and approaches to solving problems, often by younger, more tech-savvy generations. Solutions are typically developed more quickly than they would have been by traditional approaches.

In Canada, a program called the *Canadian Open Data Experience* (CODE) challenges students, technology innovators, developers, and open data enthusiasts from all across Canada to transform valuable government data into useful apps. The CODE initiative features the first national Open Data hackathon in Canada as a 48-hour competition hosted by XMG, one of the largest independant mobile gaming studios in Canada. A forum for innovation and entrepreneurship, CODE will stretch the boundaries of open data and enable technologists to share ideas, invent, research the market, and commercialize their ideas.

The *Great Canadian Appathon* (GCA) is a 48-hour game design and development competition open to Canadian college and university students. Students design and develop a mobile game according to a designated theme. The event is good for industry and for students who have the chance to network with members of Canada's growing gaming industry.

FIGURE 14.7: The Great Canadian Appethon

1.USA.gov hosts *Hack Day* events in Washington, D.C., New York City, San Francisco, and San Diego. Over 120 people have attended in the past, exploring ways to use 1.USA.gov data to help people find useful and interesting government information. The *White House Hackathon* invites programmers and tech experts to the White House to spend the day working alongside members of the White House development team. Results from previous hackathons ranged from a time-lapse visualization of zip codes where petitions are being signed to a tool that lets users create an embeddable thermometer showing how many signatures their petition needs.

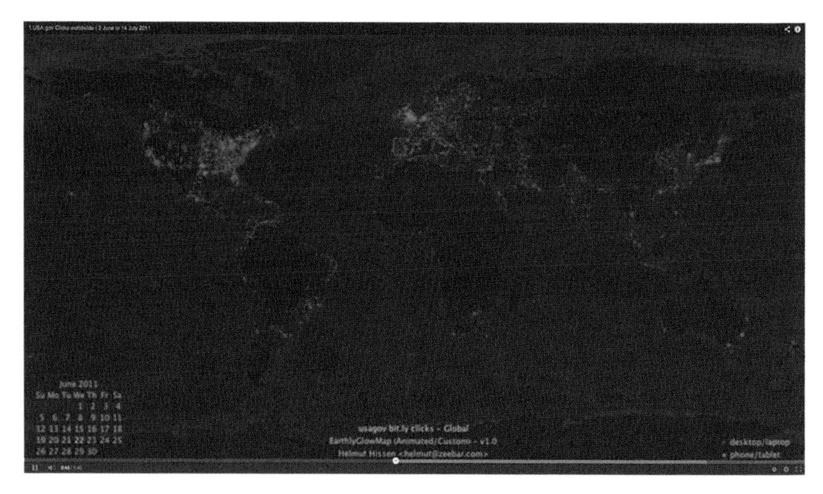

FIGURE 14.8: An Animation Created at the 1.USA.gov Hack Day—Showing Clicks on 1.USA.Gov Links from June 2 through July 14[11]

Apps für Deutschland is a nation-wide contest in Germany that recognizes the best Internet and mobile applications developed using federal data. The site showcases innovations and also demonstrates a commitment by public authorities to make data available for reuse.

FIGURE 14.9: Apps für Deutschland

[11] *"Projects Created at the 1.USA.gov Hack Day"* 1.USA.gov Blog, *http://blog.usa.gov/post/8522383948/projects-created-at-the-1-usa-gov-hack-day* (accessed February 2014).

Open Data Day brings together citizens in cities around the world to write applications, create visualizations, and publish analyses using open data to encourage the adoption of open data policies by the world's local, regional, and national governments.

Hackathons like the ones mentioned here are catalysts for change. They are a growing form of civic engagement and crowdsourcing potential solutions. Knowledge is applied to data in new, radical ways. Education is advanced as students experiment, share best practices, and are exposed to entrepreneurs and industry experts. The economy benefits from the production of new products and services. Citizens benefit through the opportunity to share ideas and engage with government decision makers. Communities benefit with solutions that are usually directly applicable to their local environments. Governments are the lucky recipients of creative concepts to help them become more efficient and stay relevant.

"It's great to see the launch of *Apps für Deutschland*, with three federal agencies, Berlin, and Bremen leading the way in contributing open data and with the opportunity for developers to show politicians, officials, and the public new and innovative ways to generate economic and social value from open government data."

ANDREW STOTT, UK TRANSPARENCY BOARD AND FORMER DIRECTOR OF DATA.GOV.UK

The Cloud and Distributed Government

Both cloud and mobile computing provide a technical framework for creating a more distributed government model. In contrast to the outdated command-and-control systems of government, distributed government offers benefits like lower costs, better delivery of services, greater transparency, and more direct access to citizens.

The adoption of cloud computing inside the private sector "continues to increase ... driven by economic conditions and a shift from capital expenditure to operational expenditure, as well as potentially more important factors such as faster deployment and reduced risk." In a survey conducted by Gartner Inc., 50 percent of respondents across all industries reported plans to adopt a public and private cloud-based services contract within the next 12 months.[12]

[12] Christine Arcaris,*"Gartner Says Worldwide Government IT Spending Flat in 2013"*,Gartner Inc., June 2013, *http://www.gartner.com/newsroom/id/2518815* (accessed February 2014).

Cloud computing by definition is a disruptive transformation of IT toward a service-based economy, driven by economic, technological, and social conditions. Cloud computing services are delivered on demand over the Internet from massive data centers. A key benefit—and the premise for how the cloud is revolutionizing IT—is the ability to "rent" computing services from a third-party provider rather than owning and maintaining physical infrastructure. In this way, cloud computing is like the traditional utility services which are consumed as a metered, pay-as-you-go service. Cloud computing demonstrates a transformation in the way governments can acquire and use technology. Key benefits are lower total cost of ownership and investments in IT, quick deployment, and access to targeted expertise and support.

TYPES OF CLOUD SERVICES:

A Public Cloud refers to services provided over the Internet, in which infrastructure or applications are hosted by a cloud- service provider on the service provider's premises.

In a Private Cloud services are hosted on a private platform in the organization's own data center.

A Hybrid Cloud is a combination of public and private clouds.

The challenges that government organizations will need to overcome in their adoption of cloud computing are security, compatibility with existing IT infrastructure, privacy, and overall performance.

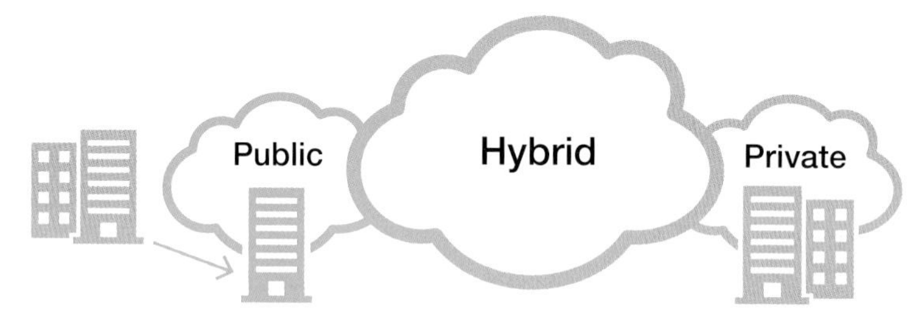

FIGURE 14.10: Types of Cloud Services

As mobile usage increases, so will our use of cloud computing. There is a strong link between mobile accessibility and the cloud. While mobility promises to increase our access to content in all formats, the cloud is able to handle this demand for volumes of information easily and cost effectively. The U.S. Department of the Interior is using the cloud to host its e-government system across the department to ensure information governance and value for taxpayer dollars.

U.S. Department of the Interior

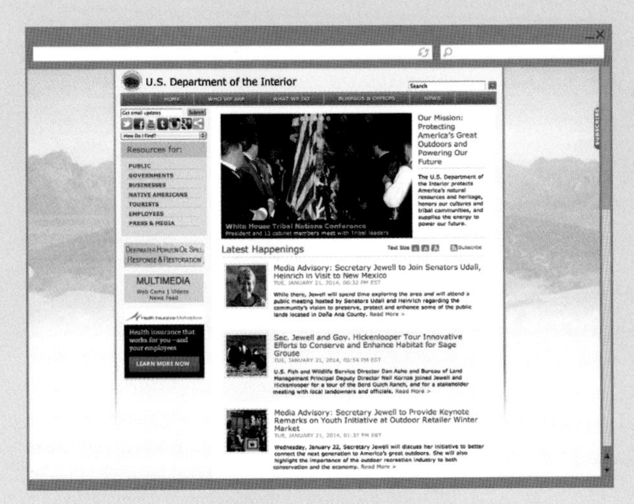

FIGURE 14.11: U.S. Department of the Interior

> "We are very pleased with how effortless it has been to deploy the EES project for the DOI. This project serves as a successful model for other government agencies looking to move their critical business information to the cloud."
>
> **MICHAEL BECK, PRESIDENT AND CHIEF EXECUTIVE OFFICER, IQ BUSINESS GROUP, FISMA-COMPLIANT CLOUD SOLUTION PROVIDER**

The Department of the Interior (DOI) is the U.S.'s principal conservation agency. It consists of 14 bureaus, and these bureaus range from the National Park Service to the Bureau of Indian Affairs to the Bureau of Land Management, Reclamation—so the Agency is managing land, minerals, and parks and national areas. DOI is a cabinet-level agency that manages America's vast natural and cultural resources.

The Agency's eMail Enterprise Records and Document Management Systems (eERDMS) is helping the DOI to optimize the management of information assets, accelerate business objectives, and reduce cost and risk. Hosted in the cloud, EES is the primary system supporting the Department's overall eERDMS Program, which will help to ensure records, information management, and legal readiness for the Department and bring together a collaborative and integrated mobile workforce for the 21st century. This single, enterprise-wide system supports the Agency's 92,000 employees and contractors, with capacity for upwards of 30,000 additional users, making it the largest cloud-based records and information governance program in the Federal Government.

The eERDMS program is a part of DOI's 2010 Information Technology Transformation (ITT) initiative to provide employees with technology designed to help reduce waste and cut costs, providing the taxpayer $100 million in annual savings from 2016 to 2020, for a cumulative total savings of $500 million. The eERDMS program has already achieved impressive milestones, as it is believed to be the first 100 percent email capture with auto classification in the federal marketplace, as well as the first Federal Information Security Management Act of 2002 (FISMA) moderate compliant, software-as-a-service (SaaS) cloud solution that addresses an entire Cabinet Federal Agency.

www.opentext.com/e-Government/USDOI

Department of Interior (DOI)

What follows is an excerpt from an interview between John Montel, Deputy E-records Officer for the Department of the Interior and Tom Jenkins, Executive Chairman of OpenText.

TOM JENKINS: You have a very novel solution at DOI. Can you give us an idea of the magnitude of your deployment?

JOHN MONTEL: *We have approximately 2,300 offices nationwide and the DOI can scale up to 240,000 employees, including volunteers, during the summertime and national events. We manage over a million square feet of offshore water area and 20 percent of the land in the U.S., and generate $12 billion in annual revenue. We are very large, very diverse, and very mobile; almost 41 percent of our entire workforce is mobile or teleworking. Our IT requirements revolve around supporting Department, Bureau, and citizen needs.*

The sheer scale of your project was extensive and very complex. Can you describe it for us?

Our project was a part of an IT Transformation initiative that started in 2010 when the Department was seeking to consolidate its IT Infrastructure and centralize its information systems, including email. A large focus was to leverage cloud technologies. We amassed over a billion and a half emails—70 million per month—and we have over an Exabyte of electronic information that we were looking to initially incorporate into the system.

I understand you have a big e-discovery component.

The original program was and will always be to support records management. However this includes being responsive to the American people and the government. We have approximately 480 attorneys in the Department of the Interior, and we're handling approximately 5,500 Freedom of Information Act (FOIA) cases a year, along with other types of discovery and legal matters. One of the benefits of our solution is the ability to search our collection of records in support of these types of needs. We wanted a technology that could not only capture content but provide this level of discovery where appropriate.

How did you communicate the value of this undertaking to your executive team?

We quickly realized that the Department was spending large sums of money obtaining discovery information from different systems. By centralizing our systems we were able to demonstrate that for half the money the Department was spending historically, we could support the entire Department with the added capability of all the assets eERDMS brings to bare.

You've done this as a cloud implementation. What are your lessons learned?

Bringing the technology in-house would have been cost prohibitive. The cloud as a solution is flexible; we can connect to our cloud securely from anywhere including mobile devices. Secondly, it allows us to quickly incorporate other technologies so it is not limiting. From a security perspective, we tend to look at protecting the cloud first then the data at the application layer. As one protects data in this manner, there is an inherent trust that comes with the cloud provider. The U.S. government and many commercial companies have done a very good job of securing information based on federal NIST standards and policies.

We're shifting from managing the device to managing the data. How did you shift your focus from the cloud to the data?

Business is moving very quickly today. We have all these technologies—from texting to social media to email to phones to fax—all on the web. We need to be able to respond in a moment's notice to our employees, citizen, and mission business needs. So the data has to follow the business process and be available to the individual regardless of location or device. In whatever we do, we have to support not only our mobile workforce, but also the 90 million people who visit us every year.

> As one protects data in this manner, there is an inherent trust that comes with the cloud provider.

Driving the Evolution of Government Apps

Using the Internet to access information and programs has enabled the development of fast, easy, and lightweight apps. The web as an operating system, combined with mobility, social technologies and the cloud, will have a lasting impact on e-government as an increasing amount of apps function to replace monolithic and siloed legacy systems.

Like popular cloud applications, lightweight apps require access and the exchange of content to be applicable and effective. Delivered when needed, they run on a mobile device but are not stored on a mobile device. In the future, the array of functions available in a mature enterprise application could be deconstructed into its sub-functions, which could be easily installed as downloadable apps. Hundreds of specific functional apps might be deployed to duplicate the functionality of a single software application.

FIGURE 14.12: Mobile Apps in Government

Mobile apps will drive the evolution of e-government. Inside the firewall, a collection of specific and targeted apps will replace legacy apps. Public servants will be able to download and personalize these apps on their mobile devices. A government-wide app store will give IT the ability to monitor, certify, and administer apps and their data, and understand better how they are used.

Building a Government App Store

The consumer mobile experience has redefined citizen satisfaction and paved the way for user adoption by setting expectations around convenience, personalization, and ease of use. Government organizations of the future will focus on developing mission-critical apps and making these available from an e-government architecture that allows for the development of mobile apps and distribution in a private-cloud. e-Government makes apps infrastructure possible by providing a set of integrated tools for managing process and information apps, while guaranteeing security and privacy.

In essence, every agency that maintains a firewall and a proprietary repository of content could create a private cloud apps environment. Self-service kiosks would provide a set of very personalized apps unique to each government department or agency.

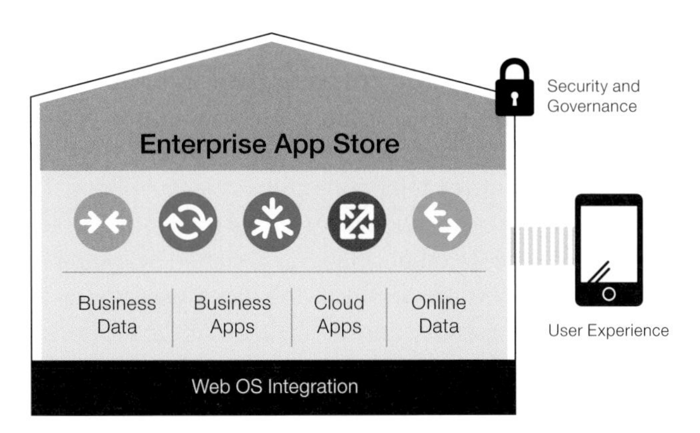

FIGURE 14.13: App Store Infrastructure

Distinctions between private and public app stores will be defined by security and regulatory requirements, especially in the context of the Bring Your Own Device (BYOD) trend. As personal and professional content becomes enmeshed, government information will need to be managed with precision so that a device cannot be wiped clean if lost—only the app and the enterprise content associated with it. For this reason, features like archiving and the control of content will occur through a secure e-government system and the app, rather than on the device itself. An e-government platform provides a solid foundation for enterprise-grade apps by delivering a secure repository that can be coupled with a rapid app authoring and deployment framework, or Smart Process Applications.

Security and the BYOD Trend

The BYOD trend is infiltrating government offices. A Forrester survey has identified that in 2012, 59 percent of U.S. government employees were using their own personal devices at work.[13] In 2013, the U.S. government issued security approval for public sector organizations to offer BYOD guidelines for employees to access government data and applications using their own mobile devices. While momentum is building for BYOD programs in government, guidelines are only just being established and many lack consistency across different departments of government.

While mobile devices promise to increase personal productivity and enhance collaboration, combining personal data and work information presents serious security threats. Government organizations need to focus on how to minimize the risk of sensitive data falling into the wrong hands when devices go astray or security breaches occur. From a technical perspective, risk can be reduced by building and managing apps on secure platforms and making apps available using a secure enterprise app center or store.

[13] *"Bring Your Own Device: How Do State and Local Governments Address the Proliferation of Employee Devices?"* Forrester Research and Cisco, 2012, *https://www.cisco.com/web/strategy/docs/employee_devices_final.pdf* (accessed February 2014).

As mobile devices and tablets are adopted by government organizations to help improve productivity, security will be a growing concern. Security on a mobile device is a combination of security over-the-air, over-the-wire, and permission-based access to the e-government system. When information is transmitted to a mobile device, it follows an extremely secure and proprietary protocol used by telephone and wireless vendors. If this information is from a secure e-government repository, security works to identify a user as a trusted member who is permitted access based on permissions assigned by system administrators. Mobile platforms will verify permissions much in the same way a web browser checks access permissions to an e-government system or intranet. As data is transmitted or collaborative spaces accessed, the platform ensures that version history, audit capabilities, reports, security, and permissions contained with the system translates directly to the mobile device. The security of an e-government system is discussed in greater detail in Chapter 3.

Who Owns the Data?

In the cloud, an organization's data and applications reside on the "cloud cluster," a centralized network of computers and services owned by the cloud provider. But who owns the data? Organizations in the public sector must maintain strict control over their data to protect against liability and comply with regulations to ensure business continuity. Privacy is a key concern. While data that a cloud-computing provider collects about its users can improve service delivery, citizens and businesses today are concerned about abuses and violation of privacy, especially in light of regulations like the USA PATRIOT Act, which increases government access to information.

Along with privacy and compliance, intellectual property is another key concern when it comes to cloud services. In some cases, the cloud provider owns the infrastructure or the applications, while the user owns the data. But this delineation is not always clear. Open source software often combines data and code, and it is not always clear who owns rights to what.

While mobile devices and cloud computing are paving the way for new opportunities and dramatic increases in productivity and efficiency, widespread usage must be metered with the robust security and privacy mechanisms inherent in an e-government system. In the feature below, e-government provides a flexible, reliable, and scalable infrastructure for the government's needs in a private cloud.

Bundesrechenzentrum (BRZ)

The Federal Computing Center (BRZ) is the IT service provider of the Austrian public administration. With 1,200 employees and a total annual turnover of 265.3 million euro, the BRZ successfully develops and provides e-government services for ministries, universities, social security providers, and public organizations. The BRZ deploys 320 IT processes, equips 1,200 locations throughout Austria with infrastructure, and services about 30,000 workplaces.

In 2000, the land and commercial registers of the Austrian Ministry of Justice were a typical example of process fragmentation. While the land registry data had been managed digitally since the 1980s, the original documents remained in the physical archives of courthouses and were inaccessible within processes. Moreover, the Ministry of Justice incurred the huge costs of archive maintenance and the risk of losing original documents. In 2004, the BRZ decided to address the issue by implementing an Enterprise Content Management (ECM) solution.

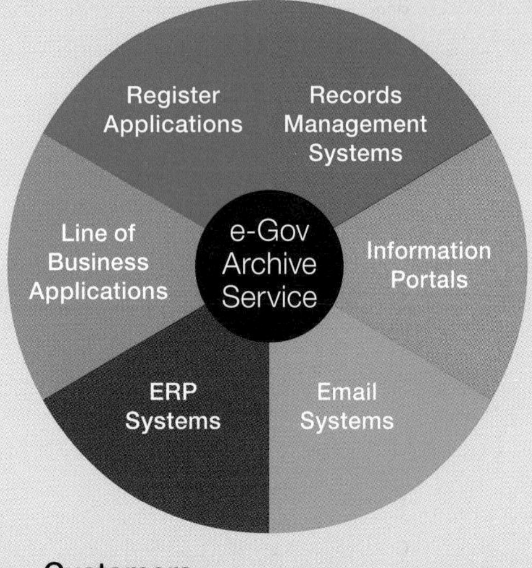

Customers

- Tax and Customs
- Administrative Courts
- Justice
- Universities
- Accounting Agency
- Federal HR Management

Documents

- Balance Sheets
- Contracts
- Evidences
- Notifications
- Invoices
- Data Archiving
- Employee Files
- Print Files

FIGURE 14.14: Cloud-Based ECM at BRZ

As the pilot study for the Land Registry was implemented, BRZ received more requests from administrations to manage documents electronically and integrate processes. In response, BRZ built a scalable ECM infrastructure called the "eGov Archive Service"—the first-ever Austrian private ECM-cloud service. Today, it provides a robust platform for 12 government customers, 40 government applications, more than 10 ERP systems, and mailing systems. The eGOV Archive Service manages 45 terabytes (TB) of data or 400 million objects, serves approximately 1 million transactions per day, and is accessed by 30,000 users (tax auditors, judges, police, customs officials, HR staff, and accountants) and potentially every Austrian citizen. Services include managing, accessing, routing, and searching to legally-compliant archiving of all kinds of documents and tight integration with line-of-business and Enterprise Resource Planning (ERP) systems for a comprehensive cloud solution.

CHAPTER 15

STRATEGIES FOR CHANGE MANAGEMENT

CHAPTER 15

Strategies for Change Management

"The biggest barrier to innovation in digital engagement is not technology, but culture and lack of imagination."[1]

For governments to stay relevant they must continually re-invent themselves. They must create an environment in which innovation thrives. They should be ready to take risks, follow coherent strategies and effective leadership, and define new models of engagement, and they also must be ready for a substantial shift in culture built on openness, inspiration, and trust. Business problems must be keenly examined and new processes created to solve them fearlessly and with imagination.

An enterprise or "whole of government" strategy is a key ingredient to government transformation based on an e-government infrastructure that delivers secure and integrated information and services. This strategy must be guided by processes, principles, and standards—and participatory, transformational leadership. While in the private sector the element of competition drives innovation, strong leadership plays a key role in driving innovation in government.

"Open Data is Canada's new natural resource. The possibilities for using this data are as infinite as our imaginations. I look forward to seeing what innovative and entrepreneurial Canadians are able to create with this newly accessible information. Part of what I'm doing is culture change. The culture of government—any government, any political party, any jurisdiction in the world—you have a certain amount of culture that is "hoard the information," information being power. We are trying to break that down."

TONY CLEMENT, PRESIDENT OF THE TREASURY BOARD, GOVERNMENT OF CANADA, POSTMEDIA, JANUARY 3, 2012

[1] Malcolm Turnbull, *"Australian Minister Calls for Innovation in Digital Media"*, FutureGov Summit Australia, December 2013, *http://www.futuregov.asia/articles/2013/dec/04/australian-minister-calls-innovation-digital-gover/* (accessed February 2014).

Transformational Leadership

The operations of e-government could not be achievable without strong leadership based on a coherent strategy. A strategy accounts for cultural diversity and technology infrastructure challenges while supporting engagement across government departments and partners. A transformational leader has to overcome outmoded government structures and old management styles to empower public servants to self-direct, make decisions, experiment, generate ideas, and take risks. Individuals and teams should be rewarded for outstanding performance. This fosters a sense of pride and ownership. The focus is more on leadership than it is on management.

Building Capacity

Transformational governments need to build capacity by bringing together people with specific skill sets to collaborate on projects—including those in private-sector organizations. A second way to build capacity is through better human capital management, specifically by offering ways for current civil servants to develop the skills required by future models of government. This would also improve overall performance. A third way to improve capacity is to adopt the recruitment and retention practices of the private sector to attract and retain talent. Finally, building up communities of practice facilitated by e-government technologies promotes access to proven approaches and preserves knowledge.

Assessing (and Taking) Risks

Strong leadership directs transformation. To effect change, government leaders should be willing to take risks and redefine processes. IT issues need to be addressed and a risk assessment completed. Where does the largest cost and risk exist? This is typically the starting point for many projects in both the public and private sectors. Significant concerns are interruption of service, disruption, and cycles that outlive the tenure of some leaders.

> The Canada School of Public Service is using technology to modernize learning and facilitate flexible courses for learners. Over 100 civil servants launch an online learning activity at the school every hour.
>
> **SOURCE: GOVERNMENT OF CANADA'S BLUEPRINT 2020**

Redefining Processes

Moving away from traditional structures, practices, and solutions often requires starting from scratch in redefining processes. Effective e-government leaders add strategic value by driving the development of next-generation processes. Governments can use e-government to rapidly create new processes that support customer service—within hours—without requiring IT support or software development skills. By combining well-structured modules with pre-built components, an application-factory approach allows a manager to build new processes easily. Alternately, an existing process can be used as a template and modified to suit business needs across customer service. This means that staff can be creative in anticipating service requirements and designing ways to address them. An on-demand environment is supported by a flexible e-government infrastructure, new technologies, and the ability to re-engineer evolving customer service processes.

Enterprise Architecture

Enterprise architecture provides a framework for organizational change and includes plans for transitioning to future government models. Before resources are committed to implementing change, enterprise architecture identifies capability and risk. Enterprise architecture should outline ways in which data and information can be integrated with services effectively. Data integration must be reliable, secure, and accessible. Government enterprise architecture helps to ensure the interoperability of systems and the sharing of information resources across agencies. e-Government systems across the public service support digitization, data integration, and records and information management.

New Models of Engagement

Collaborative e-government technologies facilitate the free flow of ideas and the exchange of knowledge. To truly transform, governments will have to create networked environments based on new engagement models to better serve the public and government customers. Government relationships are complex and difficult to manage, yet they offer a way to apply resources to projects that are beyond a public sector organization's scope. This dynamic requires a substantial shift in culture. How to create shifts in culture and support technology adoption are outlined in the feature below, in the excerpt from an interview with ClearCadence, based on their experience with change management in government organizations.

Clear Cadence

ClearCadence provides their clients with innovative and cost-effective business solutions through the efficient deployment and integration of information technology. The Company partners with large government agencies to re-evaluate, re-define, and improve their processes.

What follows is an excerpt from an interview with David Dye, Co-Founder of ClearCadence, Jim Conklin, Managing Director of the BPM Division, ClearCadence, and Tom Jenkins, Executive Chairman of OpenText.

TOM JENKINS: What do you find is the biggest challenge that a typical agency has when embarking on a project?

JIM CONKLIN: *Most of the projects span across agencies and touch multiple systems. A good example is a court system. The clerk's office is managing all the files, but the prosecution, the public defender, and law enforcement also need access to the files. Coordinating multiple agencies is the bigger challenge, more so than the technology itself.*

How do people make the decision to move from paper to electronic?

It transforms the way they're doing business, so the adoption takes a generation phase. You have the younger people, and they adapt well because they have grown up using technology. But some of the older generation may be a bit fearful of technology and are uncertain about it. So the adoption levels are completely different.

So do you run a hybrid system for a while?

No. We build a process based on what the agency needs to move forward with. When it comes to some of the traditional judiciary structures, we manage change one-on-one when necessary.

Most of your customers are government and mission-oriented. How do you find they justify the cost of the project?

Whether they're improving efficiencies, reducing cost, or adding durability to generate revenue—the closer they can get their ROI model to align with a key performance indicator—that's what gets an executive's attention. We typically ask our customers: "What is the easiest project to implement that will provide the highest KPI?" An attainable first win that's realistic to achieve in allotted timeframes is critical.

What implementation have you done recently where you found that magic?

The Court System in the U.S. has experienced budget cuts, but they still have to produce with limited resources. We implemented a paperless project in one division of the court system. Court papers need to be filed, put in a manila folder, and processed through the system. Content comes in from various sources, including electronically through an e-filing solution. But these files need to be verified with the clerk's office, processed for court review and/or signature, sent back to the clerk's office—all while keeping the attorney's office in the loop.

There is a lot of content flying back and forth across government organizations and locations. If I'm an attorney and I have an emergency case 30 miles away in a different building, when the process is digitized and automated, I can pull up the electronic file quickly and easily without disrupting my work. When the files are digitally stored, the government has an audit trail of everything. So it's much more efficient for all the agencies and the constituencies. The result is a combination of offering a better service level at a lower cost.

"When the files are digitally stored, the government has an audit trail of everything. So it's much more efficient for all the agencies and the constituencies."

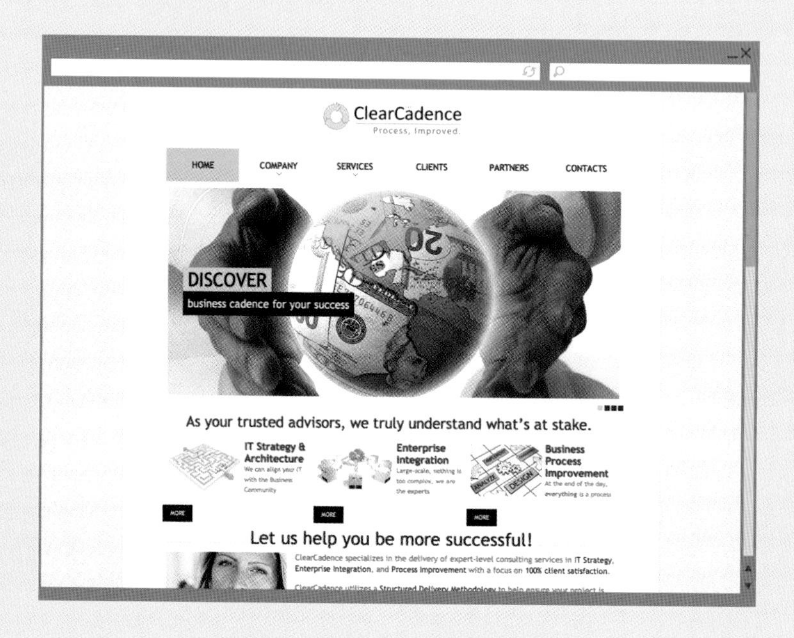

FIGURE 15.1: ClearCadence

Challenges to Change Management in Government

Government agencies have been working according to predictable, command-and-control structures and processes for years at the sacrifice of initiative and performance. The younger generations are more comfortable with the new ways of engaging and the adaptability required to respond to changing markets and citizens.

Transformation in government is an ongoing process. Transformational leaders must be flexible and organizations agile enough to accept this truism. Beyond structural adjustments, a change of attitude in public servants and citizens is already underway. They are adopting entrepreneurial, innovative approaches to communicating and collaborating to improve government operations. They are advocating for more decentralized processes and ownership of projects, both of which are contrary to working in an established government bureaucracy.

There are a number of obstacles to be overcome for transformation to occur. The central agencies of government need to loosen their detailed reporting requirements while maintaining a balance between central oversight and initiative. Department and agency heads are typically appointed based on their background in government, policy work, and connections. Once they are appointed, leaders often do not serve long enough to see change implemented. Tenures are short and depend often on parties in power; leaders tend to focus more on policy reform than process reform. And finally, many operations are under scrutiny by organizations with conflicting agendas—including opposition parties, auditors and regulators, the public, watchdog groups, and the news media.

> "Information is a government, not a departmental, asset. CIOs, like others in back-office functions, need to start thinking and acting more like enterprise leaders, providing value within the context of the bigger strategic picture rather than focusing on the day-to-day technical challenges that they have typically been concerned with."
>
> **CORINNE CHARETTE, CHIEF INFORMATION OFFICER, GOVERNMENT OF CANADA**

In many ways, public sector organizations resemble private sector companies and can be run as such. In the past decade, private-sector management techniques have been adopted based on competitive tendering, market testing, and privatization.[2] The result has been a clearer delineation between the very natures of the two types of organizations based on very different management styles. The call to arms has been for reform from the top down as well as from the bottom up.

[2] Henry Hornstein, *"Successes and potential obstacles to change management in the public service"*, Ivy Business Journal, 2010, *http://iveybusinessjournal.com/topics/the-organization/successes-and-potential-obstacles-to-change-management-in-the-public-service#_ftn4* (accessed February 2014).

FIGURE 15.2: e-Government Framework—Aligning Objectives with Capacity for Better Outcomes

Throughout government departments and agencies, there are examples of significant performance improvements. All of the stories included in this book are about e-government transformation—from its current state of digitization and transaction to a future state of interaction, engagement, and participation. The vision of transformation is being defined and recognized as one that will be in a perpetual state of flux. So structures and processes must subsume this, and forays down the path to making strategic vision a reality will be many and variant. The good news is—as we have illustrated throughout this book—the technology is available, and many governments have already taken their first steps toward implementing a comprehensive and effective e-government strategy.

APPENDIX: OPENTEXT BOOK MATRIX

APPENDIX:

OpenText Book Matrix

If you would like to read more about Enterprise Information Management technologies, please see our recently published book entitled, *Enterprise Information Management (EIM): The Next Generation of Enterprise Software.*

This book describes the EIM journey. What is the state of enterprise information now? Where are we headed? What exactly is EIM and how will you know if it's suited for your agency? The book contains all the answers to these questions, and more.

As an approach, a strategy, and an integrated suite, EIM optimizes the information flows that formulate the foundation of an agency's mission operations. Enterprise Information Management unlocks the potential for superior service delivery and performance, reduced regulatory risk and cost, optimally efficient business processes, more engaging citizen and user experiences, and effective online transactions and information exchange—on premise, in the cloud, and on mobile devices.

How to Use this Book with the EIM Book

For more detailed information, each of the EIM technologies and their related strategies and best practices can be mapped to specific chapters in the *e-Government or Out of Government* book. Please use the matrix below to cross reference chapters with the relevant chapters in *Enterprise Information Management (EIM): The Next Generation of Enterprise Software.*

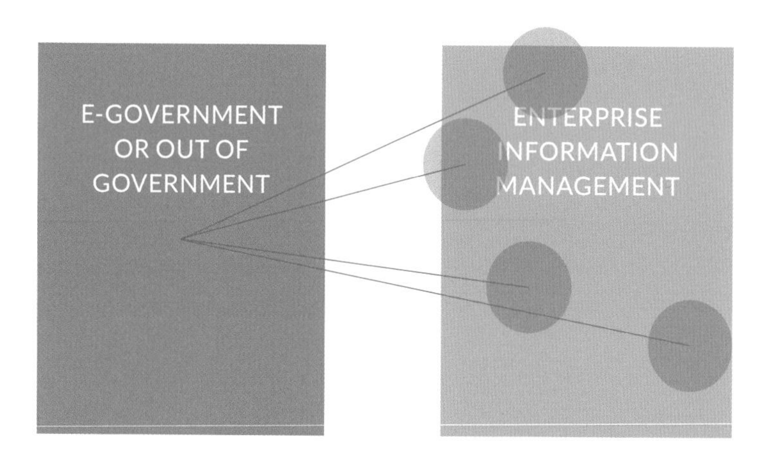

e-Government or Out of Government	Enterprise Information Management: The Next Generation of Enterprise Software
CHAPTER 1: The Business Need for e-Government	**CHAPTER 1:** The Evolution of Information Management **CHAPTER 11:** Focused on the Value **CHAPTER 12:** Information Flows and the Journey
CHAPTER 2: How Governments Are Organized	**CHAPTER 9:** The Social Enterprise
CHAPTER 3: The Government ICT Landscape	**CHAPTER 2:** Enterprise Content Management **CHAPTER 7:** Information Governance **CHAPTER 8:** Information Security **CHAPTER 12:** Information Flows and the Journey
CHAPTER 4: e-Government Drives Productivity	**CHAPTER 2:** Enterprise Content Management **CHAPTER 3:** Business Process Management **CHAPTER 4:** Customer Experience Management **CHAPTER 5:** Information Exchange **CHAPTER 6:** Discovery
CHAPTER 5: e-Government Technologies	**CHAPTERS 1 - 12**
CHAPTER 6: e-Government at the International Level	**CHAPTER 2:** Enterprise Content Management **CHAPTER 3:** Business Process Management **CHAPTER 5:** Information Exchange **CHAPTER 9:** The Social Enterprise **CHAPTER 10:** Mobile Computing and the Cloud
CHAPTER 7: e-Government at the National Level	**CHAPTER 3:** Business Process Management **CHAPTER 4:** Customer Experience Management **CHAPTER 5:** Information Exchange **CHAPTER 9:** The Social Enterprise **CHAPTER 10:** Mobile Computing and the Cloud
CHAPTER 8: e-Government at the Regional Level	**CHAPTER 3:** Business Process Management **CHAPTER 4:** Customer Experience Management **CHAPTER 9:** The Social Enterprise **CHAPTER 10:** Mobile Computing and the Cloud

e-Government or Out of Government	Enterprise Information Management: The Next Generation of Enterprise Software
CHAPTER 9: e-Government at Local Level	**CHAPTER 3:** Business Process Management **CHAPTER 4:** Customer Experience Management **CHAPTER 9:** The Social Enterprise **CHAPTER 10:** Mobile Computing and the Cloud
CHAPTER 10: Reinventing Public-Private Partnerships (P3s)	**CHAPTER 12:** Information Flows and the Journey
CHAPTER 11: e-Government and the Future	**CHAPTER 4:** Customer Experience Management **CHAPTER 9:** The Social Enterprise **CHAPTER 10:** Mobile Computing and the Cloud
CHAPTER 12: Open Government and Crowdsourcing	**CHAPTER 2:** Enterprise Content Management **CHAPTER 7:** Information Governance **CHAPTER 8:** Information Security
CHAPTER 13: e-Government and Big Data	**CHAPTER 2:** Enterprise Content Management **CHAPTER 5:** Information Exchange **CHAPTER 6:** Discovery **CHAPTER 7:** Information Governance **CHAPTER 8:** Information Security **CHAPTER 10:** Mobile Computing and the Cloud
CHAPTER 14: Mobile e-Government in the Cloud	**CHAPTER 4:** Customer Experience Management **CHAPTER 5:** Information Exchange **CHAPTER 7:** Information Governance **CHAPTER 8:** Information Security **CHAPTER 10:** Mobile Computing and the Cloud
CHAPTER 15: Strategies for Change Management	**CHAPTER 11:** Focused on the Value **CHAPTER 12:** Information Flows and the Journey

GLOSSARY

Glossary

A

Accountability - The acknowledgment of responsibility for actions, decisions, and policies by the government (civil servants and politicians) according to public standards of review and legislative bodies such as a congress or parliament.

Administration *(also Public Administration)* - The development, implementation, and delivery of government policy, or the management of public programs.

Advanced Research Projects Administration *(ARPA)* - Agency created in 1958 by President Dwight D. Eisenhower for the purpose of advancing research and development projects in technology and science for military purposes.

API - See *Application Programming Interface.*

Application *(App)* - Software or programs used to execute tasks on computers.

Application Programming Interface (API) - An interface implemented for a software program to enable interaction with other software, much in the same way that a user interface facilitates interaction between humans and computers.

App Store - A digital distribution platform for iPhone® mobile apps developed and maintained by Apple Inc. Users can visit the App Store,® for example, to browse and download apps developed by Apple.

Arab Spring - The wave of revolutionary demonstrations and protests, riots, and civil wars that took place in the Arab world beginning in December 2010.

Archive *(verb)* - The systematic transfer of valuable digital data, which no longer requires immediate accessibility, to alternate storage media. Often stored on Computer Output to Laser Disk (COLD) systems.

Archives *(noun)* - Preserved records and digital assets that have been identified as potentially valuable for future legal, evidentiary, or historical information. These records are preserved in the context of their creation as evidence of action, decision, and transaction. "Archives" also refers to the department or institution entrusted with this task.

ARPANET - One of the world's first networks to implement TCP/IP, and the originator of what was to become the Internet, funded by ARPA within the U.S. Department of Defense.

B

Baby Boomers - The generation born during the demographic Post–World War II baby boom between the years 1946 and 1964 that enjoyed a great amount of prosperity after the war.

Bandwidth - The volume of information per unit of time that a computer, person, or transmission medium can handle.

Benchmarking - Comparing business performance and processes to best practices in the industry.

Big Data - Information assets that exist in high-volume, high-variety, and high-velocity and require innovative analytics to extract intelligent information that results in improved decision-making.

Bilateralism - Refers to relationships formed between two sovereign states for economic, cultural, or political purposes. Free Trade Agreements are often based on a bilateral agreement between two nations.

Blended Learning - Combining two or more teaching methods in a hybrid form of teaching designed to benefit students.

Blog *(also Web Log)* - A chronological and topic-oriented collection of entries posted on a web page. Typically, blogs communicate an author's point of view and solicit feedback in the form of comments which can be posted with the blog.

BPM - See *Business Process Management.*

Browser - See *Internet Browser.*

Business Applications - Software programs used to solve business needs such as word processing, accounting, or customer relationship management.

Business Intelligence *(BI)* - A technology for analysis of information contained in structured data. It is the structured counter-part to content analytics.

Business Process Management *(BPM)* - Refers to aligning processes with an organization's strategic objectives, designing and implementing process-centric tools or architectures, and determining measurement systems for effective process management.

C

CEM - See *Customer Experience Management*

Channel - A communication medium to output content. It could be via the web, printed materials, video, CD-ROM, etc.

Chat *(also Instant Messaging or IM)* - Real-time instant messaging and other forms of chat within the context of an overall topic, website, or meeting space.

Citizen-centric - Integrated approach to public service delivery that focuses on meeting citizen needs across multiple channels and devices to increase levels of engagement and satisfaction. Changes are required at the cultural, organizational, and technical levels.

Citizen Participation *(also Participatory Government)* - Involvement of citizens in policy development and service delivery at all levels of government.

Civic Obligation - The responsibilities of citizens in a democratic government, such as voting, etc.

Civil Servant - See *Public Servant.*

Cloud Computing *("The Cloud")* - A metaphor inspired by the cloud symbol used to represent the Internet in flow charts and diagrams. Cloud computing describes the disruptive transformation of IT toward a service-based economy, driven by economic, technological, and cultural conditions.

Collaboration Software - Programs that link processes and individuals across different locations and time zones to create an environment where team members work together to share ideas, experiences, and knowledge.

Collaborative Workspace *(or "Conference")* - A shared workspace in a connected environment where users can collaborate and work together even when separated by geography. Users can both store content in the workspace, as well as hold discussions.

Command-and-control - Bureaucratic management structure of government.

Commenting - Adding online comments to social media to add value, including commenting on online documents, blogs, wikis, and more.

Compliance - Adherence to a body of regulations, government legislation, or standards (for example, ISO 9000).

Composite Applications - Model-driven development environments that rely on graphical process modeling tools to support direct interpretation of the models into executable code. The technical concept can be compared to mashups, however, composite applications use business sources of information, while mashups typically rely on web-based sources.

Conferencing - Real-time meetings between groups over the web. In organizations, these meetings facilitate the exchange of information as if all the users were in one room together, such as collaboration around presentations or spreadsheets, on white boards, and shared screens.

Connectors - In database management, a link or pointer between two data structures.

Content Analytics - A technology used for analysis of information contained in content. It allows customers to optimize their user experience by dynamically serving up content based on automatically evaluated content relevance.

Content Lifecycle Management *(CLM)* - The combination of document management, records management, workflow, archiving, and imaging software and hardware into a fully integrated solution to effectively manage the lifecycle of content, from creation through to archiving and eventual deletion.

Content Management - Storage, maintenance, and retrieval of HTML and XML documents and all related elements. Content management systems may be built on top of a native XML database and typically provide publishing capabilities to export content not only to a website, but to physical media and print as well.

Content Syndication *(also Web Syndication)* - A form of syndication that makes website content available to multiple sites, often in the form of web feeds delivering summaries of recently added or updated content.

Contextual Information *(Collaboration)* - Smaller services/objects that can be embedded in business applications.

Contextual Searching - Contextual search goes beyond searching on file name or key fields. It looks at the data within documents and records and supplies results based on the context of content.

Contractor - A business or individual that contracts with an organization (in the public sector for the context of this book) for the delivery of a product or a service such as the building of a facility, road, etc.

Cross-Platform - Refers to developing for, and/or running on, more than one type of hardware platform. It implies two different methods. The first method is programming source code that is compiled into different machine environments, each of which has to be supported separately. The second method uses an interpreter such as the Java Virtual Machine.

Crowdsourcing - Acquiring solutions, services, or ideas by outsourcing development and ideation to "the crowd", typically from an online community, rather than from traditional employees or suppliers.

Curriculum - A set of courses offered by a school, college, university or educational institution.

Customer Experience Management *(CEM)* - An integrated suite of CEM products delivered as a comprehensive platform to manage media, web, social, and interactive content to deliver a consistent user experience across multiple channels.

Customer Relationship Management *(CRM)* - Enterprise-wide software applications that allow companies to manage every aspect of their relationship with customers. The goal of these systems is to assist in building lasting customer relationships and to turn customer satisfaction into customer loyalty.

D

DAM - See *Media Management.*

Data Archiving - Data archiving offloads historic data from the online database and archives it for future access on a secure media.

Database - A collection of data arranged for ease and speed of search and retrieval.

Database Management Systems - Software packages that control the creation maintenance, and use of a database.

Data Capture - A method of data input that requires no data entry. Specific devices are designed to capture data such as barcode readers or magnetic stripe readers (such as those found on a credit card).

Data Center *(also called Server Farm)* - A collection of computer servers usually maintained by an enterprise to accomplish server needs far beyond the capability of one machine. Server farms often have backup servers, which can take over the function of primary servers in the event of a primary server failure.

Data Protection Act *(DPA)* - A United Kingdom Act of Parliament which defines U.K. law on the processing of data on identifiable living people. It is the main piece of legislation that governs the protection of personal data in the U.K. It was enacted to bring U.K. law into line with the EU data protection directive of 1995.

Data Protection Directive - A European Union directive which regulates the processing of personal data within the European Union.

Data Warehouse - A database designed to support decision making in an organization. Data from the production databases are copied to the data warehouse so that queries and analysis can be performed without disturbing the performance or the stability of the production systems.

Deep Web - Refers to World Wide Web content that is not part of the surface web, which is indexed by standard search engines. The Deep Web consists of content within organizations, behind firewalls, and other security processes.

Desktop - The area of the monitor screen in a graphical user interface (GUI) against which icons and windows used to run applications appear.

Digital Age *(also Information Age)* - The shift from an industrial-based economy (industrialism) to one based on information technologies.

Digital Asset - Describes any subdivision or collection of content and metadata that holds value to the owner. Digital assets may include photos, video, audio, web pages, text documents, Microsoft® PowerPoints, or graphics.

Digital Asset Management (DAM) - See *Media Management.*

Digital Divide - The gap between those with access to technology and required technologies (such as ICTs) and those without. Also a delineation between the more prosperous highly developed nations and poor developing nations.

Digital Economy - An economy based on goods and services produced through web technologies, digital media technologies, and other electronic business processes.

Digital Experience Management *(DEM)* - Using tools such as widgets to embed digital media, DEM presents significant content distribution opportunities for organizations outside the enterprise, as well as enabling emerging social collaboration tools within the enterprise.

Digital Governance - ICT-enabled governance, or the creation, implementation, and delivery of ICT-based models for better governance.

Digital Media - The term encompasses a wide variety of content types: photos, graphics, audio files, video clips, Flash® animations, PDFs, PowerPoint® files, and design layouts.

Digital Native - A person who was born during or after the introduction of digital technology and, through interacting with it from an early age, has a good understanding of its applications.

Discovery - A category of EIM offerings that helps organizations capture, combine, and transform data across information silos into formats that can be analyzed for deeper business insight.

Disposition - Final deletion of content when it reaches the end of its lifecycle.

Disruptive Innovation *(also Disruptive Technology)* - Used in business and technology, a disruptive technology or disruptive innovation is an innovation that creates a new market and value network, and eventually disrupts an existing market to displace an earlier technology there.

Distance Learning - Remote learning based on students not being physically present in a classroom, typically accessed through web-based technologies.

Document - A piece of work created with an application, such as a word processor. A computer file that is not an executable file and contains data for use by applications.

Document Management *(DM)* - Involves the capture and management of documents within an organization. The term traditionally implied the management of documents after they were scanned into the computer. Today, the term has become an umbrella term under which document imaging, workflow, and information retrieval fall.

Document Repository - A database that includes author, data elements, inputs, processes, outputs, and interrelationships.

DoD - United States Department of Defense.

DoD 5015.2 - United States Department of Defense 5015.2-STD or the Design Criteria Standard for Electronic Records Management Software Applications.

E

ECM - See *Enterprise Content Management.*

ECM Applications - Applications usually tailored to address line-of-business problems or customized for specific vertical markets.

EDI - See *Electronic Data Interchange.*

EIM - See *Enterprise Information Management.*

e-Democracy - The use of ICTs to promote democracy through citizen participation in the creation and delivery of government programs, services, policies, and resources.

e-Discovery *(or Electronic Discovery)* - Refers to discovery in civil litigation or government investigations which deals with the exchange of information in digital format.

e-Government ***(also Electronic Government)*** **-** Refers to the use of ICTs and Internet, web-based, or mobile technologies to improve operational performance, engage with citizens, and deliver government services. It encompasses technologies for e-services, e-health, e-procurement, e-voting, e-management, e-democracy, and more. In scope, e-government moves beyond providing services online and encompasses a holistic vision of electronic government that consolidates processes, resources, and information across agencies.

e-Health - Using ICTs to facilitate health care practices.

e-Invoicing ***(also Electronic Invoicing)*** **-** A form of electronic billing based on technology and streamlining the process between participants, such as customers and their suppliers.

e-Learning - The use of electronic media and information and communication technologies (ICT) in education.

Electorate - Registered, voting public.

Electronic Data Interchange ***(EDI)*** **-** A document standard that acts as common interface between two or more computer applications to better understand the document transmitted. EDI is commonly used by large organizations in e-commerce processes.

Electronic Digital Management System - In order to manage digital documents, systems created to allow users on a network to view, markup, and edit documents.

Electronic Government - See *e-Government*.

Email - One of the first and most popular uses for the Internet, email (electronic mail) is the exchange of computer-stored messages by telecommunication.

Email Management - The application of content lifecycle management to emails to manage the creation, archiving, storage and disposition of email messages.

e-Management - Using ICTs to facilitate all aspects of management, from training through to performance management.

Empowerment - Refers to supporting consumers of government information, programs, and resources (citizens and civil servants) to increase engagement, productivity, performance, and overall satisfaction.

Engagement - Extending the use of ICTs to help bring citizens, businesses, and public servants closer to their government. ICTs introduce more channels for engagement in the policy development and decision-making processes of government. Engaging citizens in the political process, for example, through open, transparent, and accountable government.

Enterprise Application - A computer program designed to perform specific functions, such as inventory control, accounting, payroll, material management, etc.

Enterprise Content Management ***(ECM)*** **-** A set of enterprise content management (ECM) technologies including a platform to unite capture, document and records management, workflow, search and archiving as well as applications and add-ons such as email, e-discovery, auto-classification, contract management and engineering document management.

Enterprise Information Management *(EIM)* - A comprehensive software suite that encompasses the capture of information; the management of structure, unstructured, and application data; the exchange and presentation of information on both sides of the firewall; intelligent business processes and solutions; information applications that parallel ERP data and process; enterprise information architecture that enables enterprise applications as well as mobile, social, and cloud; and Business Intelligence and analytics. Complete EIM consists of Enterprise Content Management (ECM), Business Process Management (BPM), Customer Experience Management (CEM), Information Exchange, and Discovery.

Enterprise Resource Planning *(ERP)* - Any software system designed to support and automate the business processes of medium and large businesses. This may include manufacturing, distribution, personnel, project management, payroll, and financials. ERP systems are accounting-oriented information systems for identifying and planning the enterprise-wide resources needed to take, make, distribute, and account for customer orders.

Entitlement - A guarantee of access to something, such as land or welfare benefits, based on established rights or by legislation.

Entity Extraction - An entity extractor locates and extracts places, people, organizations, and more. Controlled vocabularies and linguistic rules are used to identify and extract all occurrences of an entity type. Entity types can include product names, company names, proper names, geographic locations, dates, times, and more.

e-Procurement *(also Electronic Procurement)* - Purchasing goods and services over the Internet, replacing manual, paper-based processes with electronic processes and information management to improve efficiencies across all touch points in the supply (or value) chain.

European Union *(EU)* - An economic and political union of 28 member states that are located primarily in Europe.

Exabyte *(EB)* - The exabyte is a multiple of the unit byte for digital information storage. 1 exabyte is 1,000 PB. The unit symbol for the exabyte is EB.

F

FDA - Food & Drug Administration (FDA) (United States). FDA's mission is to promote and protect the public health by helping safe and effective products reach the market in a timely way while monitoring products for continued safety after they are in use.

FDIC - Federal Deposit Insurance Corporation (FDIC) (United States). Insures deposits and promotes safe and sound banking practices.

Federal Government - Pertains to a union of states under a central government distinct from the individual governments of the separate states.

Federalism - Describes the constitutional division of power between a central (or national) government and states or provinces, as determined by a constitution.

Federation - A political entity made up of a union of partially self-governing states or regions under a central (federal) government.

Federal Risk and Authorization Management Program *(FedRAMP)* - A government-wide program that provides a standardized approach to security assessment, authorization, and continuous monitoring for cloud products and services.

FISMA *(or Federal Information Security Management Act of 2002)* - A United States federal law enacted in 2002, requiring each U.S. federal agency to develop, document, and deploy an agency-wide program to provide information security.

Firewall - A firewall is a part of a computer system or network that is designed to block unauthorized access while permitting authorized communications.

Forums - Online discussion forums in which users post "articles" to forums organized around a topic, typically in question and answer format resembling an offline discussion.

FRB - Federal Reserve Board (USA).

Freedom of Information Act *(also Freedom of Information Laws)* - Full or partial disclosure of information to the general public to data held by national governments based on "right-to-know" legal process by which requests may be made.

FSA - Financial Services Authority (FSA) (U.K.). Independent body which regulates the financial services industry in the U.K.

G

G8 Countries - A forum for the leaders of eight countries with the strongest economies to discuss financial and trade matters.

G20 Countries - The Group of Twenty (G20) is the premier forum for its members' international economic cooperation and decision-making. Its membership comprises 19 countries plus the European Union.

G-20 Summit - The annual meeting for leaders of the G20 Countries. Throughout the year, finance ministers and central bank governors meet regularly to discuss ways to strengthen the global economy, reform international financial institutions, improve financial regulation, and discuss the key economic reforms that are needed in each of the member countries. Underpinning these meetings is a year-long program of meetings among senior officials and of working groups coordinating policy on specific issues.

Geospatial Analysis - Applying statistical analysis and other informational techniques to data which has a geographical or geospatial aspect.

Gigabyte (GB) - The gigabyte is a multiple of the unit byte for digital information storage. One gigabyte is 1,000 MB or one thousand million bytes. The unit symbol for the gigabyte is GB or Gbyte.

Globalization - The development of an increasingly integrated global economy, characterized by free trade, free flow of capital, migration of people, and knowledge exchange.

Governance - All processes of governing, whether undertaken by a government, organization, or industry.

Government App Store - The enterprise equivalent to the Apple App Store® as a distribution platform, only maintained behind the firewall (or in a private cloud).

Government-to-Business *(G2B)* - This relationship describes information and services that are used by entrepreneurs, businesses, and corporations for commercial use, including filing statements of incorporation, obtaining business licenses, customs declarations, and more.

Government-to-Citizen *(G2C)* - This describes the interactions and transactions that take place between a citizen and their government, including the use of public services for individual or family use, such as the payment of taxes, payments of fines to local or state governments, personal records such as a passport or a new drivers license or a change of address, social security, public libraries, student loans, benefits, and any health-related services.

Government-to-Employee *(G2E)* - This model of engagement defines the relationships between governments, employees, and contractors. It describes the exchange of information at an interagency level, between departments, management, and personnel regarding administrative tasks, performance, and mission activities.

Government-to-Government *(G2G)* - This model of engagement involves the exchange of information between government authorities regarding administration, laws, policy development, programs, and projects.

GPS or Global Positioning System - A satellite-based navigation system maintained by the US government that provides location and time information anywhere on the Earth, which is freely accessible by anyone with a GPS receiver.

H

Hackathon: An event or short duration during which computer programmers and others involved in software development collaborate on software project. Also called "appathons".

Health Insurance Portability and Accountability Act *(HIPAA)* - Enacted by the United States Congress and signed by President Bill Clinton in 1996, HIPAA protects health insurance coverage for workers and their families when they change or lose their jobs.

Hosting - Maintaining a computer system and its applications at a third-party site.

Homeland Security Act *(HSA)* - With the passage of the Homeland Security Act by Congress in November 2002, the Department of Homeland Security formally came into being as a stand-alone, cabinet-level department to further coordinate and unify national homeland security efforts.

I

Identity Theft - Stealing an individual's personal information (such as name, social insurance number, passport number, credit card numbers, etc.), and assuming this identity, without the individual's knowledge of it.

IMF *(International Monetary Fund)* - The IMF is an organization of 184 countries working to foster global monetary cooperation, secure financial stability, facilitate international trade, promote high employment and sustainable economic growth, and reduce poverty.

Information Exchange - A set of solutions within Enterprise Information Management (EIM) that facilitates efficient, secure, and compliant exchange of information inside and outside of organizations.

Information Age - See *Digital Age*.

Information and Communication Technologies *(ICTs)* - New media technologies combined with Internet users, service providers (such as telecommunications) and enterprise applications to facilitate the access, storage, transmission, and manipulation of information.

Information Governance - The set of multi-disciplinary structures, policies, procedures, processes, and controls implemented to manage information on all media in such a way that it supports the enterprise's immediate and long-term regulatory, legal, risk, environmental, and operational requirements.

Information Technology *(IT)* - The development, design, implementation, support, and management of technology-based information systems, including computer hardware and software.

Infrastructure - The physical and organizational structures required for the operation of a country, economy, or enterprise to function.

Instant Messaging *(IM)* - See *Chat*.

Intelligent Community Forum - A thinktank that studies the economic and social development of modern communities, identifies smart cities around the world, and ranks them each year. They examine the ways that communities can create prosperity based on advances in communications and technology and sharing best practices for sustainable growth.

Internet - An interconnected system of networks that connects computers around the world via the TCP/IP protocol.

Internet Browser - The program that serves as the client front end to the World Wide Web.

Internet of Things - The network of physical objects that contain embedded technology to communicate and sense or interact with their internal states or the external environment.

Intranet - An "internal Internet" configured behind a firewall to connect individuals and departments. A privately maintained computer network that can be accessed only by authorized persons, especially members or employees of the organization that owns it.

International Monetary Fund *(IMF)* - A multilateral organization that oversees the global financial system and monitors the economic and financial policies of its 188 member countries.

International Organization for Standards *(ISO)* - A worldwide federation of national standards bodies from 156 countries. Its global vision is to develop standards that support the facilitation of global trade; the improvement of quality, safety, security, environmental and consumer protection; as well as the rational use of natural resources and global dissemination of technologies and good practices, all of which contribute to economic and social progress.

Interoperability - The extent to which systems and devices can exchange data, interpret shared data, and present it so that it can be understood by a user.

ISO 9000 - A series of standards published by the International Organization for Standardization (ISO) to define, establish, and maintain a quality assurance system for manufacturing and service industries.

ISO 14000 - A series of standards published by the International Organization for Standardization (ISO) that help organizations minimize the impact of their operations on the environment, in compliance with laws, regulations, and requirements.

K

Keyword - A term used as a keyword to retrieve documents in an information system such as a catalog or a search engine.

Knowledge Management *(KM)* - An umbrella term for making more efficient use of the human knowledge that exists within an organization. The major focus is to identify and gather content from documents, reports, and other sources and to be able to search that content for meaningful relationships. Knowledge Management also concerns the ability to identify high-value individuals within an organization.

L

Legacy Software - An old, outdated method, technology, computer system, or application program.

Learning Management Systems *(LMS)* - A software application to administer, document, track, and report training programs, classroom and online events, e-learning programs, and the associated content.

M

Mainframes - Computers used mainly by large organizations for critical applications, typically bulk data processing such as census, industry and consumer statistics, enterprise resource planning (ERP), and financial transaction processing.

Media Management *(also known as Digital Asset Management, Brand Asset Management or Media Asset Management)* - Media Management consists of the ingestion, storage, management, retrieval, production, and distribution of digital assets.

Metadata - Sometimes known as data about the data, metadata describes and provides context for content.

Millenials *(also known as the Net Generation)* - The generation born after 1982, also called the Net Generation, who are technically savvy and expect to use the same technologies and tools in the workplace that they use at home, and in their leisure time, to exchange information and other media.

Mobile App - Mobile apps, also called mobile applications, are software applications that run on smartphones and tablet computers. Mobile apps are discreet programs designed to solve a specific purpose with a tether to back-office servers or new types of availability via "app content servers". They are designed to perform at the touch of a smart screen, enabling users to do things that begin to exceed what is possible with a conventional PC connected to the Internet.

Mobile Device - Includes personal digital assistants, smartphones, and tablet computers. A mobile device is a small hand-held computing device typically operated with a touch screen or miniature keyboard.

MoReq 2010 v1.1 - Short for "Model Requirements for the Management of Electronic Records", it is a formal requirements specification for an electronic records management system.

Multilateralism - International governance that involves the development of rules, policies, and organizations to resolve common issues and support collaboration among three or more sovereign countries or nations.

Multimedia - Integration of text, voice, video, images, or some combination of these types of information. Also called rich media.

Multinational Organization - A large corporation which both produces and sells goods or services in various countries, often proponents of globalization.

N

Net Generation - See *Millennials*.

Non-governmental Organizations *(NGOs)* - Organizations that are not a part of a government and are not conventional for-profit businesses. NGOs operate independently from government, but form close relationships with specific government organizations.

O

Online - Connected to or accessible via a computer or computer network. Typically refers to being connected to the Internet or to another remote service.

Open Data - Information that is accessible, available in digital machine-readable format, and can be re-used under open license terms.

Open Government - A governing principle that gives citizens the right of access to the documents, data, and proceedings of government to allow for greater transparency. The drive to open government reflects and respects the necessary balance between freedom of information and protection of privacy legislation in many jurisdictions.

Open Government Partnership *(OGP)* - The Open Government Partnership (OGP) was launched in September 2011, when the 8 founding governments (Brazil, Indonesia, Mexico, Norway, Philippines, South Africa, United Kingdom, and the United States) endorsed an Open Government Declaration.

Open Government Standards - The Open Government Standards were initiated in April 2012 to coincide with the presentation of the OGP National Action Plan.

Open Source - Refers to a computer program in which the source code is available to the general public for use and/or modification from its original design.

Operating System - A computer's master control program that manages its internal functions and controls its operation. An operating system provides commonly used functions and a uniform, consistent means for all software applications to access the computer's resources. Windows® and UNIX® are operating systems.

Optical Character Recognition *(OCR)* - Recognition of printed or written characters by computer. Each page of text is converted to a digital image using a scanner and OCR is then applied to the image to produce a text file.

Organisation of Economic Cooperation and Development *(OECD)* - International economic organization of 34 countries founded in 1961 to stimulate economic progress and world trade.

P

Paperwork Reduction Act - A United States federal law enacted in 1980 designed to reduce the total amount of paperwork burden the federal government imposes on private businesses and citizens.

Performance Management - Processes, programs, or approaches that ensure goals are consistently met in an efficient manner.

Permissions - Management of who can access a computer or network. The Access Control List (ACL) is the set of data associated with a file, directory, or other resource that defines the permissions that users, groups, processes, or devices have for accessing it.

Personal Information Protection and Electronic Documents Act *(PIPEDA)* *(Canada)* - Sets out ground rules for how private sector organizations may collect, use or disclose personal information in the course of commercial activities. PIPEDA also applies to federal works, undertakings and businesses in respect of employee personal information. The law gives individuals the right to access and request correction of the personal information these organizations may have collected about them.

Petabyte *(PB)* - The petabyte is a multiple of the unit byte for digital information storage. 1 petabyte is 1,000 TB. The unit symbol for the petabyte is PB.

Platform - The term originally concerned only CPU or computer hardware, but it also refers to software-only environments. A messaging or groupware platform implies one or more programming interfaces that email, calendaring, and other client programs are written to in order to communicate with the services provided by the server.

Portal - Within the enterprise, software that provides access via a web browser into all of an organization's information assets and applications. Portals provide a variety of services including web searching, news directories, free email, discussion groups, online shopping, and links to other sites.

Privacy Acts - Impose obligations on how government departments and agencies must handle the personal information of citizens, permanent residents, and foreign nationals.

Privatization - Transferring ownership of a business, enterprise, or agency from the public sector to the private sector, either to a business that operates for a profit or to a not-for-profit organization.

PRO - The Public Records Office of the United Kingdom of Great Britain. PRO publishes a standard for records management systems designed to ensure interoperability with the national archive and promote records management best practices throughout the U.K.

Process Management - The automation of business processes using a rule-based expert system that invokes the appropriate tools and supplies necessary information, checklists, examples, and status reports to the user.

Procurement - Process for purchasing goods and services, based on a multi-party collaboration process that spans multiple stakeholders in purchasing, financial accounting, inventory management, and other external vendors.

PSI - Public Sector Information.

Public Administration - The development, implementation, and delivery of government policy, or the management of public programs.

Public-Private Partnerships *(PPPs or P3s)* - A cooperative venture between the public and private sectors, built on the expertise of each partner that best meets clearly defined public needs through the appropriate allocation of resources, risks and rewards.

Public Service Without Borders *(PSWB)* - Public Service Without Borders (PSWB) is a dynamic IPAC (Institute of Public Administration) online community for new and experienced public sector professionals, academics, and students of public administration and policy across Canada and around the world.

Q

Quality Assurance - Applied during pre-production and manufacturing to ensure products being made will meet specifications and requirements.

R

Records Management *(RM)* - Refers to the creation, retention, and scheduled destruction of an organization's paper and film documents. Email and computer-generated content also fall into the RM domain.

Redundancy - The duplication of critical components of a system with the intention of increasing reliability of the system, usually in the case of a backup or fail-safe.

Regulatory Compliance - See *Compliance*.

Regulatory requirements - Overseen by various governmental agencies to ensure compliance with laws, regulations and established rules. Examples relevant to content management applications include: DoD 5015.2 Standard, Basel II, and HIPAA.

Relational Database - A database in which all the data and relations between them are organized in tables. A relational database allows the definition of data structures, storage and retrieval operations, and integrity constraints.

Reporting - Metrics-focused analysis of user behavior (unlike web analytics, which is experience driven).

Repository - Think of this as the enterprise library—it is a location for storage, often for safety or preservation within the enterprise. It is a trusted source of content that can be searched and retrieved.

Rich Content or Media - See *Digital Media*.

Rights and Permissions - Identifies the circumstances under which a particular asset may be used. For instance, indicates who legally owns the asset, in what mediums it may be used (web, print, TV), and the financial liabilities incurred to include the asset.

S

Sarbanes-Oxley Act - Passed by U.S. Congress to protect investors from the possibility of fraudulent corporate accounting activities.

Scalability - Ability to reach high performance levels.

Search - A technology focused on user-driven information retrieval based on statistical occurrence of search keywords in text-based content.

SEC - Securities and Exchange Commission. The SEC was established by Congress to help protect investors by administering the Securities Act of 1933, the Securities Exchange Act of 1934, the Securities Act Amendments of 1975, the Trust Indenture Act, the Investment Company Act, the Investment Advisor's Act and the Public Utility Holding Company Act.

Semantics - A term used often in the context of the Semantic Web, which typically refers to RDF-based modeling of online user experience. In the context of content analytics, the term semantics is sometimes used to refer to the connotation of information contained in content or what is the information about.

Semantic Search - Searches data beyond just word recognition, seeking to understand the intent of the user and the contextual meaning of words as it searches.

Sentiment Analysis - Sentiment analysis detects the tones in content, identifying and displaying opinions that are expressed in clusters of sentences, phrases, or entities.

Server - A server computer, sometimes called an enterprise server, is a computer system that provides essential services across a network to private users inside a large organization or to public users on the Internet. Enterprise servers are known to be very fault tolerant, as even a short-term failure can cost more than purchasing and installing the system.

Short Message Service *(SMS)* - Text messaging sent using this service, which allows a short alphanumeric message (160 characters) to be sent for display on a mobile or cell phone.

Six Sigma - Techniques and tools for process improvement and quality control developed by Motorola in 1986.

Smartphone - A mobile phone that offers advanced, PC-like functionality such as email, Internet access, calendaring and viewing capabilities, along with a built-in full keyboard or external USB keyboard and VGA connector.

Smart Process Applications *(SPA)* - Application software that supports people-intensive business activities that are very changeful, highly flexible, and loosely structured. These packaged apps incorporate current best practices and can easily be updated to reflect continuous collaborative business process improvements.

Social Media - Media designed to be disseminated through social interaction, created using highly accessible and scalable publishing techniques. Social media uses Internet and web-based technologies to transform broadcast media monologues (one-to-many) into social media dialogues (many-to-many).

Social Networks - Websites that facilitate connections of people based on self-generated user profiles. Facebook.com and LinkedIn® com are examples of social networking sites.

Software - The programs, routines, and symbolic languages that control the functioning of a computer and direct its operation.

Software as a Service *(SaaS)* - This type of computing delivers a single application through the browser to a large number of customers using a multi-tenant architecture.

Structured Data - Data that resides in fixed fields within a record or file. Relational databases and spreadsheets are examples of structured data.

Supply Chain - The system of organizations, people, information, and resources involved in moving a product or service from supplier to customer.

Supply-Chain Management - The design, planning, execution, control, and monitoring of supply chain activities to create net value, build a competitive infrastructure, leverage logistics, synchronize supply with demand and measure performance.

T

Tablet - A tablet computer, or tablet, is a mobile computer that is larger than a mobile phone or personal digital assistant (PDA) but smaller than a laptop, with a flat screen that is operated through touch and an onscreen virtual keyboard.

Taxonomies - The classification of data into groups or categories.

Terabyte *(TB)* - A unit of computer memory or data storage capacity equal to one trillion bytes or 1,000 gigabytes (GB). The unit symbol for the terabyte is TB.

Transaction - Synonymous with a specific business application, such as order entry, invoice information capture, etc. To create, change, or display business information in an enterprise application, users have to call certain transactions in the system.

Transactional Data - Orders, purchases, changes, additions, and deletions are typical business transactions stored in the computer. Transactions update one or more master files and serve as both an audit trail and history for future analyses. Ad hoc queries are also a type of transaction but are usually not saved.

Tweet - See *Micro-blogging*.

U

Unstructured Data - Data that does not reside in fixed locations. Free-form text in a word processing document is a typical example.

USA PATRIOT Act - The official title of the USA PATRIOT Act is "Uniting and Strengthening America by Providing Appropriate Tools Required to Intercept and Obstruct Terrorism (USA PATRIOT) Act of 2001." The purpose of the USA PATRIOT Act is to deter and punish terrorist acts in the United States and around the world through enhanced law enforcement investigatory tools.

User Interface *(UI)* - A user interface is the system people use to interact with a computer or other device. Typically, a system may expose several user interfaces to serve different kinds of users.

User Profiles - A collection of personal data associated to a specific user typically within an online community or corporate intranet. Profiles often contain a picture, relevant personal and professional information including knowledge, skills, abilities, department, projects, roles, other contacts and links.

V

VERS - Victorian Electronic Records Strategy (Australia). Public Record Office Victoria (PROV) runs a compliance program to test systems and products against the Standard for the Management of Electronic Records (PROS 99/007) (the VERS Standard).

Video - The technology of electronically capturing, recording, processing, storing, transmitting, and reconstructing a sequence of still images representing scenes in motion.

Virtualization - An umbrella term that describes software technologies that improve portability, manageability, and compatibility of applications by encapsulating them from the underlying operating system on which they are executed.

W

Web - A shorthand way to refer to the World Wide Web and possibly its complementing technologies. For example, a web authoring tool might be used to create documents that contain HyperText Markup Language (HTML).

Web 2.0 - Refers to web-based applications that enable new and emergent ways of searching, presenting and consuming information using the Internet. Web 2.0 is characterized predominantly by technologies that use the web as a platform for collaboration and communications. The term also covers applications that are participatory in nature, lightweight, and easy to deploy (APIs and mashups, for example) and are available online as a service.

Web Analytics - A technology for user behavior analysis (click-stream analysis). It allows customers to generate reports on user behavior on the site and to optimize user experience by dynamically serving up relevant content based on metadata.

Web Browser - See *Internet Browser.*

Web Content - The content featured as part of the user experience on websites, including text, video, images, sounds, and animations.

Web Content Management *(WCM)* - Systems designed to drive websites by separating content from presentation and providing the following capabilities—capacity planning, site design/layout, look/feel navigation, content development, production, delivery, session tracking, and site evolution.

Web Services - Web services refer to the web-based provision of services via open interfaces. This enables the integration of "third-party" applications with a website, giving rise to new sites or mashups.

Website - A collection of related web pages with supporting images, videos, or other digital assets that share a common domain name or IP address in an Internet Protocol-based network.

Widget - Highly portable web applications that allow non-technical users to add dynamic content or functionality to a web page. User-friendly websites are increasing their use of widgets to simplify and enhance the Internet user's experience.

Wi-Fi - A very high bandwidth connection. A Wi-Fi-enabled device such as a personal computer, video game console, mobile phone, MP3 player, or PDA can connect to the Internet within range of a wireless network connected to the Internet.

Wiki - A collection of articles that can be entered, edited, linked, and expanded by any authorized user. Wikis facilitate the open sharing of knowledge on a designated web page.

WikiLeaks - Controversial organization based in Sweden that discloses anonymous submissions and leaks of confidential data without identifying sources. In November 2010, WikiLeaks released U.S. State department diplomatic cables, which were then made available via BitTorrent for download.

Workflow - Using applications and technology to automate the execution of each phase in a business process.

World Wide Web *(WWW)* - An HTML-based Internet system developed at the European Center for Nuclear Research (CERN) in Geneva. Also relates to the complete set of documents residing on all Internet servers that use the HTTP protocol. The web is accessible to users via a simple point-and-click system.

Z

Zettabyte *(ZB)* - A multiple of the unit byte for digital information storage. One zettabyte is 1,000 EB (exabytes) or 10007 bytes. The unit symbol for the zettabyte is ZB.

BIBLIOGRAPHY

Bibliography

Anonymous. "*Tale of the Eloquent Peasant.*" The British Museum: Egypt, 1800. *https://www.britishmuseum.org/explore/highlights/highlight_objects/aes/p/papyrus_with_part_of_the_tale.aspx* (accessed January 2014).

Arcaris, Christine. "*Gartner Says Worldwide Government IT Spending Flat in 2013.*" Gartner, Inc.: June 2013, *http://www.gartner.com/newsroom/id/2518815* (accessed February 2014).

Arcaris, Christine, and Rishi Sood. "*User Survey Analysis: IT Spending Priorities in Government, Worldwide, 2013.*" Gartner, Inc.: January 25, 2013.

Barrenechea, Mark J., and Tom Jenkins. Enterprise Information Management: The Next Generation of Enterprise Software. Canada: OpenText, 2013.

Bartels, Andrew and Connie Moore, et al. "*Smart Process Applications Fill A Big Business Gap.*" Forrester Research: November 2012.

Beieler, John. "*Mapping Protest Data.*" John Beieler Blog: July 17, 2013. *http://johnbeieler.org/blog/2013/07/03/mapping-protest-data/* (accessed February 2014).

Bettino, Larry A. "*Transforming Big Data Challenges Into Opportunities.*" Information Management: April 18, 2012, *http://www.information-management.com/newsletters/bigdata-ROI-IBM-Walmart-USPS-10022342-1.html* (accessed 22 Apr. 2013).

Borissow, Peter. "*Forecasting Crime in Washington D.C.*" Wikipedia. *http://en.wikipedia.org/wiki/File:Signature_Analyst_Assessment_of_DC.jpg* (accessed February 2014).

"*Bridging the Gap between Levels of Government.*" Policy Brief. OECD Observer: 2009.

"*Bring Your Own Device: How Do State and Local Governments Address the Proliferation of Employee Devices?*" Forrester Research and Cisco: 2012. *https://www.cisco.com/web/strategy/docs/employee_devices_final.pdf* (accessed February 2014).

Brown, Bob. "*Google previews new privacy policy.*" Network World: January 31, 2012. *http://www.networkworld.com/news/2012/013112-google-privacy-policy-255529.html* (accessed February 2014).

"*Building a 21st Century Platform to Better Serve the American People.*" Government of the United States: May 23, 2013.

Cable, Dustin. "*The Racial Dot Map.*" Demographics Research Group: *July 2013. http://www.coopercenter.org/demographics/Racial-Dot-Map* (accessed February 2014).

"*Canada's Economic Action Plan.*" Government of Canada. *http://actionplan.gc.ca/* (accessed February 2014).

"*Canada's Action Plan on Open Government.*" Government of Canada: data.gc.ca. *http://data.gc.ca/eng/canadas-action-plan-open-government* (accessed February 2014).

Chemengich, Margaret K., "*Managing strategic change in public sector.*" Standard Research Journal of Business Management Vol 1: 1-40, April, 2013.

Chudzak, Chrystia. "*The Digital Government.*" Video: September 1, 2013. *http://www.powtoon.com/p/dzzsQTV8lil/* (accessed February 2014).

Clement , Tony. "*Remarks by Tony Clement, President of the Treasury Board and Minister responsible for FedNor, for the Launch of the Next Generation Open Data Portal and Open Government Licence.*" Treasury Board of Canada Secretariat: June 18, 2013. *http://www.tbs-sct.gc.ca/media/ps-dp/2013/0618-eng.asp* (accessed February 2014).

Diaz-Uda, Anesa, and Joe Leinbach. "*The Power of Zoom: Transforming Government Through Location Intelligence.*" Deloitte University Press: 2012.

Dobbs, Richard and Herbert Pohl, et al. "*Infrastructure productivity: How to save $1 trillion a year.*" McKinsey Global Institute: January 2013.

Eggers, William D. and Joshua Jaffe. "*Government on the go: Boosting public sector productivity by going mobile.*" Deloitte University Press: Feb 8, 2013. *http://dupress.com/articles/gov-on-the-go/?id=us:el:dc:govgo:crosspromo_mobilemicro:fed:021913* (accessed February 2013).

"*Facebook Statistics.*" Statistics Brain: January 1, 2014. *http://www.statisticbrain.com/facebook-statistics/* (accessed February 2014).

"*Family Tracker App.*" iTunes. *https://itunes.apple.com/ca/app/family-tracker/id349880412?mt=8* (accessed February 2014).

Fang, Zhiyuan. "*E-Government in Digital Era: Concept, Practice, and Development.*" International Journal of the Computer, the Internet and Management: August, 2002, Vol.10, Number 2.

Ferguson, Mike. "*Enterprise Information Protection – The Impact of Big Data.*" Intelligent Business Strategies: 2013.

"*File Archiving: The Next Big Thing or Just Big?*" An Osterman Research White Paper. Osterman Research: December 2012, SlideShare.com, *http://www.slideshare.net/emcacademics/analyst-report-osterman-research-file-archiving-the-next-big-thing-or-justbig* (accessed 6 Jan. 2013).

Fountain, Jane E., "*Building the Virtual State: Information Technology and Institutional Change.*" Washington, D.C.: Brookings Institution Press, August 1, 2001.

Frazier, Jake, and Anthony Diana, "*Hoarders: The Corporate Data Edition.*" Law Technology News: December 19, 2012. *https://www.cgoc.com/resources/hoarders-the-corporate-data-edition* (accessed February, 2014).

Frissen, Valerie, and Jeremy Millard, et al. "*The Future of eGovernment: An exploration of ICT-driven models of eGovernment for the EU in 2020.*" European Commission Joint Research Center (JRC) Scientific and Technical Reports: 2007.

Fyfe, Toby. "*New Paradigm for the CIO.*" Canadian Government Executive: June 19, 2013. *http://www.canadiangovernmentexecutive.ca/e-government/ict/item/1269-new-paradigm-for-the-cio.html* (accessed March 2014).

Gantz, John, and David Reinsel. "*The Digital Universe in 2020: Big Data, Bigger Digital Shadows, and Biggest Growth in the Far East.*" IDC: December 2012.

"*Gartner Reveals Top Predictions for IT Organisations and Users for 2013 and Beyond.*" Gartner, Inc.: October 24, 2012. *http://www.gartner.com/it/page.jsp?id=2211115* (accessed January 2014).

"*Gartner Says Solving 'Big Data' Challenge Involves More than Just Managing Volumes of Data.*" Gartner, Inc.: June 2011. *http://www.gartner. com/newsroom/id/1731916* (accessed November 15, 2012).

"*Gartner Says the Internet of Things Installed Base Will Grow to 26 Billion Units By 2020.*" Gartner, Inc.: December 12, 2013.

Gens, Frank. "*IDC Predictions 2013: Competing on the 3rd Platform.*" IDC: 2012. *http://www.idc.com/research/Predictions13/downloadable/238044.pdf* (accessed February 2014).

Goetz, Michele, Henry Peyret and Alan Weintraub. "*Data Governance Equals Business Opportunity. No, Really.*" Forrester Research: May 20, 2013.

"*Government End User Strategy.*" HM Government (U.K.): 2011.

Gupta, Tanya. "*The UN E-Government Survey: Towards a More Citizen-Centric Approach.*" The World Bank: December 27, 2011. *http://blogs.worldbank.org/publicsphere/un-e-government-survey-towards-more-citizen-centric-approach* (accessed Jan 2014).

Harris, Derrick. "*Take a look at how much the U.S. government loves requesting user data.*" Gigaom: August 27, 2013. *http://gigaom.com/2013/08/27/take-a-look-at-how-much-the-u-s-government-loves-requesting-data/* (accessed January 2014).

Hill, Kashmir. "*Blueprints Of NSA's Ridiculously Expensive Data Center In Utah Suggest It Holds Less Info Than Thought.*" Forbes, July 24, 2013.

Hornstein, Henry. "*Successes and potential obstacles to change management in the public service.*" Ivy Business Journal: 2010. *http://iveybusinessjournal.com/topics/the-organization/successes-and-potential-obstacles-to-change-management-in-the-public-service#_ftn4* (accessed February 2014).

Howe, Jeff. "*Crowdsourcing: A Definition.*" Crowdsourcing Blog: June 2, 2006. *http://crowdsourcing.typepad.com/cs/2006/06/crowdsourcing_a.html* (accessed February 2014).

"*ICT Strategy of the German Federal Government: Digital Germany 2015.*" Federal Ministry of Economics and Technology (BMWi) (Germany): 2010.

"*Infographic: 2013 Mobile Growth Statistics.*" Digital Buzz Blog: Tuesday Oct 1, 2013. *http://www.digitalbuzzblog.com/infographic-2013-mobile-growth-statistics/*

"*Intelligent Community Forum.*" *http://www.intelligentcommunity.org/* (accessed February 2014).

"*International Energy Outlook 2013 (IEO2013).*" U.S. Energy Information Administration: July 25, 2013. *http://www.eia.gov/forecasts/ieo/* (accessed February 2014).

"*ITU releases latest global technology development figures.*" ITU: February 27, 2013. *http://www.itu.int/net/pressoffice/press_releases/2013/05.aspx* (accessed January 2014).

Jenkins, Tom. "*Managing Content in the Cloud.*" Canada: OpenText, 2010.

Jerez, Sergio. "*Barcelona in the Pocket.*" City of Barcelona: PowerPoint® Presentation, June 2013.

Kappeler, Andreas, and Mathieu Nemoz. "*Public Private Partnerships in Europe - Before and During the Recent Financial Crisis.*" European Investment Bank: July 2010.

Keifer, Steve. Herding Geese: "*The Story of the Information Supply Chain.*" Self-published, 2001.

Lanvin, Bruno, and Anat Lewin. "*The Next Frontier of E-Government: Local Governments May Hold the Keys to Global Competition.*" The World Bank: Oct, 2013.

Leahy, Erin. "*The State and Local Big Data Gap.*" MeriTalk: April 29, 2013.

Lenihan, Donald G. "*Realigning Governance: From E-Government to E-Democracy.*" Centre for Collaborative Government: April 2002.

"*Major Mobile Trends Show Global Mobile Industry is now the Fastest Growing Market in the World.*" MobileMarketingWatch.com: *http://www.mobilemarketingwatch.com/major-mobile-trends-show-global-mobile-industry-is-now-thefastest-growing-market-in-the-world-16840/* (accessed June 3, 2013).

Makarenko, Jay. "*Federal Government in Canada: Organization, Institutions & Issues.*" Mapleleafweb: March 4, 2009. *http://mapleleafweb.com/features/federal-government-canada-organization-institutions-issues#federal* (accessed Jan 2014).

Manyika, James, Michael Chui, et al. "*Big data: The next frontier for innovation, competition, and productivity.*" McKinsey & Company: June 2011.

Manyika, James, Michael Chui, et al. "*Open data: Unlocking innovation and performance with liquid information.*" McKinsey Global Institute, October 2013.

McAfee, Andrew. "*Big Data, Bright Future.*" on24.com: Video, 2012. *http://event.on24.com/view/presentation/flash/EventConsoleNG.html* (accessed November 5, 2012).

McAfee, Andrew, and Erik Brynjolfsson. "*Big Data: The Management Revolution.*" Harvard Business Review: 2012. *http://hbr.org/2012/10/big-data-the-management-revolution/ar/pr* (accessed November 5, 2012).

McKenna, Barrie. "*The hidden price of public-private partnerships.*" The Globe and Mail: October 14, 2102, *http://www.theglobeandmail.com/report-on-business/economy/the-hidden-price-of-public-private-partnerships/article4611798/* (accessed February 2014).

"*MDSS: Medical Data Collection on Mobiles.*" MDSS: May 2007. *http://www.media.mit.edu/ventures/EPROM/research.html* (accessed February 2014).

MeriTalk. "*Federal Records Management: Navigating the Storm.*" MeriTalk Press Release: March 2013. *http://www.meritalk.com/pdfs/navigating-the-storm/MeriTalk_Navigating_the_Storm_Release.pdf* (accessed January 2014).

MeriTalk. "*Smarter Uncle Sam: The Big Data Forecast.*" MeriTalk Press Release: 2013. *http://www.meritalk.com/pdfs/emc-big-data/Smarter_Uncle_Sam_Press_Release.pdf* (accessed February 2012).

MeriTalk. "*State and Local Agencies Expect Data to Double in Next Four Years; Show Little Adoption of Big Data.*" MeriTalk Press Release: April 29, 2013. Milakovich, Michael, E. Digital Governance: New Technologies for Improving Public Service and Participation. New York: Routledge, 2012.

Miles, Doug. "*Making the Most of Mobile - content on the move.*" AIIM/OpenText: 2011.

Mzekandaba, Simnikiwe. "*Big data may help streamline Abidjan bus routes.*" Web Africa: May 7, 2013. *http://www.itwebafrica.com/ict-and-governance/379-ivory-coast/231010-big-data-could-help-streamline-abidjan-bus-routes* (accessed February 2014).

"*National Pipeline Mapping System.*" *https://www.npms.phmsa.dot.gov/PublicViewer/* (accessed February 2014).

"*Obama Administration Unveils 'Big Data' Initiative: Announces $200 Million in New R&D Investments.*" The White House: March 29, 2012. *http://www.whitehouse.gov/sites/default/files/microsites/ostp/big_data_press_release.pdf* (accessed January 2014).

O'Brien, Adelaide, and Mark Yates. "*IDC MarketScape: U.S. and EMEA Government Records Management 2013 Vendor Assessment.*" IDC Government Insights. IDC: April 2013.

"*Open Definition.*" *http://opendefinition.org/* (accessed February 2014).

"*Open Government Partnership.*" *http://www.opengovpartnership.org/* (accessed February, 2014).

"*Organization for Economic Development and Co-operation (OECD).*" *http://www.oecd.org/statistics/* (accessed February 2014).

"*Ottawa restricts use of data collected through government websites.*" CBC News: March 13, 2013. *http://www.cbc.ca/news/technology/ottawa-restricts-use-of-data-collected-through-government-websites-1.1307853* (accessed January 2014).

Paquet, Ray. "*Technology Trends You Can't Afford to Ignore.*" Gartner, Inc. *http://www.gartner.com/it/content/1503500/1503515/january_19_tech_trends_you_cant_afford_to_ignore_rpaquet.pdf* (accessed February 2014).

Poeter, Damon. "*Microsoft Joins Ranks of the Tragically Hacked.*" PC Magazine: February 22, 2013.

"*Projects Created at the 1.USA.gov Hack Day 1*." USA.gov Blog. *http://blog.usa.gov/post/8522383948/projects-created-at-the-1-usa-gov-hack-day* (accessed February 2014).

Rauf, David Saleh. "*PATRIOT Act clouds picture for tech.*" Politico: November 2009, *http://www.politico.com/news/stories/1111/69366.html* (accessed February 2014).

"*Recap 2013: Most discussed Geospatial News.*" Geospatial World: December 2013. *http://geospatialworld.net/Paper/Business/ArticleView.aspx?aid=30791* (accessed February 2014).

Reynolds, Neil. "*Ottawa should do the math: Productivity trumps head counts.*" The Globe and Mail: April 23, 2013. *http://www.theglobeandmail.com/globe-debate/ottawa-should-do-the-math-productivity-trumps-head-counts/article4101797/* (accessed February 2014).

Richter, Felix. "*Mobile Phones Account for 17% of Global Web Usage.*" Statista: August 20, 2013. *http://www.statista.com/topics/779/mobile-internet/chart/1380/mobile-web-usage/* (accessed February 2014).

Ried, Stefan, and Holger Kisker. "*Sizing the Cloud.*" Forrester Research: April 21, 2011.

Rodman, Richard, Renee Romulus, and JR Milone. "*The Waves of Change in Federal Human Capital Management.*" PWC: 2012.

Schroder, Maria and Christian Heise. "*From OpenGovData to GovData: Why Germany needs the OGP (and the OGP needs Germany).*" Open Gov Blog: February 15, 2013. *http://blog.opengovpartnership.org/2013/02/from-opengovdata-to-govdata-why-germany-needs-the-ogp-and-the-ogp-needs-germany/* (accessed January 2014).

Shah, Anup. "*Poverty Facts and Stats.*" Global Issues: January 7, 2013. *http://www.globalissues.org/article/26/poverty-facts-and-stats* (accessed February 2014).

Sharma, Chetan. "*2013 Mobile Industry Predictions Survey.*" Chetan Sharma Consulting: January 2013. *http://www.chetansharma.com/MobilePredictions2013.htm* (accessed May 7, 2013).

Singel, Ryan. "*Whistle-Blower Outs NSA Spy Room.*" Wired Magazine: July 2006. *http://www.wired.com/science/discoveries/news/2006/04/70619* (accessed February 2014).

Smith, Craig. "*By the Numbers: 64 Amazing Facebook User Statistics.*" Digital Marketing Ramblings: December, 2013. *http://expandedramblings.com/index.php/by-the-numbers-17-amazing-facebook-stats/#.UtMD3_v5OXM* (accessed February 2014).

Smith, Gayle, and Nick Sinai. "*Open Government Progress.*" The White House Open Government Initiative Blog: October 31, 2013. *http://www.whitehouse.gov/blog/2013/10/31/open-government-progress* (accessed February 2014).

Sowmya, Jayakumar and Hussain Shafiq Pyarali. "T*he Effective Use of Crowdsourcing in E-Governance.*" Nanyang Technological University: March 22, 2013.

"*State and Local Agencies Expect Data to Double in Next Four Years; Show Little Adoption of Big Data.*" MertiTalk Press Release: April 29, 2013. *http://www.meritalk.com/pdfs/state-and-local-big-data/State_and_Local_Big_Data_Gap_Release.pdf* (accessed February 2014).

"*Stolen Facebook and Yahoo passwords dumped online.*" BBC News: December 4, 2013. *http://www.bbc.co.uk/news/technology-25213846* (accessed January 2014).

"*Strategic Sourcing: Improved and Expanded Use Could Save Billions in Annual Procurement Costs.*" United States Government Accountability Office: September 20, 2012.

Sweden, Eric. "*Transforming Government through Change Management: The Role of the State CIO.*" NASCIO: 2007.

Tellier, Paul, and David Emerson. "*Seventh Report of the Prime Minister's Advisory Committee on the Public Service.*" Clerk of the Privy Council: March, 2013. *http://www.clerk.gc.ca/eng/feature.asp?pageId=314* (accessed December 2013).

"*The Canada Council for Public Private Partnerships.*" *http://www.pppcouncil.ca/* (accessed February 2014).

"*The Domesday Book.* National Archives." *http://www.nationalarchives.gov.uk/education/focuson/domesday/take-a-closer-look/* (accessed January 2014).

"*The Expanding Role of Mobility in the Workplace.*" Forrester Research and Cisco Systems: February 2012.

"*The President's SAVE Award.*" The White House: *http://www.whitehouse.gov/save-award* (accessed February 2014).

"*The United Kingdom Report on the Re-use of Public Sector Information 2013.*" National Archives: 2013.

"*The World in 2013: ICT Facts and Figures.*" International Telecommunication Union: 2013. *http://www.itu.int/en/ITU-D/Statistics/Pages/facts/default.aspx* (accessed December 2013).

"*Top 5: Oldest Examples of Crowdsourcing.*" Article One Partners: September 16, 2011. *http://info.articleonepartners.com/top-5-oldest-examples-of-crowdsourcing/* (accessed February 2014).

Tumin, Zachary and Archon Fung. "*From Government 2.0 to Society 2.0: Pathways to Engagement, Collaboration and Transformation.*" Harvard Kennedy School: 2011.

Turnbull, Malcolm. "*Australian Minister Calls for Innovation in Digital Media.*" FutureGov Summit Australia: December 2013, *http://www.futuregov.asia/articles/2013/dec/04/australian-minister-calls-innovation-digital-gover/* (accessed February 2014)

"*United Nations E-Government for the People: E-Government Survey 2012.*" United Nations: 2012. *http://unpan1.un.org/intradoc/groups/public/documents/un/unpan048065.pdf* (accessed February 2014).

"*U.S. Postal Service in trouble, losing $25 million daily.*" CNN: Dec 10, 2012. *http://outfront.blogs.cnn.com/2012/12/10/u-s-postal-service-in-trouble-losing-25-million-daily/* (accessed January 2014).

"*What We've Heard: Blueprint 2020 Summary Interim Progress Report.*" Government of Canada. November 2013.

Whitfield, Karl. "*Fast growth of apps user base in booming Asia Pacific market.*" Portio Research: March 2013. *http://www.portioresearch.com/en/blog/2013/fast-growth-of-apps-user-base-in-booming-asia-pacific-market.aspx* (accessed February 2014).

"*Why Open Data?*" Open Data Handbook: 2012. *http://opendatahandbook.org/en/why-open-data/index.html* (accessed February 2014).

"*Wikipedia.*" Wikipedia. *http://en.wikipedia.org/wiki/Wikipedia* (accessed February 2014).

"*Wikipedia survives research test.*" BBC News: December 15, 2005. *http://news.bbc.co.uk/2/hi/technology/4530930.stm* (accessed February 2014).

"*YouTube Statistics.*" YouTube. *http://www.youtube.com/yt/press/statistics.html* (accessed February 2014).

Innovator Story and Interview Bibliography

Alabama Gas Corporation, Alabama Natural Gas Distributor Energizes Sales Force with OpenText, OpenText, 2012, *www.opentext.com/e-Government/Alagasco.*

Belgian Railways, Belgian Railways on the Right Track with OpenText Extended Solutions for SAP,® OpenText, 2012, *www.opentext.com/e-Government/BelgianRailways.*

Bundesrechenzentrum (BRZ), ECM as a Service: eGovernment Platform for the whole of Austria, OpenText, 2008, *www.opentext.com/e-Government/BRZ.*

Calgary Police Service (CPS), Calgary Police Service Secures Documents and Records, OpenText, 2013, *www.opentext.com/e-Government/CPS.*

Care Assessment Agency (CIZ), Video, OpenText, 2013.

CARE Canada, OpenText ECM Strengthens CARE Canada's I Am Powerful Campaign, OpenText, 2008, *www.opentext.com/e-Government/CARECanada.*

City of Barcelona, City of Barcelona - OpenText Customer Case Study, Video, May 14, 2013, *http://www.youtube.com/watch?v=hlv_IRX70Do.* (accessed January 2014), *www.opentext.com/e-Government/CityofBarcelona.*

City of Edmonton, A Site for All Citizens, Success Story, OpenText, 2009, *www.opentext.com/e-Government/CityofEdmonton.*

City of San Francisco, Human Services Agency, Human Services Agency of San Francisco Streamlines Processes to Improve Public Assistance, OpenText, 2010, *www.opentext.com/e-Government/HSA.*

City of Surrey, City of Surrey Uses OpenText to Create a Richer, More Interactive Online Experience, OpenText, 2013, *www.opentext.com/e-Government/CityofSurrey.*

ClearCadence, Video, OpenText, 2013.

Clerk of the Circuit Court, Pinellas County, Florida County Enhances Services to Citizens, OpenText, 2013, *www.opentext.com/e-Government/PinellasCounty.*

Department of Canadian Heritage: Vancouver 2010 Winter Games, Canadian Heritage Goes for Gold with OpenText's Records, Document, and Information Management System, OpenText, 2009, *www.opentext.com/e-Government/VANOC.*

Derby City Council, Derby City Council Setting New Standards for Document and Record Handling with OpenText Content Server and Capture Center, OpenText, 2013, *www.opentext.com/e-Government/DerbyCityCouncil.*

Derbyshire County Council, *Taking Control: 250,000 Vendor Invoices at Derbyshire County Council,* OpenText, 2013, *www.opentext.com/e-Government/DerbyshireCountyCouncil.*

DOMEA, *DOMEA Government Content Management,* OpenText, 2004, *www.opentext.com/e-Government/DOMEA.*

European Court of Human Rights (ECHR), *Open Text eDOCS Improves Access to Human Rights Knowledge Around the World.* Open Text, 2008, *www.opentext.com/e-Government/ECHR.*

G20 Summit, *Social Media and the G20: How Canada Modernized International Meetings,* OpenText, 2013, *www.opentext.com/G20Summit.*

GCDOCS, *Are You Ready for GCDOCS,* Canada School of Public Service, (Accessed February 2014), *www.opentext.com/e-Government/GCDOCS.*

Geisinger Health System, *Moving Medical Information Mountains,* OpenText, 2013, *www.opentext.com/e-Government/Geisinger.*

General Council of the Judiciary, *Consejo General del Poder Judicial Proyecto WEM: Portal www.poderjudicial.es,* (Presentation), Consejo General del Poder Judicial, November 26, 2013, *www.opentext.com/e-Government/CGPJ.*

Global Public Health Intelligence Network (GPHIN), *GPHIN Uses Text Mining for its early warning system that detects human threats around the world,* Open Text, 2010, *www.opentext.com/e-Government/GPHIN.*

Government of Aragón, *El Gobierno de Aragón moderniza su presencia en la Web con las soluciones de OpenText,* OpenText, 2011, *www.opentext.com/e-Government/GovernmentofAragón.*

Hong Kong Polytechnic University, *Hong Kong Polytechnic University Deploys OpenText EIM Solutions to Better Manage University Records and Information,* 2013, *www.opentext.com/e-Government/HongKongPolyU.*

Institute of Public Administration of Canada (IPAC), *Public Service Without Borders Promotes Open Government, Excellence in Public Service,* OpenText, 2013, *www.opentext.com/e-Government/IPAC.*

International Organization for Standardization Central Secretariat (ISO), *How ISO built one of the world's leading extranets,* OpenText, 2006, *www.opentext.com/e-Government/ISO.*

International Post Corporation (IPC), International Post Corporation, GXS/OpenText, 2007, *www.opentext.com/e-Government/IPC.*

IQ Business Group (IQBG), Video, OpenText, 2013.

Junta de Andalucía, Junta de Andalucía, Open Text, 2009, *http://www.ot.co.uk/Customer-Stories/Customer-Story-Detail?sys_action=show&id=648* (Accessed 2014), *www.opentext.com/e-Government/JuntadeAndalucía.*

Karlsruhe Institute of Technology, *Exzellenz im Internet: Karlsruher Institut für Technologie setzt auf Web Content Management von OpenText,* OpenText, 2011, *www.opentext.com/e-Government/KIT.*

Library of Parliament Canada, *The Library of Parliament Streamlines Research Services Using OpenText ECM Suite,* OpenText, 2012, *www.opentext.com/e-Government/LibraryofParliament.*

LUKOIL Overseas Holding GmbH, *OpenText Expands the Capabilities of LUKOIL Overseas Corporate Document Management Systems,* OpenText, 2012, *www.opentext.com/e-Government/LUKOILOverseasHoldingGmbH.*

Melbourne Water, *OpenText ECM Suite Provides Enhanced Information Management for Melbourne Water,* Video, OpenText, 2012, *www.opentext.com/e-Government/MelbourneWater.*

Metro Vancouver, *Metro Vancouver Establishes Comprehensive Lifecycle Management of Corporate Records,* OpenText, 2013, *www.opentext.com/e-Government/MetroVancouver.*

Mumbai International Airport, *Consortium Manages Modernization of India's Busiest Airport,* OpenText, 2010, *www.opentext.com/e-Government/MIAL.*

Naval Sea Systems Command (NAVSEA), Video, OpenText, 2013.

Netherlands Ministry of Defense, Video, OpenText, 2013.

Oakland County Michigan, *Oakland County Deploys OpenText Media Management On Demand to Manage Media Assets,* OpenText, 2013, *www.opentext.com/OaklandCounty.*

Office of the Superintendent of Financial Institutions (OSFI), *Case Management at the Office of the Superintendent of Financial Institutions,* LiveLinkUp Orlando 2003 Proceeding, OpenText, 2003, *www.opentext.com/e-Government/OSFI.*

Pennsylvania State University, *Penn State Researchers Discover Reliable, Manageable Remote Access with OpenText Exceed OnDemand®,* OpenText, 2012, *www.opentext.com/e-Government/PennStateU.*

RBS 6 Nations Championship, Sotic deliver new digital platform for the RBS 6 Nations Championship, January 2014, http://www.sotic.net/media/3219.php (Accessed February 2014), *www.opentext.com/e-Government/ RBS6NationsChampionship.*

Regional Municipality of York, The Regional Municipality of York Migrates to eDOCS for Improved Business Processes, OpenText, 2010, *www.opentext.com/e-Government/YorkRegion.*

State Council of the Canton of Valais, State Council of the Canton of Valais Implements Paperless Office File Management with OpenText Solutions, OpenText, 2012, *www.opentext.com/e-Government/CantonofValais.*

State Lotteries of Spain (SELAE), Loterías y Apuestas del Estado gestiona la experiencia Web con OpenText, Computing España, September 1, 2012, *www.opentext.com/e-Government/SELAE.*

Suffolk University, Suffolk University Attains a Higher Degree of Web Content Management with OpenText, OpenText, 2009, *www.opentext.com/e-Government/SuffolkUniversity.*

SWK STADTWERKE KRFELD AG, Transparent Energy Bill, Internal Success Story, OpenText, 2013, *www.opentext.com/e-Government/SWKSTADTWERKEKRFELDAG.*

The Lend Network, LEND Network: Leaders Engaged in New Democracies, U.S. Department of State Press Release, March 27, 2012, http://www.state.gov/s/sacsed/communitydemocracies/c51361.htm (Accessed 2014), *www.opentext.com/e-Government/LEND.*

Transport Canada, Transport Canada Drives Information Management, OpenText, 2010, *www.opentext.com/e-Government/TransportCanada.*

U.S. Department of Defense, Video, OpenText, 2013.

U.S. Department of Justice, U.S. Department of Justice Consolidates Case Management, OpenText, 2012, *www.opentext.com/USDOJ.*

U.S. Department of the Interior (DOI), U.S. Department of the Interior Sets the Bar High with Groundbreaking eERDMS Program, OpenText, 2013, *www.opentext.com/e-Government/USDOI.*

Western Cape Government Health, Western Cape Government Health Uses OpenText Solutions for Healthcare Enterprise Information Management, OpenText, 2013, *www.opentext.com/e-Government/WesternCapeGovernmentHealth.*

INDEX

Index

A

B

C

D

J

K

L

M

N

P

R

S

T

U

V

W